HOW AMERICA'S
BEST PLACES TO WORK
INSPIRE EXTRA EFFORT IN
EXTRAORDINARY TIMES

RE▸ENGAGE

LEIGH BRANHAM, SPHR, AND MARK HIRSCHFELD

New York   Chicago   San Francisco   Lisbon   London
Madrid   Mexico City   Milan   New Delhi   San Juan   Seoul
Singapore   Sydney   Toronto

The *McGraw·Hill* Companies

1 2 3 4 5 6 7 8 9 0 DOC/DOC 1 0 9 8 7 6 5 4 3 2 1 0

ISBN   978-0-07-170310-9
MHID   0-07-170310-1

McGraw-Hill books are available at special quantity discounts to use as premiums and sales promotions, or for use in corporate training programs. To contact a representative, please e-mail us at bulksales@mcgraw-hill.com.

This book is printed on acid-free paper.

≈

We dedicate this book to our loving families, whose support, encouragement, and love engages, and re-engages.

▶ CONTENTS

▶ FOREWORD

T he authors paint a bleak picture that is all too familiar. Yet, their solutions to the disengaged workforce go beyond the simplistic panaceas offered by so many who have not done their homework. If you thoroughly read what Leigh and Mark offer—rather than scan it, looking for a quick fix—you will come to realize that engagement is not a program, a survey, a software package, or, worst of all, a motivational speech. True sustainable engagement is a function of an organization's culture, which is the result of leadership's vision and behavior.

A culture of engagement prevails through the worst of tragedies. It is a way of life, a family of values that does not waver. The problem for most companies is that their cultures, perhaps workable in good times, cannot carry the load or resist the forces that cataclysms bring. Time and again, between the lines as well as explicitly, the authors show the research that lays out the true path to sustainable engagement.

Leadership that spawns and supports a naturally engaging culture; culture that is the bedrock for policy; policy that leads system design; systems that run engaging processes—all leading to individual objectives based on an understanding of the whole. This is the formula for engagement that the authors are describing.

Where do you start? Read carefully and think deeply about what Leigh and Mark are telling you. This is not a get-it-quick-and-go scheme. It is the very antithesis of so many supposed cure-alls that are flooding the market. This is real. This is difficult. This works, provided you have the courage and persistence to make it work. The formula is here. Now it is up to you.

Jac Fitz-enz

▶ PREFACE

Bumbling leaders and grumbling workers
Dropping stocks and drooping dividends
Crumbling morale and stumbling managers
Fleeting jobs and retreating markets
Helpless Boomers and hapless Millennials

S ound familiar? For many, these are now everyday workplace realities. Whether we like it or not, they are, in a sense, the "new normal."

Consider the tumultuous times facing us:

▶ Significant financial stresses, not seen in a century, have caused record unemployment, with the realization that many of those jobs are never coming back.

▶ Thousands of workers have seen their retirement accounts wither, and many are forced to stay in the workforce beyond their intended retirement dates.

▶ We have a health-care crisis where the skyrocketing costs of care are rising much faster than salary increases, leaving more people with a fool's choice—taking care of their health or paying for other basic needs.

▶ The public's trust of company leaders continues to erode, fueled by greed, mismanagement, and the financial collapse that began in 2008 and that many blame on the "corrupt corporation," a disease that has stricken nearly every industry.

▶ Many of our greatest corporate icons—including those in the banking, finance, and automotive industries—have dissolved and disappeared almost overnight, leaving many to wonder what level of security they may have in any occupation or with any employer.

▶ For the first time in history, the pace of change has produced four distinct generations in the workplace, and conflicts among them have gone beyond clever drama in the movies.

The work setting where we felt a sense of entitlement to our jobs has vanished. We can no longer count on lifetime employment the same way our parents did. We can no longer feel secure that our business leaders are generally honest and trying to do the right thing for all of us. We can no longer rely on the bootstrap mentality that if we just work hard enough, everything will be all right.

And when our workplace is bad, we suffer. When inept leaders turn our company to rubble and threaten our retirement funds, we no longer think about leadership as a concept that doesn't impact us, because it's hitting us right in the wallet. When a self-absorbed, petty supervisor makes the life of our spouse miserable and he comes home stressed and angry, we know our family life is directly hurt by what goes on at work.

When a loved one tells us she's been harassed at work and gets no support from the company to address the complaint, we know her spirit has been wounded. When we receive dawdling service from an establishment that we've paid good money to patronize, that is staffed with employees who clearly don't care, we wonder whether we'll ever again "get our money's worth."

It's sad, really, how a negative workplace can impact our lives and the way we feel about ourselves. The situation is reaching pandemic heights—most people go to work at jobs they dislike, supervised by people who don't care about them, and directed by senior leaders who are often clueless about where to take the company.

Sad, indeed.

The glimmer of hope in this malaise is a small but growing group of employers who are creating remarkable workplaces, where employees are nurtured and, as a result, thrive—achieving exceptional results for all. These elite employers seem to be cutting against the grain, steadily and confidently going about the business of engaging their employees.

They've often carved their paths in the face of adversity and doubt. Some stock analysts, for example, can't see past their noses to understand that investing a little extra in engaging the workforce will pay for itself with happier and more loyal customers in the long run. This relatively new breed of premier employers is second-guessed even by the well intentioned, who tell them that "employees will just take advantage of you if you give them the chance." Other skeptics admonish that those "people programs" may be nice when business is riding high, but they need to be the first things to go when the bottom falls out of the business.

The companies profiled in this book have a very different mindset about all of this. They're a principled bunch, and when the economy gets shaky or market analysts get nervous, they know that "when the going gets tough, the tough work even harder to maintain a great place to work." They don't set aside core principles in turbulent times—"they don't drop the aircraft in order to fly the microphone," as the aviator would warn. They challenge employees to keep themselves engaged even as they challenge all leaders to be accountable for engaging employees. When other leaders are hiding away in their plush executive suites, these true leaders are out in front of employees and customers, talking openly and honestly. And when they must make job cuts or put salary freezes in place, they do so in a professional and dignified manner—no ducking and running in this all-too-exceptional group.

Nor is there anything willy-nilly about their approach to building a great workplace. To begin, there actually *is* a plan—that alone sets them apart. Moreover, their plans are tightly bound to the organization's key values. This allows their leadership to make clear decisions about what actions are important where people-related investments are being considered. Many of these better places to work even create their own language, which serves as a shorthand for the human capital values they so passionately treasure, a language that functions to clarify, guide, and inspire.

The passion they invoke with their employees nears cultlike fervor in the best possible sense. Stories of employees choosing a longer commute or making a lateral career move to stay with a winning workplace are common. And the way these employees consistently work harder and take extraordinary steps to serve customers, a great challenge for most businesses, displays the true differences between so-so and outstanding employers.

Remarkably, these successful employers are willing, even eager, to share their stories, including some of the "company secrets" that have helped them create great places to work. Lest you think them selfless in their efforts to share, many, on the contrary, see this as a way to build their brand in the marketplace, knowing that great workplaces tend to attract more of those they would like to have on their payrolls. You see, they understand that creating a great workplace is a strategic advantage, one that is within their control and can help insulate them from competitive threats. It is best that you beware of these winning workplaces—they may be attracting your best and brightest as we speak!

In some cases it's clear to us that those who lead these great places to work are almost daring the rest of us to take on this challenge, goading those who only pay lip service to the tenets of great workplaces. They seem to be saying:

▶ *"Stop pretending to care about your employees, and actually . . . care."*
▶ *"Stop telling your employees they are valued and then treating them no better than a disposable soda can—for limited use and then tossed away."*
▶ *"Stop throwing unnecessary bureaucracy into the way of smart people who, for the most part, will do the right thing by you and dazzle customers."*

The stories we chronicle in this book can act as a beacon for those who are weary of those old and tired ways. Another path awaits you.

At the heart of what's chronicled in *Re-Engage* is a company's culture—how it is led, what is valued, how folks come together to get things done, how people really listen to and talk openly and honestly with each other, and how they resolve and often celebrate differences. One executive lamented his employer's performance on such matters: "We have vastly underestimated how deeply ingrained are the organizational and cultural rigidities that hamper our ability to execute." The leader who wrote this was Elmer Johnson, who penned these words in a memo dated January 21, 1988.

His employer? General Motors.

Mr. Johnson may have foretold the ultimate destiny that lay before GM and became reality some 20 years later—its loss of market leadership and product innovation that led to a government bailout and the company's eventual slide into bankruptcy court.

Think this stuff doesn't matter? Think again.

We've titled this book *Re-Engage*. To some it might sound like clever wordplay, especially since "employee engagement" has become one of the most overused and least understood buzzwords of this still-new century. But to us it has multiple layers of meaning. The outstanding employers we introduce you to in this book are effectively re-engaging employees in several ways.

The best places to work know how to re-engage:

▶ Those who have become disengaged because of a disappointing work experience or bad boss.

▶ Employees who have been traumatized by an event outside their control, such as an economic recession or the tough times their current employer may be facing.

▶ Those who are already engaged and must be effectively led, managed, and supported every day lest they slip into a state of disengagement. The best workplaces see this as a task that cannot be taken for granted; even their best and brightest may suddenly or gradually lose their passion and commitment to the business.

Some of what we gleaned from our research and present here is quite novel, adding new insights that have emerged in recent years about the elements that create a first-class employment experience.

We are just beginning, for example, to see the impact of having four generations at work, and our insights should go a long way in advancing the discussion of how the generations can work, dare we say thrive, together. And our studies showing how company growth and consequent increases in employee populations can negatively affect employee engagement—and what can be done to fight that "tipping point"—also break new ground.

In other parts of this book we offer gentle reminders of approaches that have served successful leaders well for many years. Caring leadership, compensation that is fair and justly administered, great teamwork—these basics of leadership haven't changed, but they deserve to be revisited, particularly through the eyes of winning employers.

In the course of writing this book, we've heard the voices of over 2 million employees, many of whom you'll read about. We go to great lengths to give them a platform from which they can help you understand how the actions of their leaders affect them. You'll hear many who work in highly engaged workplaces speak of how lucky they feel to work there. And you'll hear others who are so disillusioned and disgusted with their employers they can hardly wait to find another position. It is quite apparent these good folks are giving us their verdicts about their places of work. These verbatim quotes express raw and heartfelt emotions that reflect the way they have been led and the workplace cultures they have experienced. The good news from our point of view is that we can influence for the better how employees feel about their workplaces. Many of the outstanding employers we highlight tell us that "things weren't always this good" and that they needed to change their ways to become great workplaces. Therein lies our hope.

The longshoreman-philosopher Eric Hoffer wrote, "In times of change, learners inherit the earth while the learned find themselves beautifully equipped to deal with a world that no longer exists." In the course of writing this book we have been reporters, observers, and, importantly, learners, looking deeply into how we can manage the change that is in front of us from "the world that no longer exists." These remarkable employers are helping us to clearly see what that new world is all about.

We invite you to join us on the journey.

▶ CHAPTER ONE

Employee Engagement

The Key to Building a *Best Place to Work*

*The best companies now know, without a doubt, where productivity—
real and limitless—comes from. It comes from challenged, empowered, excited, rewarded teams of people. It comes from engaging every single mind
in the organization, making everyone part of the action, and allowing
everyone to have a voice—a role—in the success of the enterprise. Doing
so raises productivity not incrementally, but by multiples.*

—Jack Welch, former CEO and Chairman, General Electric

▶ MARY: FEELING THE DIFFERENCE

As a single mom supporting two children, Mary needed reliable work
that helped her make ends meet. Before starting at her latest employer,
Mary never felt much satisfaction in her work beyond the paycheck.
"To me," Mary reflected, *"work was just something you had to do in order
to enjoy the other parts of your life. It never occurred to me that work could
be a place where I could have fun, be valued for what I do, and feel like I'm
really making a contribution."*

When asked about what has made the biggest difference in her current job compared with other places of employment, Mary boiled it down to three things: a caring manager, great coworkers, and a feeling that she is part of something.

Her family has noticed her attitude change. *"When I used to come home from work, I was tired and moody. Although I still have a bad day every now and then, I'm much more positive and energized when I get home. It's funny, but I never realized how draining my old job was. Now that I'm here, I just feel better about myself, and that's making a difference at home."*

Mary continued: *"I can honestly say that I look forward to going to work in the morning. Some of my friends think I'm crazy, but I really do feel that way. I've been here for six years now, and I can't imagine going to work anyplace else."*

When asked about her company winning the *Best-Places-to-Work* designation, Mary told us: *"It was easy giving them good ratings on the survey. Our leadership works hard to create this culture, and the survey results reflect that. All of us love this company and want to see it grow. I know people who could make a little more elsewhere or find a job closer to their home, but we stay here because we love it. That's why we're a great place to work!"*

▶ NOT ENOUGH EMPLOYEES ARE SAYING, "I FEEL SO LUCKY TO WORK HERE!"

Although Mary's story is inspiring, it is certainly not unique, at least to the employees who work for employers that have been recognized as *Best Places to Work*. Indeed, we hear many employees from these special organizations offering the same all-too-rare sentiment—we feel *lucky to work here* because *it's a pleasure to go to work each day.*

This book is based on in-depth research of winning workplaces, including an extraordinary number of employee surveys—2.1 million— along with more than a million verbatim comments, from the *Best-Places-to-Work* competitions and awards events conducted annually in 45 cities across the United States. The survey research conducted in these events has been collected annually since 2004 by Quantum Workplace of Omaha, Nebraska.

As surveys began to flow into the servers at Quantum Workplace in 2004, we immediately began noticing results and trends we found interesting. We were occasionally inspired by reading the positive employee comments at winning companies and often horrified at comments from companies where employee engagement scores were low. (After reading remarks from employees at a hospital in one small town, we resolved that if we ever find ourselves driving through that community and happen to take ill, we'll just pop a couple of aspirin and keep driving!)

▶ THE *BEST-PLACES-TO-WORK* DATABASE

With millions of surveys collected from over 10,000 employers, we believe our analysis of Quantum Workplace's ongoing research to be, in some respects, the most comprehensive analysis of employee engagement in the United States.[1] According to Greg Harris, president of Quantum Workplace: *"Other researchers may have collected as many or more individual surveys, but the* Best-Places-to-Work *project has allowed us to view a larger and more diverse sample of employers, especially with regard to company size."* The breadth of the Quantum Workplace database has had a significant impact on the insights we present in this book. Simply stated, with this wider perspective of employee engagement from so many employers—small, medium-size, and large—we were able to glean insights that other researchers may not have been able to uncover because of the more limited scope of their data.

▶ CAN A *BEST-PLACE-TO-WORK* BE ANYPLACE?

Conventional thinking might suggest that *Best-Places-to-Work* winners must come from trendy, high-profile industries, such as fast-growth, high-technology businesses. Wouldn't the best and brightest want to go where the "hot jobs" are? And wouldn't those industries have a head start in creating a highly engaged workforce? We note that high-profile companies like Microsoft and SAS have indeed made the *Best-Places-to-Work* winner's circle, and they are to be congratulated for the reviews their employees have provided that brought them this recognition.

And, you may well think, some industries must be at a distinct disadvantage when it comes to creating great workplaces. For example, how could companies with employee populations that are paid less, or are less skilled, or are less well educated be expected to create highly engaging workplaces? And for some "less desirable" industries, it may seem almost impossible to attract and retain great talent.

And yet we found survey comments like this from an employee at one winning company: *"Few people say, 'I want to work for a moving company when I grow up,' yet here we are and here we stay."*

Four researchers recently published a study of "dirty work" occupations that are viewed by society as physically, socially, or morally tainted."[2] The notion has been popularized by a television show on the Discovery Channel called *Dirty Jobs*. The show's host, Mike Rowe, places himself in jobs that most of us would not consider doing—exterminator, hot tar roofer, alligator farmer—you get the picture. We can chuckle at his exploits and privately be thankful we don't have one of these roles as our daily occupation.

Society in general may view many industries and lines of work as less prestigious, but we can emphatically state that this does not mean that employers in these industries are precluded from creating high-morale, engaging, and productive workplaces.

In a recent *Best Places to Work in Omaha* (Nebraska) recognition event, two of the companies that were recognized in the large-company category were Quality Living, Inc., and Greater Omaha Packing. The winner, Quality Living, which we will profile in greater length because of its outstanding leadership practices, is a long-term nursing-care facility for individuals with severe brain injuries; and Greater Omaha Packing is a locally owned meat-packing plant. The employee engagement scores of these two companies were outstanding—any employer from any industry would be delighted to have their results.

At the conclusion of the awards luncheon, a number of guests were heard to remark, *"Well, I guess if a nursing home and meat-packing plant can win, we don't have any excuse for not creating a great workplace in our line of work."*

Some of the stereotypes we have about certain jobs, and the companies that provide them, may be well-founded in some respects. But the leaders at places like Quality Living and Greater Omaha Packing knew that great leadership and a positive culture could trump any preconceptions their communities may have had about their respective businesses. And because they declined to buy into those predispositions, they are thriving in achieving their respective missions.

In short, becoming a *Best-Places-to-Work* winner is not about whether your industry is cutting edge or whether you are located in an area of the country that has a mild climate. It *is* about embracing and committing to a set of principles about how people should be managed and about executing those principles with passion.

Take This Ship and Re-Engage It!

From time to time we'll draw upon a story or image related to navigating one vessel or another—rough waters, keeping on course, watching for crosswinds, that kind of thing. We chose the sailing metaphor to explain some of the critical concepts in this book because we believe it fits the turbulent times we now live in.

We were also inspired by a great contemporary leader, Captain D. Michael Abrashoff, who took over a U.S. Navy destroyer that had very low morale and high crew turnover and, in his two-year tour, turned it into one of the most successful, highly decorated ships in the fleet. In his book, *It's Your Ship*, he summarizes the sense of accomplishment that came from re-engaging a seemingly ragtag crew:

As I departed, I thought about how far we had all come in two years. Once divided and troubled, the ship I left to my successor was all a captain could wish for—the gem of the ocean. I was hugely proud of these soldiers, who had become such a tight, accomplished, effective team, and I was unabashedly proud of myself. I came far as both a leader and a person. I will never forget the excitement of commanding the Benfold, *of watching it improve every single day.*

Be it on land or sea, re-engagement is more than possible: it is within our reach.

▶ GREAT WORKPLACES: IT'S ALL ABOUT THE PERKS, RIGHT?

In the articles that appear in the popular press from time to time about winning workplaces, we often hear about the wonderful perks these employers provide—volleyball courts, massage chairs, laundry service—the list could go on. We suspect that the editors of these publications believe such benefits are worth highlighting and newsworthy. And although we too find it useful to be aware of them, we are quite convinced these perks are not the essence of what makes highly engaged workplaces, particularly those that sustain employee engagement over a prolonged period.

We are further convinced that these perks, although no doubt appreciated, simply represent a deep commitment on the part of the employer to create a great workplace. An editorial in *PR Week* mirrors our sensibilities on the matter: "What's missing is clear direction for all companies and insights into how to measure their employee efforts concretely. . . . Being the ideal employer has less to do with what goodies are lavished on employees and more with how employees feel about themselves and the organization."

So if you are looking for a silver-bullet benefit or a "plug-and-play engagement-in-a-box program," we strongly suggest you may be reading the wrong book. This is a book about the true substance of employee engagement, those enduring and endearing elements that may include a few cool perks but encompass so much more.

▶ DISENGAGING MANAGEMENT BEHAVIOR STILL RAMPANT . . . WHY?

If there is one thing company leaders know for sure, it's that they want motivated, enthusiastic, productive workers. Yet, by their actions, many demonstrate daily that they do not know how to bring out the best in people. These actions include:

▶ Cranking up the negative consequences instead of recognizing positive results
▶ Setting goals so unattainably high that workers burn themselves out, reducing the effectiveness of customer interactions
▶ Conducting employee surveys, then failing to take action
▶ Giving performance feedback just once a year, or even less often
▶ Making promises and not keeping them
▶ Ignoring and failing to solicit their employees' ideas

The list can go on and on. The *Dilbert* comic strip has thrived for years by humorously, and often cynically, documenting the many failures and foibles of so-called leaders. The curious thing to us is that leaders and managers behave in so many ways that produce the exact opposite of the response they desire. It is an important and vexing question: why do leaders act counter to their own best self-interests and the best interests of the organizations they are charged with leading?

Here are some examples of self-defeating management behavior from our own experience:

▶ A manager attempted to justify a salary inequity by telling an underpaid employee, "You're lucky you have room to grow."

▶ A manager failed to confront a poorly performing worker who was reducing the effectiveness of the team and causing good performers to leave. The poor performer was not a bad person, just someone who was in the wrong job but had come to realize he could be "willfully useless" without having to pay a consequence. Yet the problems he created continued year after year.

▶ A large consulting firm acquired a small regional firm that over the years had built a sterling reputation based on delivering more than clients expected. When representatives from the acquiring firm came in to address employees of the newly acquired firm, instead of commending them for the market-leader reputation they had built, they berated the assembled managers and staff for "overdelivering" and left a proud team of professionals feeling devalued, demoralized, and resentful.

These are management sins of both commission and omission. The result in either case: disengaged employees who must now be re-engaged . . . or may never be.

▶ SO, WHAT IS EMPLOYEE ENGAGEMENT?

Here are two definitions:

▶ ". . . a heightened *emotional and intellectual connection* that an employee has for his or her job, organization, manager, or coworkers that, in turn, influences him or her to apply additional *discretionary effort* to his/her work."[3]

▶ ". . . the extent to which employees commit to something or someone in their organization and how hard they work and how long they stay as a result of that commitment."[4]

In terms of observable behavior, engaged employees have been described by the following actions:

▶ They give more discretionary effort, defined as the expenditure of effort solely at the discretion of the worker (what we do because we *want* to, not because we *have* to).

▶ They consistently exceed expectations, doing more than what is minimally expected.

▶ They take more responsibility for and "ownership" of the organization's interests and objectives.

▶ They receive better customer service ratings.

▶ They voice more ideas for ways to improve and innovate.

▶ They promote and model teamwork.

▶ They volunteer more for extra assignments and duties.

▶ They anticipate and adapt better to change, and they facilitate change.

▶ They resist changes they see as harmful to the organization.

▶ They persist at difficult work over time.

▶ They tend to tolerate limited periods of lower work satisfaction.

▶ They speak well of the organization to their friends and family.

▶ They are more likely to stay employed with the organization.

What Percentage of Employees in Your Work Unit Is Fully Engaged?

The employee who does all these things all the time would be the perfect employee, and we all know there is no such person. Take a moment to reflect on this question—how many employees in your own place of work consistently demonstrate the behavior described in the bullets above? Would you say 20 percent, 40 percent, 60 percent— or more? Do certain employees come immediately to mind? Do you count yourself among them? Most people, when asked to point out the engaged people in their work units, are able to do so without having to think too hard about it.

In some work teams, almost everyone is engaged. In others, almost no one is. Either way, the consequences are significant. The higher the percentage of engaged employees in your organization, the more likely it is that customers are being served better or that better products are being made.

How many of the actions above do *you* display on a consistent basis? Are you as engaged as you would like to be? If you are, good for you and your employer. If not, why not?

Can a Person Be Too Engaged?

We believe full engagement is always of benefit to the individual and the employer. But as we know, a strength carried to an extreme can quickly become a weakness. Workaholism is not engagement. Employees who constantly push themselves hard to perform well may become burned out. We all need periods of "rejuvenative disengagement" (or downtime) in the form of regular breaks, free evenings and weekends for rest and recreation, and periodic vacations.

Employers also need to guard against taking undue advantage of a highly engaged employee's willingness to take on more work. The "job creep" phenomenon results when managers load up dependable high performers with so much work that opportunities for downtime become less and less available. At the same time, these same managers, instead of confronting their poor performers, choose to give them fewer assignments, which further undermines the engagement of top performers who see and experience the injustice of the situation. This is a recipe for disengagement and turnover of our most valued talent.

How Do We Know an Engaged Employee When We Hear One?

Survey findings reveal that engaged employees tend to have better things to say about their workplaces than employees who are not engaged. Here are a few illustrative comments from some of the employees surveyed from the winning companies featured in this book:

▶ *"I genuinely enjoy working for this company. I look forward to coming in to work every day."*
▶ *"I love it here—I love contributing to make it a better place and knowing what I do is important. I love putting the needs of the*

customer first and taking an interest in assisting them to understand about our products and company."

▶ "At most of my previous jobs, I felt like I was just a number and
all my hard work was not truly recognized and appreciated. At
(our) company, I have been given the opportunity to express my
creativity to the maximum level. In doing so, I have created some
very useful Excel templates that the company has been using since
my hire date."

▶ "This is the best company I have ever worked for. The people and
the management make the environment the best I have seen. People help each other and seem to enjoy working with each other. The
goal that I see is, everyone is working to produce the best product
available. People want to come to work because it is such a good
environment."

How Do We Know a Disengaged Employee When We Hear One?

By contrast, here are some comments from employees at companies
with some of the lowest scores on the *Best-Places-to-Work* engagement
survey:

▶ "My supervisor is a person that I have trouble with. He has no
trust in anybody. He makes the job hard for everybody. He takes
credit for everything. Makes it hard to want to do your best."

▶ "We also work in cubicles that have broken desks, some are missing
drawers or the drawers do not open. It makes employees feel positive
and encourages better productivity when they feel like they are valued.
It does not make me feel valued to come to a desk that is broken."

▶ "If you no longer value your employees and what they can do for
you, they see this and in turn don't work as hard for you or leave
the company (as we have seen recently, losing good people) for
somewhere they can be valued."

▶ "I feel I now cannot give the customer service inside and outside
the organization that I once was so proud of. Due to reducing my

current team, the workload has become tremendous and has placed
a lot of stress on the remaining team members."

So, Where Does Engagement Come From—the Employee or the Employer?

The short answer is that it comes from both. Although the majority of our focus will be on the elements that leaders can address to create a great workplace, we have also included an important chapter on self-engagement. The ideas and practices offered there can help all readers increase their levels of engagement, regardless of (or perhaps in spite of) the quality of management they experience.

Still, the question is an interesting one that business leaders, academicians who study employee motivation, and HR practitioners have thoroughly examined and discussed for decades. Either way, how we answer the question has consequences. If the individual employee is the party most responsible for his or her own engagement, then employers need to focus on finding, recruiting, and selecting engaged employees. If the employer is the party most responsible for employee engagement, then it must put the focus on training, managing, and coaching for optimum engagement. Fortunately, it is not an either-or choice we have to make; smart employers will focus on "both-and."

Why Not Just Hire Employees Who Are Already Engaged?

An executive called recently and asked the following question:

> *I've been reading a lot about employee engagement and how important it is to the success of a company. We've had a lot of employee turnover, and it's having a negative impact on our customer service. Our senior leadership team is now on board with this engagement thing; engaged employees are definitely what we want. **So can you help us develop a preemployment selection assessment process that will help us know the level of engagement of prospective employees?** [Our emphasis.] We want to hire only engaged people.*

It is certainly true that picking the right people in the first place goes a long way toward creating an engaged workplace. But as sincere as the executive's question was, it is really the wrong question. We know what was behind her query: if she could just find people who are, by nature, motivated, energetic, and enthusiastic, then she could largely solve the engagement, retention, and customer service problems at her company. Although it is true that you can use preemployment assessments to learn about the general motivation of an individual, just because the person has that innate drive does not mean he or she will be motivated or engaged at your workplace.

Some employees *are* naturally more engaged than others. One employee engagement researcher (Crant) has rightly pointed out that there are two dimensions of employee engagement behavior: personal and situational.[5] The personal dimension entails the individual's natural predisposition to have a good work ethic, energy, and enthusiasm—in other words, to be self-engaging. The situational dimension covers all factors and conditions within the workplace, such as culture and management practices, that enhance—or reduce—the employee's desire to sustain that engaged behavior. It is the situational dimension that, except for Chapter 10 on self-engagement, will be the focus of this book.

Employee Engagement: Clearly a Two-Way Street

Employee engagement is created and sustained partly by the employee and partly by the employer. Hiring more engaged employees will raise the overall level of employee engagement in your team or organization, but it will not be enough to reach peak levels of employee engagement. If the executive mentioned earlier were to start hiring more naturally self-motivated and enthusiastic employees, and the company did not provide the right leadership, her turnover problem might well get worse. Perhaps there exists a small minority of employees who will stay fully engaged regardless of poor leadership and other negative situational factors, but we cannot recall meeting any. You may have heard it said that "sharp knives are harder to handle than dull ones"—

the upshot is that employers who hire more naturally motivated employees usually must become even more adept at leading them.

What does a motivated employee stuck in a poor work environment sound like? Here are the words of an employee who works at a company that scored in the bottom quartile of *Best-Places-to-Work* survey results:

> *I have no mentor-person to be in contact with when I have problems. When I do discuss difficulties I am having with coworkers and ask for possible solutions, I have not had much success. No feedback, either positive or negative, has been given upon request. I have asked for help from my superiors, but have received marginal help at best. I really love working with the customers and I believe I am helping them, but I feel like I do not fit in with the department.*

It appears that this employee wants to perform, wants to take care of the company's customers, and exhibits the internal motivation to improve and do well in the job. Clearly, this individual has not received the coaching and feedback needed to be fully effective.

This respondent either is already disengaged or is on the slippery slope. It is always disappointing when managers don't work to help individuals who want to be successful in serving their customers and, in turn, find genuine satisfaction in what they do. Our studies reveal that managers are generally more engaged than frontline workers, but in this case, the root of the problem may well be a disengaged manager's indifference to an employee's needs.

In short, the employee needs to be re-engaged. Our fervent belief is that with a different management approach, that can be achieved.

Can Disengaged Workers Be Re-Engaged?

The following story provides insight into this question:

Charlene, a new call center manager, had noticed that one of her direct reports, Jason, a call center analyst, was obviously not engaged in his work. Two of Jason's peers had reported that Jason had been spending lots of time browsing the Internet. Charlene herself had observed Jason returning late from lunch and playing Internet games. She believed that Barry, a former coworker and friend of Jason, had been a negative influence on him. Barry had been in the habit of spending time on the phone making personal calls, playing games on the Internet, and taking long breaks and lunches with Jason.

Charlene knew she had to confront Jason about his behavior. She sat down with him, told him what she had observed, and described the negative impact it was having on coworkers. Jason at first professed not to care, but he finally admitted he was bored in his job. He agreed to change his behavior. In the meantime, Charlene told him she would try to find him a more challenging assignment. After taking stock of some unmet needs in the call center, Charlene assigned Jason to a "quality trending" role where the center was experiencing significant challenges. Jason expressed confidence that he could do the new job well. As things turned out, he blossomed in the new position. Monitoring results, creating new worksheets and handouts, and coming up with new ideas were strengths that had lain dormant in his previous role. Jason had been re-engaged.

Charlene reflected with pride and satisfaction on her successful intervention:

I just let him know he could step outside the previous negative impression he had created. I had seen that he had strong case knowledge and liked to come up with new ideas. He got so much recognition in his new assignment that he later posted for a training position and is doing an outstanding job. Many employees don't get esteem-building in their personal lives, so they are starved for encouragement. We team leaders get so caught up in our tasks sometimes, we can forget to focus on our people.

Who was the prime mover in this story? Clearly, it was Charlene, the manager. As we have asserted, both employees and managers are responsible for self-engagement. But there is a key difference that is also a basic premise of this book—that in addition to keeping themselves engaged, leaders and managers are paid to engage those who report to them.

Engaging and re-engaging employees—as leaders, *this* is our charge.

"Leaving with a Sack in Their Hands"

Mark enjoys telling a story about his father, a successful small-town Nebraska clothier with a passionate customer base and employees whose tenure often surpassed 50 years. As Mark was headed to college in the late 1970s, he sought his dad's counsel on the topic of success in business and in life. One admonition stuck with Mark all these years: *"Son, it's really pretty simple. Success in business starts with caring deeply for your employees so they, in turn, care deeply for your customers. And when your customers feel cared for, they tend to leave the store with a sack in their hands."*

This fatherly advice succinctly captures the relationship between an engaged workplace and customers. Want more customers to "leave with a sack in their hands"? Care deeply for your employees.

▶ LINKING EMPLOYEE ENGAGEMENT TO KEY BUSINESS SUCCESS

It is reasonable to ask, "If we invest more time and money into moving a higher percentage of our employees into the fully engaged category, what business benefit, if any, can we expect from this investment?" The simplified cycle shown in Figure 1.1 shows how engaged workers lead to business success.

Employees Feel
"I'm very lucky because
I love working here."

Customers Return
Customers reward the
business by returning
and telling their friends.

Employees Engage
"I'll work hard to take
care of customers."

Figure 1.1

Indeed, we believe this model reflects exactly what is happening with greater frequency at *Best-Places-to-Work* winners. These elite employers simply seem to have a higher percentage of employees who come to work more excited about doing their jobs and are doing those jobs at a level of enthusiasm not commonly seen at most other employers.

This model suggests that increased employee engagement is a major contributing factor to the success of an organization. Some might look at a successful business and argue that it works the other way around—that the business's success contributes to high employee engagement. This is undeniably true as well, as much of the business-linkage research shows. It's really one of those "which-came-first, the-chicken-or-egg" kind of arguments. Whether employee engagement begins with business success or business success begins with employee engagement matters little since success and engagement are mutually reinforcing. The point is to begin the process wherever the opportunity presents itself.

Academic and popular literature is filled with studies that explore and provide evidence of this relationship. We trust that most of you who are reading this book are aware of this work, so for us to expand on it here would be "preaching to the converted." But if you would like to dig further into these studies, we have included a detailed list on our Web site, www.re-engagebook.com.

▶ BEYOND BUSINESS SUCCESS: EMPLOYEE ENGAGEMENT AS A PREDICTOR OF ECONOMIC WELL-BEING

A study from our research partner, Quantum Workplace, shows that employee engagement is capable of predicting directional movements of the Dow Jones Industrial Average four months ahead of time.[6]

According to Greg Harris, Quantum Workplace president, *"If our Engagement Index is up in June, there's an 83 percent probability that the Dow will be up four months later—in October. To our knowledge, this relationship has never been discovered before."* The study showed how employee engagement is not only a tool for measuring workplace dynamics but also an indicator of economic well-being.

"The results of this analysis for the most recent 12 months was that the engagement trends accurately predicted upward or downward monthly changes correctly in 10 out of 12 months, further providing evidence that employee engagement is indicative of what the Dow will do," adds Mr. Harris.

"Our research includes 24 months' worth of engagement scores among 6,117 companies with valid engagement scores that were measured alongside four different indicators of economic well-being: unemployment, fuel prices, the Dow, and consumer sentiment." Harris's conclusion: *"There exists a significant relationship between employee engagement and each of the four economic indicators."*

Employee engagement—it's not just for breakfast anymore—it's a key predictor of our economy. Let's turn our attention to how one of our winning companies, Gaylord Hotels and Resorts, sees the relationship between employee engagement and its success as a business.

Gaylord Hotels—How Great Workplaces Achieve Great Success

One of the employers we feature is Gaylord Palms Resort and Spa in Orlando, Florida, a beautifully themed 1,406-room luxury hotel located just 1 mile from Walt Disney World. This over-the-top resort offers a variety of restaurants, two pools, a spa club and salon, and a lavish 4.5-acre indoor atrium, which is glass enclosed and air-conditioned for comfort. The atrium includes four sections, each representing a different region of Florida: Key West, St. Augustine, the Everglades, and Emerald Bay. Without leaving the hotel, guests can wander through the misty Everglades, party on a boat in the Keys, explore a Spanish fort, or even watch live alligators being fed in the atrium waterways.

The Gaylord Palms was opened in 2002, the second of four upscale Gaylord Hotels in the United States. The meetings-focused resorts are located near Nashville, Tennessee; Orlando, Florida; Dallas, Texas; and Washington, D.C. Each of the Gaylord properties celebrates the geographical heritage of the destination in which it is located, with regional themes and attractions designed exclusively for that resort.

The Florida resort, which has 1,400 full-time and more than 600 part-time employees, on-call temps, and contract partners, has won an impressive list of awards over the years, including being named one of the Top Five Employers for Working Families in Orlando and a Top 5 Gold Key and Gold Platter Elite Award for Banquet and Convention Services in North America. The Gaylord Palms has received top 10 recognition as a *Best Place to Work* by the *Orlando Business Journal* for three straight years.

We interviewed the hotel's general manager, Kemp Gallineau, and Gaylord's vice president of corporate culture and training, Emily Ellis, to find out how the Palms has attained and sustained its premier-employer status and especially how it has achieved such high survey scores. We'll feature Gaylord throughout the book. Its views on how employee engagement links directly to key business outcomes mirror the sentiments of the other *Best-Places-to-Work* employers we've studied:

Gallineau: *We believe that if we get the right people on the bus and in the right seats, and we then invest in those people, it will pay off in great service to our customers. We explain to our Stars (the company's term for its employees) that our success starts with them. They understand that we will make money if we invest in them. Our assets—the hotel itself and all its attractions—are first class, but it is our staff that makes the difference. So, that basic philosophy is a major factor.*

Ellis: *When we opened the hotel in 2002, it was our first venture outside of the Opryland Hotel in Nashville. Our CEO, Colin Reed, saw the opportunity for us to build a strong brand from the inside out as a great place to work. He was also a true believer in the service-profit chain—that taking care of employees equates to taking care of customers, which results in better profits. That means it's important that we create emotional connections with our people so they will do the same with our customers. That's my role—to help people make connections. The other thing I need to point out is that even though both Colin and Kemp are very results driven and have a head for business, they both have a heart for people. They are both very committed to creating those emotional connections.*

Gallineau: *Our turnover is the lowest in the entire hotel industry—28 percent here at the Gaylord Palms and in the low 30s nationwide. Part of that has to do with the property itself and how impressive it is and the rest of it about our culture, I think. If you asked the average person in the community* *what our "employer brand" is, I think they would simply say "Wow!" People in Orlando know it's a great place to work. The people who work here are happy, and our guests can see that. We are in the number two hospitality market in the United States after Las Vegas. But it's hard to get hired here. There are few openings because people don't want to leave, and when positions do come open, we try to fill them from the inside if we can, though hiring the best available candidate is the key. We promoted 167 people last year.*

▶ FINAL THOUGHT

To be sure, creating a highly engaged workplace doesn't solve all ills, but you have to like your chances of surviving and prevailing better, particularly in this more competitive and turbulent environment, with an engaged workforce than without one.

The Oracle of Omaha, Warren Buffett, once said: *"Time is the friend of the wonderful company, the enemy of the mediocre."* By creating more engaged workplaces, many employers are putting time on their side.

▶ **CHAPTER TWO**

Crosswind Factors

Why It's Harder Than Ever to Build a Winning Workplace

Kites rise higher against the wind.
—Sir Winston Churchill

▶ ANNA'S JOURNEY TO A BETTER WORKPLACE

Anna was guarded about trusting her new employer.

You couldn't blame her, really. In just over four years she had been through a merger—which cost her one great job—only to be downsized at another financial services company because of the severe recession that hit the industry particularly hard. She told her husband she felt betrayed. She and her team in finance had worked very hard, putting in extra time—far beyond what had been expected, in spite of working for a boss she didn't respect. She had also built several friendships that were difficult to leave behind.

The experiences had left her jaded about the corporate world, so when she accepted a new position with a smaller, family-owned company, she promised herself that she wouldn't get too involved "I'll do what is expected," she thought, "but not get in so deeply with what I'm doing that it will make it easier if the hammer drops again and I lose my job."

After a few months, her worries began to go away. She enjoyed her new team members, many who had been with the company for years. They seemed genuinely happy and committed to doing quality work.

Her new manager has been supportive and friendly. He even came to her a few weeks into her tenure and said, *"Anna, I know you've had some bad breaks with other jobs. Although I can't promise what the future holds for any of us, I promise to keep you and the rest of our team informed about what's going on. Personally, I see a great future for you here, either as a manager or, if you think it would be best for you, growing into a senior financial analyst. It's up to you how far you want to take this, and I'll certainly do what I can to help you."*

Anna is now reconsidering her more reserved approach to the workplace. On the recommendation of her boss, she attended a "lunch and learn" hosted by human resources that offered various ways employees could better themselves, either in their current roles or for future opportunities.

In an e-mail to her sister she wrote: *"After a few bad apples I think I may have finally found a home."*

▶ WANTED: ENGAGED EMPLOYEES . . . NOW MORE THAN EVER

If you are a called to be a leader or manager of people, or have been thrust into such a role, it is important that you not underestimate the challenge you are facing. Even before the economic cataclysm of 2008, the following factors had already combined to increase the complexity and difficulty of leading and engaging employees:

▶ The corporate downsizings that began in the 1980s and continued through recent years had all but killed off the idea of long-term loyalty.

▶ The workplace expectations of most Generation Xers (born 1965–1980) and Millennials (born 1981–1994) are so different from those of Traditionalists (born 1945 and before) and Boomers (born 1946–1964), that many long-standing management philosophies and practices are no longer effective.

▶ The continuing retirement of 78 million Boomers, combined with a limited pool of 44 million rising Gen Xers, is expected to result in a long-term talent shortage that (assuming reasonable levels of economic growth) will give more power and leverage to the employee.

▶ Leaner organizational structures have continued to fuel the pressure to "do more with less" at the very time when younger generations (and many older workers) are seeking more work-life balance.

▶ The quickened pace of technological and economic change has made most jobs more complex, requiring greater skill levels and literacy at the precise time when workforce skill levels are dropping.

▶ Facing higher health-care costs, many companies have cut back on benefits without providing compensatory improvements in overall quality of working life.

These challenges will continue to significantly affect how we engage our employees and ourselves.

▶ CROSSWIND FACTORS: CHALLENGES TO EMPLOYEE ENGAGEMENT

We can now report groundbreaking research into three trends that, in whole or in part, make creating a great workplace more difficult. Because they are so relevant, we will reference them frequently throughout this book (identifiable by three icons) and make note of how they impact all aspects of creating a great place to work. In a sense, they will modify, or alter, how you approach literally every strategy you may wish to implement to create a more engaged workplace. They are:

1. **Diseconomies of scale.** As your *company grows in employee size,* it will become increasingly more difficult to create an engaged workplace.

2. **Generational diversity.** As your company *becomes more age diverse,* it will become more difficult to create a highly engaged workplace.

3. **Turbulent times.** When an *economic crisis grows in severity,* impacting your employer and perhaps the greater community in general, employee engagement will be negatively affected.

A former associate of ours, who is a pilot, speaks often of the challenges the aviator faces when there are crosswinds. Additional planning is required. There is a need for additional conversations with air traffic controllers. Pilots may have to put contingency plans into effect that they would never consider in friendlier weather.

It's the same with these three workplace realities. We can still succeed. We can still have highly engaged employees. We can still enjoy the benefits of greater productivity and customer loyalty. It's just going to take more time and more effort, that's all.

We'll introduce you to these three crosswind realities and then discuss how we can face and overcome them as we seek to engage, re-engage, and build better workplaces.

Crosswind Factor #1: Diseconomies of Scale

In his best-selling book *The Tipping Point,* Malcolm Gladwell offers a number of remarkable theories about how little things can make a big difference in our lives, in our work, and even in how products can be marketed. One of those theories has direct application to this work of employee engagement—that the number of employees in the organization can make a big difference in how effectively people relate to and work with one another.[1]

Gladwell cites the research of anthropologist Robin Dunbar, which indicates that we humans may have a limited capacity to effectively work in groups. Dunbar's theory—called channel capacity—suggests that our brains have a channel capacity of roughly 150: "The figure of 150 seems to represent the maximum number of individuals with whom we can have a genuinely social relationship, the kind of relationship that goes with knowing who they are and how they relate to us. Putting it another way, it's the number of people you would not feel embarrassed about joining uninvited for a drink if you happened to bump into them in a bar."[2] Dunbar found many instances where societies that had, without necessarily understanding this dynamic, worked to maintain a group size below this number.

The Tipping Point offers examples of this theory that have likely impacted the design of military units as well as other organizations, including a religious order called the Hutterites, whose communities split as they neared that magic number of 150. In the latter case, a leader in one of the communities indicated that "when things get larger than that, people become strangers to one another."[3] He continues: "If you get too large, you don't have enough things in common, and then you start to become strangers and that close-knit fellowship starts to get lost."[4] Aside from relationship building, Gladwell also suggests that knowledge can be more easily transmitted, shared, and stored in smaller groups.

In the world of business, Gladwell turns to the W. L. Gore Company in Newark, Delaware, as an example of an enterprise that has applied this rule of 150 to its workplace. W. L. Gore is a very successful business that has been recognized as an employer of choice by various sources. As Gladwell explains, the company's founder, Wilbert "Bill" Gore, saw the value of keeping things small. Quoting Gladwell: "'We found again and again that things get clumsy at a hundred and fifty' he [Gore] told an interviewer some years ago, so 150 employees per plant became the company goal. In the electronics division of the company, that meant that no plant was built larger than 50,000 square feet, since there was almost no way to put many more than 150 people in a building that size."[5] It appears the company has kept to this standard, reporting 7,000 associates in 45 locations. If you do the math on that, it works out to just about 155 employees per location.

Our Tipping-Point Research

Limiting unit size is one way a larger enterprise can maintain connectivity and defy the tipping point. Our goal was to see if the tipping-point phenomenon held up under the light of a more rigorous scientific study of employee engagement. Figure 2.1 shows the results of *Best-Places-to-Work* employers ranked by size and their overall engagement scores. As you can see, the overall mean score goes down as the average employer size goes up—our data support Dunbar's theory. These results are statistically significant beyond luck or chance; they truly represent a new reality, particularly for those employers that are large or growing in employee population.

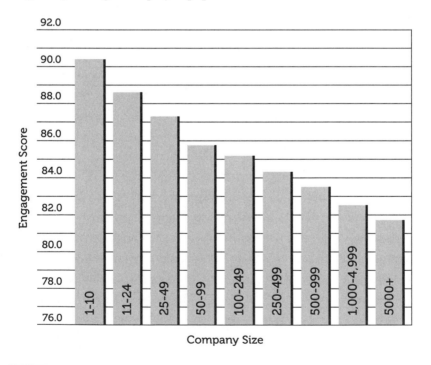

Figure 2.1

But surely, you might say, don't large companies have resources at their disposal to counteract this trend? For example, isn't it common knowledge that employee benefits are better at larger employers? According to our studies, the answer is no—Figure 2.2 shows the total mean score of the two employee benefits survey items on the Quantum Workplace survey. Even in this area, where one might assume larger employers have an advantage, we find this crosswind factor serves to penalize larger employers.

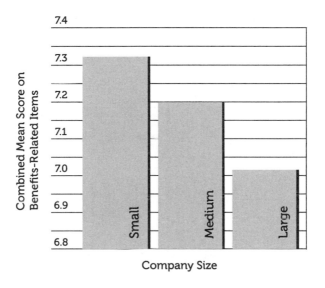

Figure 2.2

This finding goes against what we initially expected. How could smaller employers have an advantage over larger employers when it came to benefits? It turns out that a number of our initial thoughts were off the mark regarding the power of the tipping point.

An additional dynamic that comes with increasing employee populations is the distance between the top leaders of the company and other employees—the layers of hierarchy from the "boardroom to the mailroom," so to speak. Our studies indicate marked differences of employee engagement by position level, as shown in Figure 2.3.

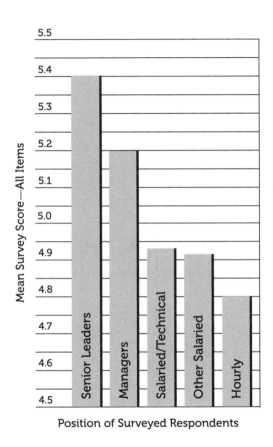

Figure 2.3

As an employer grows, these differences become even more pronounced. There is a greater sense of "haves" and "have-nots" as the distance between senior leaders and other employee levels and groups widens. As an employee of one fast-growing company lamented: "*This used to be a great place to work. Everyone knew each other, and if you had a problem, you knew who to talk to. Now there are so many layers of management that it's a miracle anything gets done around here.*"

Balancing the Diseconomies of Scale

We now consult the comments of employees at *Best-Places-to-Work* employers to gain insights into this business of the tipping point. We wondered if there are winning employers where the pull of the tipping point is being reduced by an equal or larger force, that counterbalances the negative effects of size.

The answer, thankfully, is yes.

We start with a comment or two from smaller employers to get a sense of how the tipping-point phenomenon is experienced in the life of an average employee; and then we move to larger employers, where, in theory, the tipping point should be working to reduce levels of engagement.

This first employee works for a company that has 40 employees and that is experiencing significant growth:

> *I love being part of a small, growing organization and feeling like my contributions count toward its progress in some way. I also value getting to see the inner workings of a business gaining its ground. I know working here is a valuable experience people don't get every day, and the company has taken chances on me that other more-established companies would not.*

This next employee works for a larger employer with roughly 90 associates. Yet the positive comments about her work experience still resonate:

> *This is a great company to work for. It is a great environment where everyone knows each other and everyone gets along. It's big enough where you get a wide variety of people, but small enough for everyone to know each other. The management is leading this company in the right direction. This is a place I would like to work for many years.*

Our next employee works for a winning *Best-Places-to-Work* large employer—with over 10,000 employees in various locations. These are the companies that Gladwell believes are at most risk of losing the same connective power that a smaller employer can offer:

> *Our company strives for the small-company friendly and family-oriented atmosphere despite having thousands of employees all over. I was going to only work here for two years and move to another state, but I have changed my mind. I am going to stay with the company now since I am well aware how hard it is to find a job you enjoy and a company you love.*

In the eyes of this last employee the tipping point has been kept at bay, and as a result he is choosing to engage and stay.

And finally, we identified an employee in a larger company (700 employees) that acquired the smaller company where she worked. Surely, you might think, the transition into a larger company would break the spirit of one who had cherished that family feeling with a smaller company. Not so:

> *I joined this company through an acquisition. I was nervous at first about joining such a large company, but I have never regretted it. Despite the difference in size, the company has just as intimate a feel as my former company. The senior leaders know people's names and what's happening in their daily lives and truly care about us as people as well as employees. This really trickles down into the rest of the company, and that makes it a wonderful place to come to work in the morning. Thank you for giving us an opportunity to participate in this survey.*

A story begins to emerge from these comments about what *Best-Places-to-Work* employers are doing to create winning workplaces—they are about creating a sense of family, building personal connections between the senior leadership and employees, and eliciting the feeling that you're part of something special in which you have a significant measure of influence. In later chapters we will explore these themes that, in total, generate the conditions where engagement and re-engagement can happen.

The Boardroom-to-Mailroom Engagement Gap

And that engagement gap that we spoke of between senior leaders and hourly employees? The two examples in Figures 2.4 and 2.5 show the marked contrast. As you can see in Figure 2.4, when levels of employee engagement are low—in this case from an employer scoring in the bottom quartile—the difference in scores between senior leaders and other employee groups can be quite stark.

Position Level	No.	Mean Item Score	Agree	Neutral	Disagree
Executive Level	11	5.0	100%		
Manager Level	32	4.5	67%	16%	17%
Professional/Technical Level	101	4.0	36%	46%	18%
Other Salaried	39	2.7	33%	67%	
Hourly	276	3.3	22%	46%	33%

Figure 2.4

By contrast, the results in Figure 2.5 show what happens when an employer has very high employee engagement scores, in this case from a winning *Best-Places-to-Work* employer. Higher overall levels of engagement act as a buffer to the diseconomies of scale.

Position Level	No.	Mean Item Score	Agree	Neutral
Executive Level	9	5.9	100%	
Manager Level	57	5.9	100%	
Professional/Technical Level	193	5.9	98%	2%
Other Salaried	107	5.7	90%	10%
Hourly	310	5.7	95%	5%

Figure 2.5

Crosswind Factor #2: Generational Diversity

It is a fact of life that growing up in different eras causes people to see the world (and other generations) differently. Many would agree with the following stereotypes:

▶ *Traditionalists (born 1945 and before)* are duty bound and hardworking but may be inflexible and resistant to change.
▶ *Boomers (born 1946–1964)* are ambitious and participative but may be overly political and self-interested.
▶ *Gen Xers (born 1965–1980)* are independent and resourceful but may be cynical and disrespectful.
▶ *Millennials (born 1981–1994)* are self-confident and technically sophisticated but may be dependent and naïve.

Of course we all know many people in each generation, including ourselves, for whom these stereotypes are absolutely untrue. *This point cannot be overemphasized: the unique combination of one's personality, life experiences, education, ethnicity, and upbringing trumps generational membership.*

There can be no doubt that the sweeping changes of the last 30 years, such as new technologies, the increasing divorce rate and growth in the rate of single parenthood, and global competition, have uniquely and powerfully shaped the development and character of different generations. Experts have cited the increasing prevalence of video games, computer access, and texting and their effect on the brain conditioning and personality development of large numbers of Gen Xers and Millennials. Stereotypical perceptions, even if they are not applicable to many, are part of the reality we must deal with daily in managing our workplaces.

Employee Engagement by Generation

We hypothesized that if differing generational views about engagement and loyalty are as real as we think they are, they would show up in the survey data. Our analysis produced a clear conclusion:

> Overall employee engagement levels differ by age group and trend toward older employees being more engaged. Of all employee age groups, Traditionalists generally report the highest levels of employee engagement, followed by Boomers, then Gen Xers, then Millennials.

Figure 2.6 represents our findings related to employee engagement by age. Although the youngest of employees (less than 25 years of age) report higher levels of engagement, the trend otherwise shows employees becoming more engaged as they age.

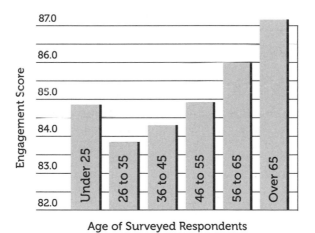

Age of Surveyed Respondents

Figure 2.6

The data suggest that younger generations are more likely to say: *"I'm not really crazy about the job I'm currently in, and if I don't find something that fits my career plans, I'm going to get my résumé updated and see what else is out there."* Younger employees, as a rule, don't appear to have the same commitment to their employers as older employees, and are seemingly more willing to pick up and move elsewhere if their current job does not provide a high level of interest and satisfaction.

A recent newspaper article quotes a young woman regarding her lack of work commitment: *"If people don't even go into something like marriage with the thought that they are stuck in it forever, I don't think they are going to enter a corporate institution or some other place of employment thinking that they have to stay there."*[6] Her sentiments mirror the survey results. This general lack of engagement can severely diminish both employee performance and retention.

AND AS WE BECOME MORE DIVERSE . . .

We conducted a novel analysis of the results from *Best-Places-to-Work* surveys to determine whether the more age-diverse employers had lower engagement levels. In other words, we asked: "Does having a broader and more balanced spectrum of ages represented in the workforce reduce an employer's chances of creating a highly engaged workplace?"

The results of our analysis—after controlling for other company characteristics such as age, position type, company size, and tenure—showed us that *greater variation in age within a company actually has a negative impact on engagement.* The statistical results were quite eye-opening. It turns out that, after controlling for the variables described above, the level of generational diversity accounts for more than 25 percent of the variance in employee engagement. Said another way, this single variable, what we call the Generational Diversity Indicator (GDI), is a significant factor in the ability of an organization to create a highly engaged workplace.[7]

Generational Diversity Indicator
How much of an impact does this single factor have on employee engagement? **The greater the age diversity (the higher the GDI), the less likely the employer will have high engagement scores.**

For example, according to our study:

If an employer has a slightly age-diverse workforce (more than 1.5 on our scale), it is three times more likely to have a lower overall engagement score.

If the employer has a moderately age-diverse workforce (more than 2.0), it is five times more likely to have a lower overall engagement score.[8]

If an employer has a highly age-diverse workforce (more than 3.0), it is six times more likely to have a low overall engagement score.

Even the best of *Best-Places-to-Work* employers find generational diversity challenging. The CEO of one winning company, who has primarily hired younger employers at his technology-based services company, has admitted to failures in assimilating older employers into the culture. He states: *"Older employees often have perceptions of work which aren't necessarily wrong, but are very different than our culture. We've had a few who didn't make it because they were rejected by younger employees before they even had a chance to succeed."*

The correlation between greater age diversity and lower engagement applies to employers regardless of average workforce age—in other words, regardless of which generation is predominant in the organization. Thus a relatively homogenous company of mostly Boomers or mostly Generation Xers is more likely to have a higher level of employee engagement than an employer with more generational diversity.

In summary, a company's GDI is a revealing demographic, potentially indicating a significant challenge to its efforts to develop a highly engaged workforce. Most employers aren't going to resist the demographic trend and economic necessity of generational diversity just because it makes employee engagement more challenging. The tide cannot be turned. We all will need to accept this phenomenon while working to lessen any negative effects and turn increased diversity to our advantage where we can.

NARROWING THE GENERATION GAP

We asked the obvious question: "What, if anything, are employers with higher engagement scores doing differently to lessen the negative effects of generational diversity?"

Our research revealed that employers with significantly higher levels of overall employee engagement—recognized as *Best Places to Work*—have significantly smaller gaps in engagement scores among the four generations.

According to our studies, employers who score highest in overall employee engagement have engagement score gaps between generations that are half the size of lowest-scoring employers.[9]

This means that employees in workplaces where overall engagement is high, regardless of age, are more satisfied with the kind of work they are doing, experience higher levels of teamwork, feel more valued and recognized, and are less likely to be searching for a higher paycheck. To be sure, the generation gaps still exist, but creating a great workplace seems to act as a governor on negative feelings about differences of age and perspective.

We present the remarks of three young people just starting their careers in nursing, accounting, and construction, respectively. They all work for employers selected as *Best Places to Work*, based solely on employee survey results. It is clear that their employers have created superior work environments where employees in their twenties can be excited about what they do and feel committed to staying there.

▶ **THE YOUNG NURSE**

This is my first professional job. I have worked at two other hos-
pitals before I completed nursing school and can say that I feel
lucky to start my nursing career here. My nursing orientation was
excellent, and now that I am fully oriented, I can confidently say
that I am where I need to be. I have intelligent mentors who are
approachable and knowledgeable. I have only positive things to say
about the hospital and plan on working here for years to come.

▶ **THE YOUNG ACCOUNTANT**

The firm has provided me with more opportunities to grow my
skill set than I would have received at many other organizations.
I am allowed to grow and expand my areas of competence based on
performance, not age or any other factor.

▶ **THE YOUNG PROJECT MANAGER**

I have worked for the company just over a year, and I have learned
more than in college or graduate school. As a young person in the
company, the management really takes you under their wing and
they place a lot of trust and responsibility in you. . . . They realize
that the best way to learn is through challenges. Every person at
the company is open to any question you may have. The company
is extremely focused on the development of their young staff. I love
my job, and I have grown to be extremely confident in my career.
I have no plans to leave because I really feel that it is the best place
for me.

There were a hundred more quotes in this same vein that we could
have cited, most from respondents whose employers are creating highly
engaged workplaces. These three young people are anything but indifferent about their work experiences, and their attitudes stand in sharp contrast to the way many research studies have characterized Millennials:

- ▶ Instead of indifference, you hear passion.
- ▶ Instead of doubts about staying, you hear commitment.
- ▶ Instead of "I'm in this just for me," you hear the embrace of community.

Despite complaints to the contrary among "we with the graying hair," this younger generation *can* be engaged, and the variable that makes the difference is the quality of our leadership. Engaging leadership closes the generation gaps by sowing harmony instead of discord, cooperation instead of conflict, and understanding instead of bias.

We must acknowledge the reality that there is a generation gap in the world of work, one that likely impacts overall morale and productivity. Aspiring "employers of choice" must address and close the gap as part of an overall business strategy.

Margaret Mead, who first pointed out the generation gap in the 1970s, knew that any challenge, including this one, can be solved. She said: "Never doubt that a small group of thoughtful committed citizens can change the world; indeed, it's the only thing that ever has."

Leaders of progressive organizations are creating workplaces where each generation can learn to live and work together effectively. We can choose to be part of that smaller group that is bridging the generation gap, and make our places of work more joyous and productive as a result. Those companies that have created truly remarkable workplaces, and have been honored for their efforts through the *Best-Places-to-Work* program, are showing us the way.

Crosswind Factor #3: Turbulent Times

As a result of a number of misguided business and economic practices, the United States began to suffer a severe economic crisis in the fall of 2008 that sent many companies to their demise, as well as thousands to the unemployment lines, and provoked a governmentwide struggle to head off a national depression.

The magnitude of this economic challenge can be expressed by a few sobering facts:

- More than 4.7 million U.S. workers lost their jobs between November 2008 and June 2009.[10]
- At the beginning of 2008, the Dow-Jones Industrial Average was over 12,400. By February 2009, it had dropped below 7,200, a net loss of over 42 percent. By October, the national unemployment rate had reached 9.8 percent, the highest in years.[11]
- More than 150,000 layoffs were announced among America's 500 largest companies in January 2009 alone, including cuts by stalwart employers such as Boeing, Starbucks, Target, Caterpillar, Pfizer, Home Depot, General Motors, Disney, Xerox, GE, Motorola, Best Buy, Walgreens, and Google.
- By February 2009, one in four American companies had instituted salary freezes.[12]
- Some industries, such as domestic automobiles, were suffering and nearing collapse. The National Automobile Dealers Association predicted that roughly 900 of the nation's 20,770 new-car dealers would go out of business in 2009, and automobile analysts predicted that the number of failed dealerships would rise into the thousands.[13]
- American stores dropped prices, reducing profit margins and leading to the closure of stores such as Circuit City, Linens 'N Things, and Sharper Image.[14]

We knew on the day of the financial meltdown (September 13, 2008) that it was a watershed moment. In most of our lifetimes, and certainly in the previous five years that *Best-Places-to-Work* contests have been held yearly in dozens of U.S. cities, nothing of this magnitude had happened. We saw the potential that these concussive events could drive down levels of employee engagement across all industries. The research we have conducted into U.S. employers who participate in *Best-Places-to-Work* competitions clearly shows that employers can significantly influence, if not control, how motivated and satisfied their employees are. Still, we couldn't help wondering how such a "tectonic shift" beyond employers' control—the economic crisis—might affect employee feelings and perceptions about their workplaces.

ENGAGEMENT SCORES UP . . . UNTIL MID-2008

One of the unique aspects of the *Best-Places-to-Work* surveys is that the annual awards events are conducted in 45 different cities at different times of the year, but at the same time of the year in each location. In Omaha, Nebraska, for example, *Best-Places-to-Work* polling begins each February, while in Kansas City, Missouri, survey responses are collected in August. We had access to year-over-year survey results for hundreds of employers, allowing us to compare what employees said about their employers in the fall of 2008, in the midst of an economic "perfect storm," with their responses in previous, calmer years.

Most previous employee engagement research had focused on internally stimulated employee engagement drivers and had not considered externally influenced factors. In a survey conducted by Hewitt Associates early in 2008, the Conference Board sought to find out if the economic conditions at that time were having an impact on employee engagement. Among the questions asked was "Is there a recession?"

"The short answer is that, based on Hewitt research on employee engagement and motivation in more than six thousand organizations, we don't see a psychological recession overall. During the last five years, overall levels of engagement have remained relatively stable, at just over 50 percent globally."[15]

So the general consensus, at least through the first half of 2008, was that employee engagement in the United States was stronger than in most countries and apparently immune to the reports of a coming recession. Economists later reported that the recession technically began in December 2007, but as we now know, the worst was yet to come.

In September and October of 2008 the economic conditions in the country and worldwide began a dramatic decline. That's when we asked ourselves, "Would the shock-and-fear-inducing economic news make it harder for *Best-Places-to-Work* employers to retain their premier-employer status?"

CAN EMPLOYEE ENGAGEMENT WITHSTAND A SEVERE RECESSION?

In November 2008, Quantum Workforce collected data from *Best-Places-to-Work* employers where surveys had been conducted during the fall of both 2007 and 2008. Out of the hundreds of employers that participated in several events across the United States, 210 of them had participated in both years. Among those 210, a sufficient percentage of their employees completed the survey to establish that overall results were reliable within a margin of error of plus or minus 3 percent.

Figure 2.7 shows how the 210 employers' engagement scores fared from the late third quarter and early fourth quarter of 2007 to the same time period of 2008. By an almost 2-to-1 margin (134 to 76), more employers received lower overall employee engagement scores in 2008 than in 2007. This result was a definite departure from the previous five-year trend and strongly suggested that the external circumstance of the foundering economy was negatively influencing employees' attitudes about their jobs and workplaces.

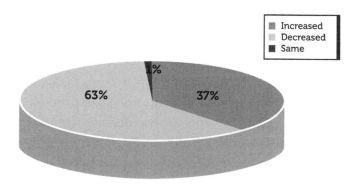

Figure 2.7

Another study documented that survivors of layoffs have difficulty staying productive, again revealing the clear loss of engagement brought on by actual layoffs or by doubts about how the economy might affect one's own employer. Three-fourths of 4,172 workers who have kept their jobs say their own productivity has dropped since their organizations let people go. The findings were based on a Leadership IQ survey of workers who remain employed at 318 companies following corporate layoffs conducted since June 2008.[16]

Thankfully, employee engagement began to stabilize in the first quarter of 2009 (Q1 2009 average engagement score was 86.68 compared with Q1 2008 average score of 86.58). One employee reflected the sentiment of many who were caught in the midst of this crisis:

> *In this economy, you can't find yourself putting all your eggs in one basket. It's not the company's fault entirely, but I do feel that [the company] is doing everything they can to protect not only the interest of their company but also the valuable and skilled workers that are here. In the end, who knows what will transpire? I have qualms with certain practices, but overall I am happy with the effort of the organization; I am impressed with the dedication to uphold their philosophy in these tough times; and I am delighted to walk down the hallways in the morning.*

The object lesson, however, is quite clear: if a crosswind, such as an economic recession, suddenly shifts across an employer's glide path, it can have a predictably negative impact on employee engagement.

ENGAGING LEADERSHIP IN TURBULENT TIMES

In the course of writing this book we profiled several outstanding organizations that have consistently shown themselves to be a cut above—the best of the best. We'll offer a more in-depth treatment of their mindsets and associated actions later, but first we'll look at how they've dealt with crisis. How do winning workplaces go about helping employees keep sight of where the business is going? Meet Nalley

Automotive, an Atlanta-based firm in an industry (car dealerships) that has seen its share of ups and downs:

> We have asked our 80 service advisors what they are noticing with customers, and we will be hearing back from them soon. We have had to lay people off since the economy started its downturn in December 2007. But we know we are going to make it through tough times because we do things right. We are also very open about the business and what's happening during times like these, **and we paint a very vivid picture of what the good times will look like after we get through this.** We ask our associates, "How would you like to be a competitor of ours at that point in time?"[17]
> —RYLAND OWEN, TRAINER/RECRUITER, NALLEY AUTOMOTIVE, OCTOBER 2008

And what about recognizing and celebrating employee successes? Surely such practices must suffer when times get difficult, right? The budget might be trimmed a bit, but one of our featured winning companies, Joie de Vivre Hospitality of San Francisco, sees recognition as a critical component of its success, particularly in difficult times:

> We decided this year not to pony up to reserve the nightclub where we had held our big holiday party for 1,000 associates as we had done in past years. We chose to have it at one of our own hotels instead. It will be a more conservative party, but it is still a big deal because **it's where we recognize our associates for all their contributions during the year and hand out a few awards that are very important to us as a culture.**[18]
> —JANE HOWARD, CHIEF PEOPLE OFFICER, JOIE DE VIVRE HOSPITALITY, NOVEMBER 2008

And from Kemp Gallineau, General Manager of Gaylord Resort Hotel and Spa in Orlando comes another creative way to help employees through tough times, using one of the natural and readily available assets of the hotel—food:

> In 2008 we saw that the economy was starting to change, and we realized we had to find ways to give back to employees in less costly ways. **So we started asking ourselves how we could focus on helping employees save time, which is increasingly precious to them.** So we came up with the idea for what we call "Star-mart" in the hotel, where we give staff . . . whom we call Stars . . . the opportunity to buy food staples on their way home rather than have to take the time to stop at a grocery. So every day we have a site where people can buy the quality grocery items that we buy in bulk—meats, milk, cheese, pizzas, roasted chicken, turkey for Thanksgiving Day, and so on, all at reduced rates. This has helped them save gas money as well. They can also order meals to go from our restaurants at cost.[19]

> *Postscript*
> We contacted Kemp Gallineau a few months after our original interview to ask him how the deep and continuing recession had affected the hotel and the engagement of employees. His response: *"It was a tough call, but because of the severity of the recession, we had to reduce our workforce by 10 percent. We provided career transition services for them, and we held several meetings with remaining employees to address their insecurities. We were simply honest; we let them know that we did what we had to do because of business realities. Since then, because of staff reductions, we have had to do some work sharing. For example, because we have fewer front-desk people, we found out that some of our employees in other departments, like catering, setup, and room service had front-desk experience with other previous employers, and they now cover the front desk during their*

less busy times of the day. The interesting thing is that our guest satisfaction scores and percentage of profit are both up. We believe that's because our Stars have responded to the challenge with an all-hands-on-deck mentality. They have stepped up like good athletic teams do when a star player is injured. We think they are more engaged than they were before. They also know we're doing everything we can to bring in new business. One way we do that is to have a map showing where our salespeople are traveling on any given day to call on corporate customers. The locations light up electronically, and there's a small photo of that salesperson, so our people can see that they, too, are on a mission."

We'll offer more practical tips for managing in difficult times as we present each of six key engagement drivers in later chapters. For now we want to be clear about one thing: a highly engaged workforce is important when business is going well, but your efforts will be doubly rewarded in a crisis.

▶ WHAT'S NEXT? HOW THE BEST EMPLOYERS ADDRESS THESE REALITIES

So now we have an understanding of the depth of these crosswind realities—how employee size, generational diversity, and economic turbulence can throw us off-course. We also know that some employers are trimming their sails, plowing head-on into these crosswinds, and continuing to succeed in our ever-changing business and social landscape.

But how do they go about doing this? What approaches have they found most successful in dealing with these challenging realities? What principles, practices, and practical actions do they take to attain and sustain their elite-employer status? What do they avoid, knowing certain actions can be very harmful to maintaining an engaged workforce? And what can we do to more effectively engage ourselves where we work?

We now turn our attention, and devote the rest of this book, to answering these very questions.

▶ **CHAPTER THREE**

What Separates the Best from the Rest?

Six Universal Engagement Drivers

The effect of sailing is produced by a judicious arrangement of the sails to the direction of the wind.

—WILLIAM FALCONER

▶ ARMAND'S DISCOVERY: "BEST PLACES" *REALLY DO* EXIST

Armand was proud that he and his family had gained citizenship in the United States after coming from Mexico 12 years ago. His family insisted he get his high school diploma, and after graduation Armand secured an entry-level position at a local manufacturing company. A good friend of the family who had worked there for several years encouraged Armand to apply and sang the company's praises: *"Maravilloso,"* he would frequently say.

But Armand was still leery. In his home country he had grown up to fear many employers, who often were harsh and cruel to workers. His father had told him stories that made the hair on the back of his head stand up. But this employer was different. It seemed like the manager, the "*jefe*," was actually nice to employees. Sure, there were times when he was frustrated when things weren't going as well as he would have liked. But he never seemed to take it out on the employees; rather, he quietly corrected employees and encouraged them to do better next time.

Armand also grew to admire his coworkers, who taught him how to work as part of their team. In the distribution area where he was assigned, he learned that some employees were better at certain tasks, so they were given the work that best fit them. For example, Nancy excelled at talking to customers, so that task usually fell to her. When it came time to train Armand in this important task, Nancy was his coach.

Armand was also thrilled that he had decent employee benefits, which were important to him and his wife as they made plans to start a family. In addition, the company was interested in helping Armand get his college degree, and the tuition reimbursement program helped him pick up a couple of night courses every semester.

Armand knew he was very lucky, finding an employer who was interested in him and could help him be successful. He plans to return the favor with hard work and loyalty, two qualities that have helped him and his family achieve the American Dream.

▶ WHAT DIFFERENTIATES WINNING *BEST-PLACES-TO-WORK* EMPLOYERS?

Armand's account is one of the many success stories from winning employers, those companies that, day in and day out, are making a positive difference for the Armands of the world.

But getting to the happy ending for Armand and others like him is a complicated task, and many leaders often ask us where they should start in their journey of making their organizations better places to work. One leader made the point: "*Look, I've only got so much time and resources to help this business, just like everyone else. Where do I start, and what's going to give me the best return on my investment?"* We realize that looking for the best "return on investment," so to speak, will be important for all employers in building, or rebuilding, their status as a great workplace.

Certainly, we reasoned, the impressive engagement scores of the winning companies did not happen by luck or chance—winners must be doing something better than or different from companies with lower engagement scores. Since 2004, several hundred employers have been recognized in various communities, so we knew we would have plenty of companies to ask about their "secrets of employee engagement." Our job was to glean insights from our in-depth data analysis and through discussions with winning employers, to ascertain "the set of their sails."

▶ "LEADING" VERSUS "LAGGING" INDICATORS

We often hear experts in the fields of economics and accounting talk about "leading" and "lagging" indicators. The so-called lagging indicators help to explain what has already happened, while leading indicators help to predict what *will* happen. In business, for example, a company's profitability is a lagging indicator, because it is a measure of what has already happened in a business related to its relative profitability.

In human resources we might also talk of leading and lagging indicators. A company's yearly turnover rate, for example, would be a lagging indicator, because it tracks historical data—the number and percentage of employees that have already left the organization. This and other lagging indicators are important to be sure, but we wanted to help identify the leading factors that could help predict the future, especially about critical business outcomes such as employee turnover, profitability, or customer loyalty.

We have abundant evidence that the factors we are about to describe are leading indicators of employee engagement. How well we manage these factors can, with some level of accuracy, help us predict the future of what our workplaces will look and feel like when it comes to achieving and maintaining that select and enviable status—their targeted talent's "employer-of-choice." Several studies cited in Appendix B on our Web site, www.re-engagebook.com, show a strong correlation between highly engaged employees and key business outcomes. They predict with some level of certainty the success of the business based on organizational features and management practices that lead to more engaged employees. Our goal in the following chapters is to more fully characterize those important elements that truly differentiate the "best from the rest" when it comes to building engaged workplaces.

▶ HOW WE ANALYZED THE DATA

We had at our fingertips a treasure trove of information to be analyzed. The conclusions we offer are the distillation of several years of study, including:

- ▶ **Quantitative analysis.** A comprehensive statistical analysis of the Quantum Workplace engagement survey, looking for items that clearly differentiate winning from nonwinning employers. This included the use of sophisticated regression models that help to identify what factors explain the greatest level of variance among the overall engagement scores. We also looked at the impact that certain demographic characteristics—age, tenure, position type or level, and company size—may have on overall employee engagement.

- ▶ **Qualitative analysis.** Together, we have carefully read verbatim survey comments from over 150,000 individual employees. These comments provide richness and perspective and have served to greatly amplify and clarify the quantitative results. The insights in this book, and the associated recommendations, would be of significantly less value if not for our efforts to read, categorize, and analyze these candid comments. On reflection, it has been a little like hanging out at America's "electronic watercooler." (For additional information about the rigorous approach we took in analyzing and categorizing anecdotal comments in relationship to the overall employee engagement scores, see Appendix A on our Web site, www.re-engagebook.com.)

We have been privileged to view the thinking and, more important, the feelings of employees in thousands of companies across the United States and, in particular, those recognized as *Best Places to Work*. This research has allowed us to clearly visualize what it's like to work in these environments, assess the state of morale in various work groups, or simply appreciate how excited an employee can be in going the extra mile to help a coworker or serve a customer.

▶ WHAT OUR ANALYSIS REVEALED: SIX UNIVERSAL ENGAGEMENT DRIVERS

As we analyzed the data, a series of themes or elements began to emerge, along with a narrative so clear and compelling that we marveled at its logic, at how simple and intuitive it seemed. It is a story in six parts, each an important building block of a highly engaged workplace culture. We will tell that story in the next six chapters, each revealing the dynamics and interplay of six Universal Engagement Drivers (Figure 3.1).[1] They are:

- ▶ **Caring, competent, and engaging senior leaders.** The bottleneck is never at the bottom. Employee engagement starts with a senior leadership team that truly cares about employees, is committed to creating a great place to work, and is trusted by employees to lead them to future success.
- ▶ **Effective managers who keep employees aligned and engaged.** Senior leaders can't do it alone. They need competent

managers who also care about employees and help them stay motivated and aligned to where the company is going and to its current objectives.

▶ **Effective teamwork at all levels.** These great companies know that outstanding work isn't done in a vacuum. It is done in a team environment where the individual members are encouraged and supported to be at their best. And these winning companies reject "us versus them" in any form.

▶ **Job enrichment and professional growth.** Within those effective work teams, employees are not just allowed but encouraged to do jobs they find satisfying and rewarding. They are also given plenty of opportunities to grow and develop in their current roles or in future assignments.

▶ **Valuing employee contributions.** As employees work to contribute to the organization's success, the company knows how to acknowledge, recognize, and reward them in ways that are most meaningful to the individual and relevant to organizational goals.

▶ **Concern for employee well-being.** Last but not least, great employers know that the productivity of their associates relies on their general health and well-being and do everything they can reasonably do to demonstrate their genuine concern.

One definition of "driver" captures the concept nicely—"a part that transmits force or motion." At the winning employers we have had the privilege of studying, there clearly are forces that propel engagement forward. It is not happenstance. It is not an activity that is only occasionally considered once "the real business of our business" is done. Each driver acts as one of six carefully set sails that catch the wind of human effort to thrust the organization forward.

One leader shared with us his fear that organizational entropy can set in, when the business, if left to its own devices, will degenerate to its lowest common denominator of service without an intentional process in place to guard against it. To create, and maintain, high levels of engagement requires significant drive and resolute purpose.

Figure 3.1   The Six Universal Engagement Drivers

The six drivers are universal in the sense that all six are to be found at high levels in the cultures of the most highly engaged workplaces in our study. Indeed, because the six drivers are intertwined with one another and woven into the fabric of an organization's culture, it is almost inconceivable that a premier employer would score low on one or more of these drivers.

Our research indicates that these six drivers work in concert to amplify overall employee engagement. Other factors have an impact on employee engagement, but none rise to the same level of primacy. They create a gestalt, a whole that is more than the sum of its parts. The absence of one driver may easily cancel out the benefits gained by the presence of another, as these examples show:

If You ...	But ...	Then ...
Have committed, caring senior leadership	Have poorly trained managers who can't help employees be successful	The efforts of the senior leaders are thwarted
Genuinely care about the career growth of your employees	Don't recognize or reward them when they make important contributions to the success of the business	They may become discouraged and look for employment elsewhere
Have excellent health and retirement benefits	Don't offer employees leadership they trust	They may watch the clock more than they think about their productivity
Have a meaningful way of recognizing employees	Don't offer opportunities for them to grow and develop	They will find those opportunities elsewhere
Have effective managers who want to do right by their employees	Cut back on or don't provide competitive benefits	They may feel forced to seek a position with better benefits
Have employees who like working with their team and have strong team accountabilities	Are poorly managed by their team leader	The team will underperform, and team members will be disengaged

▶ COMPARING UNIVERSAL ENGAGEMENT DRIVERS TO RETENTION RISK FACTORS

In 2005, Leigh Branham's book, *The 7 Hidden Reasons Employees Leave*, reported the results of his analysis of thousands of "employee post-exit surveys" that were collected by the third-party Saratoga Institute. In 19,700 such surveys, individuals who had voluntarily left their employers voiced the reasons they chose to move on. Leigh's research identified seven factors that most frequently drove good employees to put that first foot out the door.

In the table that follows, we compare the list of retention risk factors (turnover root causes) identified in Leigh's book with the list of engagement drivers described here:

Retention Risk Factors	Universal Engagement Drivers
Loss of trust and confidence in senior leaders	Caring, competent, and engaging senior leaders
The mismatch between the job and the person	Job enrichment and professional growth
Too little coaching and feedback	Effective managers that align and engage
Too few growth and advancement opportunities	Job enrichment and professional growth
Feeling devalued and unrecognized	Being valued for contributions
Stress from overwork and work-life imbalance	A genuine concern for the well-being of employees
The job or workplace was not as expected	An employee may have expected any of the above drivers and not found or sustained them in the job or workplace

Although the studies were done independently using data from different sources, they come to remarkably similar conclusions about the hallmarks of employee engagement. As you see in the table, six of the negatively stated risk factors on the left are mirror images of the drivers on the right—the six positive contributors to engagement. In other words, the retention risk factors and engagement drivers are flip sides of the same coin: the list of things that disengage, deenergize, and drive people away from a particular workplace are almost the exact inverse of those that get them excited about being highly productive on the job.

As we have previously defined it, engagement is much more than employees just showing up or going through the motions. It's about employees taking the extra steps necessary to provide great customer service. It's about one employee at a time working hard to achieve the desired result even when a supervisor isn't hovering. It's about the promise of going to work in a job that becomes a true expression of self and feeling genuine pride when the opportunity arises to tell someone where you work.

We see a causal sequence in the synthesis of these two studies, as illustrated in the pyramid in Figure 3.2. We believe that paying attention to, and leveraging, the six drivers will increase your chances of building and maintaining highly engaged work teams. Not only that, but the increased employee retention you realize will arrive as a welcome bonus.

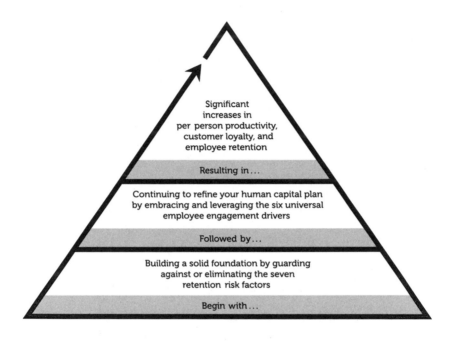

Figure 3.2

▶ EMPLOYEE ENGAGEMENT—EVOLVING VIEWS OF SENIOR LEADERSHIP AND BENEFITS

In 2004, Quantum Workplace began *Best-Places-to-Work* studies in several U.S. cities. After the inaugural year closed, Quantum conducted an analysis to identify whether there were any factors that seemed to be having a significant impact on retention risk and a desire on the part of employees to go the extra mile at work. The initial research was not as exhaustive as the work that went into the collaboration that led to this book, but it gives some longitudinal insight into changing employee perceptions through the years about what engages them at work.

Although the highest-ranked engagement drivers have remained relatively unchanged over the last five years, there are two significant exceptions: in *employee perceptions about senior leadership* and in *personal well-being and employee benefits*. To be sure, winning companies are doing a far better job of meeting these needs, as reflected in their higher scores.

Regarding *perceptions about the senior leadership* of organizations, employees most commonly would say:

Ten Years Ago . . .	Today . . .
I'm interested in having senior leaders that are competent and have a plan to move us forward. I'm probably more connected to my direct supervisor and whether she or he cares about my growth and development.	*I am keenly aware of the senior leadership of our company; and when I feel I can trust and be confident in them, that they care more about the company than their self-interest, and that they care about me as a human being, I'm much more willing to trust where they're trying to take our company.*

How to explain the higher standards and expectations of today? In the past few years, as companies have failed, many in the workforce have come to see CEO compensation as bloated and undeserved. News media have fed the public a steady stream of images featuring leaders being "perp-walked" to jail for corporate abuse. So it is certainly easy to see why employees take a more jaundiced view of their leaders. Likewise, it is also interesting to note that feeling cared for by top leaders has now become a rising expectation and part of the employee engagement narrative. We will pursue this further in the next chapter, but for now it is clear that employees trust leaders far more easily when a relationship based on genuine mutual caring is in place.

Regarding perceptions about their *own well-being and the well-being of their families,* employees most commonly would say:

Ten Years Ago . . .	Today . . .
Employee benefits are important, particularly when I change jobs or when I have a significant claim related to myself or a member of my family. I also want a fair contribution to my retirement from my employer.	*Health-care benefits are extremely important because they are eating up more and more of my take-home pay. I'm also very concerned about my retirement, particularly when the stock market is in the tank. I also have an interest in maintaining some semblance of work-life balance, and I expect my employer to honor that.*

In Chapter 9 we will examine the transformation that is going on in the world of work related to employee benefits and whole-person and lifestyle needs. We know that health and retirement benefits have always been important, but their priority has clearly risen in the minds of most employees. Survey comments in particular reflect an increase of employee interest in work-life balance, something not spoken of with the same level of frequency just a few years ago.

We know that some employee engagement drivers are timeless and will not likely go out of style. For example, keeping employees aligned with company goals, making sure they are in the loop, and inspiring their trust are enduring conditions that have been emphasized as essential leadership competencies for decades. It doesn't shock us that the quality of leadership was an important driver of employee engagement five years ago, was still important five years later, and will likely be important five—or fifty—years from now.

▶ MAKING UNIVERSAL DRIVERS INTO "SIGNATURE" DRIVERS

Although winning companies consistently score high on all six drivers, there are marked differences in how each company goes about achieving those levels of excellence or where it places the emphasis. We use the term "signature" to describe the two or three of the six drivers that combine to reflect each employer's culture, lend it a distinguishing style, and serve to support its business objectives. This is an extremely important concept for those who aspire to become employers of choice like those featured in this book.

Rackspace, a remarkable company you'll learn more about in Chapter 7, has a unique culture typified by what might seem to be an outlandish approach to creating a workplace where its employees, called "Rackers," love both the work and the environment. Rackspace understands that the Universal Engagement Driver of job enrichment and career growth is, for the company, a *signature* driver—particularly critical to the success of the business. And Rackspace allocates talent and resources toward making this driver real and alive within the company so it can authentically brand itself as a magnet for talent and customers. As we will see, Rackspace implements that driver in its own way, as an expression of its unique culture. Just as we all have our own inimitable ways of signing our names—our signatures—Rackspace has brought this key driver to life in a way that supports a critical customer service objective, and as a result, the company has thrived.

Winning Companies Tooting Their Horns

What do kazoos, harmonicas, and trumpets all have in common? Aside from being wind instruments, they are frequently used by celebrants at the *Best-Places-to-Work* events held each year across the United States and in the United Kingdom. These proceedings are becoming an annual rite for companies that embrace the charge of building great workplaces.

But if you can get beyond the din of the noisemakers, you will also notice quite remarkable moments. You'll see top executives of companies laughing and being good-naturedly teased by their entry-level cohorts. You'll see seemingly staid professional types hugging and sharing stories of how fortunate they are to have found their "home." You'll note a valued employee tearfully telling how her employer supported her through a difficult patch, which made her want to return the kindness with increased dedication. You'll hear inspirational speeches from leaders who know the real payoff for their efforts is not in the trophy they lug home but the pride in knowing they are having a profound impact on the lives of both employees and customers of the organizations they feel privileged to lead.

These are, in short, the sounds of pure joy. Kazoos and all, these are the signs, the glimmers if you will, of a culture worth striving for.

▶ CASE STUDIES OF THE SIX ENGAGEMENT DRIVERS

In the following six chapters we present detailed profiles of six *Best-Places-to-Work* employers that recorded the highest survey scores on each of the six drivers. These companies not only achieved high overall employee engagement scores, but recorded particularly outstanding scores on one of the six drivers, thus revealing it as a "signature" of their respective cultures. We wanted to fully explore how they went about creating the conditions that led to their outstanding results. The featured companies are:

Quality Living, Inc., located in Omaha, Nebraska	Chapter 4: Steering the Ship and Inspiring the Crew: Trust and Confidence in Senior Leaders
Winchester Hospital, located in Winchester, Massachusetts	Chapter 5: The *Real* Job of Managers: Keeping Employees Aligned and Engaged
Nalley Automotive Group, headquartered in Atlanta, Georgia	Chapter 6: The Power of "We" to Magnify Engagement: Building Team Effectiveness
Rackspace, headquartered in San Antonio, Texas	Chapter 7: Job Enrichment and Professional Growth: The Present and Future Driver
Joie de Vivre Hospitality, headquartered in San Francisco, California	Chapter 8: The Never-Ending Source of Engagement: Valuing Employee Contributions
Vertex Pharmaceuticals, located in Cambridge, Massachusetts	Chapter 9: Employee Well-Being: The Ultimate Benefit

Each chapter will provide a list of engagement practices that *Best-Places-to-Work* employers have used to build and hone their status. Each chapter will also present you with insights about the three engagement "crosswind" forces we presented in Chapter 2. Represented by the icons below, the insights will help you manage the effects of:

▶ Diseconomies of scale (organization headcount)

▶ Generational diversity

▶ Turbulent times

Consider your business objectives and the people practices that will best serve to attract, engage, and retain the talent you need to achieve your objectives now and in the future. You may not have the opportunity to take advantage of all the ideas from winning *Best-Places* employers listed in a chapter, but you can leverage the six universal drivers and your organization's strengths and natural advantages to build a more engaging workplace.

▶ ASSESSING YOUR EMPLOYER'S PERFORMANCE ON INSPIRING ENGAGEMENT

To best set the stage for your understanding of these universal drivers, we invite you to complete an online self-assessment of your perceptions of your current employer, as well as a similar assessment of your own level of engagement. There is no cost or obligation for completing these assessments. The task will only take a few minutes. You can then print the results for your review as you read the remainder of the book.

To complete the assessments now, which we recommend you do, go to www.re-engagebook.com.

▶ CHAPTER FOUR

Steering the Ship and Inspiring the Crew

Trust and Confidence in Senior Leaders

People join companies, but they leave managers.
—Conventional wisdom

Commitment is not to an organization, it is to the leader's vision and to the culture that follows on that vision.
—Jac Fitz-enz

▶ JOE: THE CEO TAKES A RISK

Joe had started out his career as a mechanical engineer, quickly worked his way into project management, and had held a series of progressively more responsible engineering management positions. Respected for his technical knowledge and trusted by clients, he had been recruited to head up a growing design engineering firm.

After two years as CEO, Joe had watched the firm's business pipeline dwindle as it began to lose projects to the competition. He had made some key outside hires into senior business development positions but was starting to lose faith in their ability to produce results. Employee turnover rose dramatically over one two-month period, and when the engineering manager resigned, it really got Joe's attention. He realized he needed to listen to what his employees were thinking, and against the advice of the board chairman, he decided to authorize two focus groups and an employee engagement survey.

These revealed that employees had lost faith in the entire senior management team, including Joe. They also doubted the capabilities of the business development team, believed that the firm was not sufficiently staffed to break into new markets, and felt that *senior leaders are not present on the floors with people and are not providing leadership.* One comment in particular was hard for the proud but introverted CEO to hear: *"Joe is so out of touch with employees that he has no idea what we are all about."* And there was this: *"Management doesn't share info on plans for new work, and that causes a lack of confidence."* There were other pressing issues as well, but loss of confidence that Joe and his team could turn things around was the most critical.

Joe knew something bold was called for. He scheduled an all-hands off-site meeting. Over the course of a morning Joe and the board members reported results of the employee survey, sent functional units away to breakout rooms to come up with specific ideas for improvement, and then brought all employees back into the room, inviting them to step to microphones with specific suggestions for change. Joe and the board conferred and responded to the ideas with "yes," "no," or "tabled for further study." Joe won considerable respect from his workforce for making himself so vulnerable that day and showing the courage to face the harsh realities of employee questions and comments. He had also allowed employees to vent, and some very workable ideas were presented.

Within a year, Joe had implemented many of those ideas, including making some key staff changes and being a lot more visible and communicative about plans for new business that he realized he had failed to share with staff. The firm had won a big project, stopped the bleeding of key talent, and was back in the hiring mode once again.

▶ WHO DRIVES EMPLOYEE ENGAGEMENT MORE, MANAGERS OR SENIOR LEADERS?

Anyone who stops to seriously consider the question, "Who drives employee engagement—the supervisor or senior leader?" must inevitably answer, "Both, of course!" And yet hundreds of companies around the world, including many Fortune 500 multinationals, continue to use a popular 12-question employee engagement survey that contains not a single question about senior leadership.

Inherent in the design and widespread use of this survey is the assumption that direct managers and supervisors hold all the cards and are the "dealers" in the employee engagement card game. There is no disputing that direct supervisors have a powerful impact on the employees they supervise. They hold many critical powers: to hire the right people; to assign the work that uses the employees' talents; to communicate clear expectations; to coach, care for, listen to, confront, develop, recognize, and reward their employees—or not do these vital tasks. Managers control the levers available in the everyday interactive moments when they choose to behave in ways that either engage the employee or have the opposite effect. Managers and supervisors also have the power to act as transmitters, interpreters, and enforcers of the strategies, policies, decisions, and directives of senior leaders.

In our experience, however, it is the senior leadership team (often with input from the board of directors) that creates the culture, sets the tone, inspires trust and confidence, or undermines it. We believe that senior leaders—CEOs and their direct reports—most strongly influence the very managers they hold accountable for engaging employees. If engaging employees were a card game, the senior leaders would be dealing the face cards.

By conducting employee surveys that fail to take into account these higher levers, we do a disservice to those senior leaders who sincerely want to create more engaging workplaces and need to be confronted with the sometimes painful-to-hear workplace realities that candid survey feedback provides. Why? Because it tells them exactly how they can do better in very specific ways. Of course, there are some senior leaders who choose not to conduct employee surveys, partly because they prefer not to face the uncomfortable truths reflected at them in a mirror. And there are even consultants who are themselves reluctant to report those truths for fear of being the messenger who gets shot for doing so.

▶ THE BLAME GAME

The specter of blame is a constant threat to teamwork in corporate life. Managers blame senior leaders for not sharing more of the wealth, for imposing demands to do even more with even less, and for tying their hands when it comes to rewarding employees. Senior leaders blame managers for not getting better performance from their people and for poor time management and cost control. Senior leaders and managers both blame human resources for not understanding the business and for failing to be strategic. Employees blame all the above, and get blamed for not giving their best efforts. As one frustrated manager complained, *"Why doesn't the company conduct an engagement survey that holds employees accountable for engaging themselves? It's not all on the manager, you know!"* Our research confirms that indeed it is not.

In most of the *Best Places to Work* we have studied, a spirit of partnership prevails. Senior leaders, managers, frontline supervisors, human resources staff, and employees in general realize that they all have their roles to play in an enterprise where business goals transcend blame and self-justification and where all are accountable. All parties know they are responsible for creating a highly engaged workforce. Senior leaders drive strategy, business objectives, culture, and management practices. Managers and supervisors transmit cultural values, align employees with business objectives, and drive daily results through task motivation and people skills. Like a great sports team, all the players know their roles and recognize that the team comes before the individual. Many employee engagement initiatives, such as the implementation of a new compensation system, require the support and teamwork of all employees, including supervisors, senior leaders, and HR staff.

▶ THE CHANGING CHALLENGES OF LEADERSHIP AND MANAGEMENT

In many ways, it can be argued that distinctions separating leaders and managers are artificial ones. Leaders must manage, and managers must lead. The classic distinction—that leaders do the right things and that managers do things right—is valid to an extent, but simplistic.

Leaders and managers face significant challenges and changes:

▶ In the post–Enron era, only about 40 percent of the work-force believes that senior leaders hold the best interests of the organization over their own self-interest.[1]

▶ A survey of U.S workers indicated that 56 percent are not proud of company leaders.[2]

▶ The advent of flatter organizations, along with the related reduction in the ranks of middle managers, has increased the average supervisor's span of control to unreasonable numbers of direct reports in many companies.

▶ The increased (and proper) use of 360-degree developmental feedback now serves as a check against ineffective, disrespectful, abusive, and weak leaders and managers.

▶ Managers are themselves increasingly disengaged as a result of heavier workloads.

▶ Manager-employee conflicts are made worse because of significant differences in what younger workers expect to receive and what many older managers are prepared to give, especially with regard to frequency of coaching, feedback, and recognition; work-life balance; learning opportunities; and the exercise of one's strengths in meaningful challenges.

▶ The growing reliance on teamwork, self-managing units, lateral instead of vertical information flows, and collaborative decision making has made good communication even more essential.

These challenges have put unprecedented pressure on both company leaders and direct supervisors to manage talent more effectively at the very time it has become more difficult to do so.

▶ WHAT THE SURVEY RESULTS SAY: IT'S MORE ABOUT SENIOR LEADERS THAN SOME MAY THINK

Our analysis of survey items about senior leaders, when compared with survey items about managers, revealed these findings:

▶ Of the 11 survey statements with the biggest engagement score gaps between winning and nonwinning employers, 5 of them reflected issues over which senior leaders exercise more influence, while only 2 fell more under the manager's sphere of influence.
▶ Item correlations indicate that senior leaders appear to be having a somewhat stronger relative impact than direct managers in influencing the engagement of employees.
▶ The 7 survey items reflecting issues over which *both* leaders and managers share influence served to distinguish winning from nonwinning workplaces far better than the other 30 survey items.

For a more detailed look at survey item comparisons, see Appendix D at www.re-engagebook.com.

Best-Places-to-Work survey comments mirror the quantitative results. They also support conclusions reached by other survey firms about the importance of senior leaders in the employee engagement equation. The Kenexa Research Institute, for example, recently conducted a survey of workers in six countries that found only 54 percent held favorable views of their senior leaders. These results indicated that a worker's opinion of overall senior management effectiveness is driven by the extent to which senior managers gain employees' confidence through their decisions, actions, and communications; keep employees well informed regarding company direction; and conduct business in an ethical fashion.[3]

▶ EMPLOYEES DESCRIBE THE IMPACT OF SENIOR LEADERS

Our analysis of *Best-Places-to-Work* survey comments confirmed the aspects Kenexa identified to be relevant. Survey comments, which we've categorized by theme, also revealed several additional dimensions of employees' views about senior leaders that most assuredly impact, for better or for worse, the employees' daily decisions about whether to expend or withhold discretionary effort.

Theme A: Senior Leaders' Power to Inspire and Engage

Here are two sets of comments, each illustrating the impact that senior leaders have on a workforce, for better and for worse.

POSITIVE COMMENTS

One significant take-away from the positive comments is the degree to which employees appreciate the inspirational effect that leaders can have on individuals and the organization as a whole:

> ▶ *"I have been at (the) company for 18 years and can't imagine having a better work situation. The company president has tremendous vision and integrity and sets the tone to treat the staff well in every regard. My work is professionally rewarding and appreciated by supervisors, peers, and staff. I don't be-*

lieve too many people can say that they LOVE coming to work each and every day. (The company) deserves the recognition as not just one of the best, but THE best place to work in the state."

▶ *"The company is a fantastic place to work. Our fearless leader and CEO is doing an amazing job. He is brilliant, has integrity, and never loses perspective of the work the staff is doing and what they are being asked to do. He welcomes feedback, responds to e-mails, and visits patients in the hospital on a regular basis. We love our CEO, and I personally feel fortunate to be a part of the ABC team."*

▶ *"The president takes time to develop the employees. He works on your weaknesses and plays to your strengths. The company is a very family-oriented organization and puts family first. I am very happy here and would like to stay here as long as I can!"*

Negative Comments

Contrast the comments above with the following ones, which clearly show that senior leaders can deflate the engagement balloon as well:

▶ *"One of the worst companies I have ever worked for in my career. Terrible leadership— to call them incompetent is to insult the incompetent. No forward-looking thought; completely focused on money and not on the people who make them successful."*

▶ *"I'm out of here as soon as possible. I think it's a big joke that they were even nominated as a best place to work. . . . When your organization loses five of your top managers and/or directors in the last year, something's seriously wrong. . . . It's their way or the highway, and there is one member of the senior management team that will proudly tell you that!"*

Theme B: Confidence in Senior Leaders' Decisions and Direction

Recent research reveals that the "cognitive" engagement of employees—whether they think the company's strategy and the direction it is taking makes sense—can be as important as emotional engagement.[4] One study revealed that 73 percent of employees in high-performance firms agreed that the management of their company provided a clear sense of direction, compared with only 46 percent in struggling firms.[5] You can easily argue that this cognitive factor also contains an emotional element—the feeling of security an employee experiences knowing the company actually has a clear direction.

Our own analysis of survey items supports the above conclusions. As we discussed in Chapter 3, the survey item that ranked as the fifth-highest contributor to overall engagement scores was employee trust in the leaders of an organization to set the right course. When this dimension of clear and consistent direction is missing, it undermines the very foundation of employee commitment—confidence that the captain is steering the ship to success.

NEGATIVE COMMENTS

The following selected comments drive home the point:

▶ *"I feel that senior and middle management are unsure where they are steering the company . . . and morale is low."*

▶ *"Within our department there are too many reorganizations. Senior leadership needs to get a better vision as to how the organization should be structured and stick with it."*

▶ *"I love my work, but lately I'm miserable working for this company and planning to leave. There is no top-down structure, and everything is reactive rather than proactive. As a result of the reactive tendencies of the company, things change too frequently and there is no solid, dependable component of my job. It's chaotic, and I don't have faith that the senior management is thinking about the most important aspect of the business: the people who deliver the product."*

▶ *"I continue to feel like I'm punched in the gut with continuous changes coming from upper management, unclear motives and agendas."*

POSITIVE COMMENTS

There were also these very positive observations about the confidence-building impact of competent leaders who *are* sure of their direction and strategy:

▶ *"ABC Company's senior leadership always seems to have clear goals and a well-defined strategy to achieve these goals."*

▶ *"This is a great company to work for. Our leaders are effective, they communicate goals well, and they stay the course. I have worked for other restaurant companies in the past whose yearly goals changed every quarter."*

▶ *"Even new employees straight out of school are given the opportunity to propose new directions to the company, and are given direct support from executives at the company in pursuing those directions. The company encourages every employee to take ownership for the company's direction by giving everyone the ability to change the company's direction."*

▶ *"As a long-term employee, I have enjoyed being part of the changes implemented by our current leadership. Longtime issues are being addressed, and I understand their vision for the future."*

Senior Leadership and the Tipping Point of 150

The two engagement drivers that had the largest drop in engagement scores as employee population increased were *having trust and confidence in senior leaders* and *feeling valued for one's contributions*, both factors that are strongly influenced by senior leaders. We would argue that company headcount growth puts even greater pressure on leaders to make sure they are (1) perceived as being trustworthy, (2) are taking the organization in the right direction, and (3) are providing the right resources to help employees feel valued and be successful.

GROWTH COMPANY A

In 2006 Company A was recognized as one of the top *Best-Places-to-Work* employers (in the medium-size category) in its market. At that time the company had, by coincidence, 150 employees. Its overall score was truly outstanding, a tribute to the quality of its leadership.

Over that year Company A grew significantly, doubling its workforce to more than 300. All the same leaders who were part of the company's success in 2006 were still there in 2007, but the overall engagement results dropped significantly when they moved beyond the tipping point of 150. In the table that follows, the columns to the right show the percentage of employees who responded favorably to each of the survey engagement factors (a perfect score would be 100), and the column in the far right shows the difference between the 2006 and 2007 results.

Engagement Factor	2006	2007	Difference
Team Effectiveness	92%	82%	−10%
Retention Risk	94%	81%	−13%
Alignment with Goals	92%	82%	−10%
Trust with Coworkers	92%	88%	−4%
Individual Contribution	91%	82%	−9%
Manager Effectiveness	86%	77%	−9%
Trust in Senior Leaders	95%	79%	−16%
Feeling Valued	89%	74%	−15%
Satisfaction with Current Role	87%	78%	−9%
People Practices (Benefits)	83%	77%	−6%

To be clear, this company still has outstanding results—it did place high in its employer category. But the tipping point phenomenon has begun to affect this company, and a number of things that used to be in abundance—a sense of family, caring, and connections—are now in shorter supply.

Interestingly, the survey results indicate that the drop in employee engagement was felt by all employees in Company A, regardless of tenure.

One area where company size is *not* relevant is the variation of engagement by position level. Executives, regardless of company size, are very engaged. Managers are the next most engaged, again regardless of company size. Hourly employees, regardless of company size, are the least engaged employees.

Theme C: Trust in the Honesty and Integrity of Senior Leaders

Nothing quite undermines employees' willingness to give their best effort each day more than the loss of trust that leaders are dealing honestly and in good faith.

NEGATIVE COMMENTS

Here are some of the comments that sadly attest to the undermining of trust:

▶ *"Although the CIO says he has no plans for outsourcing, there have been at least two meetings with large international outsourcing companies."*

▶ *"Executive leadership has changed, is constantly changing, and goals are not being met, yet company spins things to make it sound like everything is going according to plan."*

▶ *"There's an expression that 'the fish rots from the head down.' I never lent much credibility to that statement until I worked at my employer for over two years. I've seen my managers lie to their employees about their loss of benefits and other issues."*

▶ *"Corporate core values are ignored. I feel the company is just paying lip service to these statements. As an individual, I am constantly blocked by management in doing something that would be client focused. Excellence and quality are consistently downplayed for the sake of metrics—the more calls handled more quickly, the better, regardless of the outcome for the client."*

POSITIVE COMMENTS

On the other hand, organizations whose leaders work to build trust reap the benefit of more committed and enthusiastic workers, as these comments show:

> ▶ *"After working at other companies, I don't think that I can ever see myself working for another organization, and particularly for any other people. The trust that I have in our general manager and president is beyond anything that I have ever experienced."*
>
> ▶ *"I've worked in environments where I didn't entirely trust the CEO and management, which is why working at ABC Company is so refreshing. I really believe that the management team has a lot of integrity, and it's genuine. The CEO is a focused, inspirational leader."*

We noted with interest that the themes and comments above are remarkably similar to the factors Kenexa found to be most important for senior leaders: having confidence in their decisions and actions, keeping employees informed, and following ethical business practices. Still, they were not the only key themes we found that were directly related to senior leaders.

In analyzing the *Best-Places-to-Work* survey comments, several additional themes surfaced that have their own power to increase or decrease a given employee's willingness to give discretionary effort.

Theme D: Open, Two-Way Communication by Senior Leaders

It comes as no surprise that most employees view openness and two-way communication from leaders as a key factor in their willingness to engage. When leaders provide it, employees' anxieties tend to lessen and their trust is renewed. When leaders withhold it, fear, anxiety, doubt, and distrust often prevail.

NEGATIVE COMMENTS

Numerous employees, including many middle managers, wrote comments expressing frustration with how little senior leaders listened to their concerns and how reluctant the top leaders were to share information with them, as shown below:

> ▶ *"The leaders in this company direct things and make all of the decisions without the opinions of the employees. Most of the time*

we are just told what to do and are expected to jump and do it no matter how long it takes."

▶ *"They offer this whole 'open and honest communication' policy, but they never honor it, not to the call center and support staff. I am currently in the process of looking for a new job, but while I am still here, I will gladly put my two cents in about how I feel about working here, because others should be warned as well."*

▶ *"I believe management is pretty opaque around here. I've been here for four years, and I generally go to people who hang out with managers socially to find out what's coming down the pike. There's very little effort to engage others outside of management. There were questions on this survey about trusting leaders and manage-ment; I don't have that trust. Very little explanation is given for the why of things."*

Positive Comments

There were also many comments expressing appreciation for senior leaders who make the effort to be more open, less "close to the vest" with information, and who focus on listening to their employees and taking their ideas seriously:

▶ *"Our CEO meets with people in small groups to find out how they can better the company, and implements suggestions we make. I have never worked for a company where the CEO took time to sit down with us and actually wanted our feedback."*

▶ *"I began researching ABC Company about six months ago. I was impressed when I found the direct phone numbers to the CEO and senior management team listed clearly on the Web site. Only a handful of companies have enough confidence in their quality of service to do that."*

▶ *"There's definitely a sense that managers at all levels listen to their employees. . . . For instance, our CEO typically schedules an off-site breakfast called 'How to Make XYZ Company a Better Place to Work' at the beginning of every year. He invites small groups of employees from different areas to give open feedback on how things could be made better. Discussions run the gamut from topics about cleaning out refrigerators to questions on benefits programs. The CEO takes copious notes, then posts action items derived from those meetings onto our company intranet."*

Senior Leaders and the Multigenerational Workforce

The Advanced Management Institute conducted a survey in 2007 that found that 96 percent of managers and senior executives agreed that intergenerational teamwork was very or extremely important to their firm's success. Yet 76 percent of respondents also said that generational differences have created significant challenges, such as poor communication, reduced quality and productivity, loss of teamwork, and lower morale.[6]

Because the four generations came of age in different times, they may not value the perspectives of the others, which we believe is the greatest challenge of leading a multigenerational workforce. Most senior leaders are either Traditionalists or Boomers, and many have yet to accommodate the expectations of Millennials and Gen Xers. The reverse is true in many cases as well.

We cannot emphasize enough that the needs of individuals transcend generational membership and that the stereotypes about the generations may not be true for many. One of the key lessons of this book is that individual employees must be engaged and re-engaged one person at a time. Still, generational and life-stage differences are real and need to be acknowledged, understood, positively leveraged, and, often, overcome.

Here are some of the most constructive ways that leaders of premier employers are engaging and re-engaging employees in all four generations:

▶ **Seek first to understand** the most common issues of difference between the generations.

▶ **Commit to creating an engaging workplace culture** that provides for the universal needs of employees—as represented by the six engagement drivers.

▶ **Recognize that a shortage of talent that will** recur as more Boomers retire and the economy returns to respectable growth rates. Encourage Traditionalists and Boomers to stay on as consultants, offer flexible and part-time arrangements as they approach retirement eligibility, put them in mentoring roles, and capture their critical knowledge before they leave. *Remember:* When a universally mission-critical resource is scarce, the first to act gains a dominating and irrevocable competitive advantage.

▶ **Create continuous opportunities for employees in different generations to work together on projects,** share work spaces, mentor each other, provide training and opportunities for open dialogue about generational differences, socialize together, and seek to meet one another halfway with regard to differing expectations.

▶ **Identify emerging leaders, and provide them with the training and development they need** to stay engaged and be better prepared to step into leadership positions as more-senior leaders retire.

▶ **Train managers** in principles and techniques of effective people management and employee engagement, and hold them accountable for appropriate measurable outcomes.

▶ **Emphasize the importance of collaboration and teamwork** to all staff regardless of their generation.

> ▶ **Promote the idea that the generational filter is only one way to
> look at the world,** and that understanding and accommo-
> dating gender, racial, ethnic, and cultural differences is
> just as important.
>
> In each of the next five chapters on the other engage-
> ment drivers, we will present additional practices for
> promoting engagement and teamwork among the four
> generations.

Theme E: Perceptions of Executive Greed and Pay Inequity

Events of the first decade of the century have convinced many employees that CEOs and other senior executives cannot be trusted to
keep the best interests of the organization foremost in mind—a perception that is essentially incompatible with employee engagement.

NEGATIVE COMMENTS

Many employees were not reluctant to express their perception of
unfairness and outrage about what they see as the disproportionate
gap in pay levels between senior leaders and the average worker:

▶ *"There's a fair amount of dissension within the engineering ranks.
Most of it revolves around compensation. Executives at this company continue to be awarded large bonuses, pay raises, and cheaply-
priced stock options. Meanwhile, raises are rare among engineers."*

▶ *"The leader of our organization was given $687,000 in raises.
Not a bad income when the average employee is bringing home
less than $30,000 per year. Also, they increase annual goals and
demand more, and yet our annual income stays the same year after
year, except for our CEO."*

▶ *"I feel the company does not share the wealth. . . . The bonus structure should include all levels, not just management. You get the
feeling, 'Why should I bust my butt for my boss to get his incentive
bonus?'"*

POSITIVE COMMENTS

Survey comments such as the following ones, praising senior leaders for their generosity, were fewer and farther between:

▶ *"XYZ Company is a great company to work for. Leadership always finds ways to give to the employees."*
▶ *"Senior leadership takes every person who meets their quarterly goals to Las Vegas (four times a year). I don't know a lot of companies that take care of their sales producers like this."*

Theme F: Feelings of Being Generally Devalued by Senior Leaders

This theme is similar to pay inequity, but broader. It transcends the issues of pay inequity, greed, and excessive self-interest and encompasses the felt offense of devaluing the employee in more basic and larger ways.

NEGATIVE COMMENTS

There was no shortage of comments from survey participants along these lines:

▶ *"Senior executives and managers do not acknowledge your capabilities when speaking to the client."*
▶ *"Management makes everyone feel as though they are replaceable. Our chairman came out and said that shareholders come first, customers second, and employees third. How do you think that makes the employees feel?"*
▶ *"There is a lack of support for minorities. Not a lot of people here are open to those who are different from what they are used to. As a result, people are singled out for being who they are. I think once people start to respect you for your work rather than acting like they are in high school or hazing for a fraternity, then this company will be a much better place to work."*
▶ *"This organization consistently views employees as fiscal liabilities to be limited as much as possible; until we are perceived as*

assets rather than liabilities, it will never be a great place to work."

POSITIVE COMMENTS

Yet when senior leaders do show they value and care about employees and their development, the positive effects are obvious, real, and emotionally powerful—as evidenced in several striking comments we came across:

▶ *"ABC Company is really a great place to work. . . . If I have a problem, I feel confident going directly to one of the managing partners because I know they truly care. They know who I am and are always willing to help in any way."*

▶ *"Overall, I feel valued every day. This is the best workplace I've ever been a part of. It's also important to point out that the management team goes out of their way to know all employees personally. They always stop by and ask how things are going or even to ask for advice. Actually, hardly a day goes by when the CEO doesn't stop by. It's reassuring to know they all really care about me and want to get to know me better."*

▶ *"They make sure that our work stations are comfortable and that our equipment is in top shape and updated on a very regular basis. The atmosphere with the leadership is very open and casual, and one feels free to talk to or even e-mail the CEO, knowing they will receive a personal reply. Quite unusual!"*

The positive impact of such senior leader behavior on direct managers and supervisors can only serve to have a cascading effect on the engagement of employees throughout the organization.

Theme G: Feelings of Being Coerced by Fear, Control, and Intimidation

Unfortunately, many senior leaders rule rather than lead, and because their employers have always tolerated their harsh behavior, they continue to have a negative impact on the very people they are charged to lead and engage.

Negative Comments

A few examples of how coercive leaders are viewed by those they purportedly lead:

▶ *"Morale is so low, and there is no trust in management in this system for fear of reprisal."*
▶ *"The new chief executive manages by condescension, humiliation, and disrespect of employees for what I perceive to be no good reason. This has made people too risk averse and too focused on immaterial details for fear of (unnecessary) criticism. You could work on a project and do 39 of 40 things right, but the one thing that may not have met his standards of thoroughness will get all of the attention, and you'll come out of a meeting feeling less enthusiastic than you should."*
▶ *"Those who dare to raise an objection or a new way of looking at things are immediately labeled as negative and basically kept from ever progressing in the company. Our director has made his prejudiced and misogynistic views known to his employees. He once dope-slapped an employee in front of the entire department and cafeteria and suffered no consequences. At ANY other company he would have been fired."*
▶ *"I'm disappointed in the decision of the EVP to hire such a harsh, nonsocial human being as the current senior IT officer. Everyone in the department has been walking on eggshells for eight months."*

Evidence of "Servant Leadership"

Several survey respondents went out of their way to express their appreciation for leaders who lead not by coercing, but by serving employees' needs:

▶ *"This organization has a beaten path of proven success with a true servant leadership attitude exemplified from right at the top."*

▶ *"I think it is quite a rare and beautiful thing when the CEO/ chairman refers to himself as Your Humble Servant—and he lives up to it!!! I can honestly say that I love coming in to work every day—and truly mean it!!!"*

▶ *"Phenomenal place to work. Leadership is second to none, and several relationships formed within the company will be lifelong. The company truly cares for the individual over the company and is exemplified first and foremost through our gracious and humble CEO."*

▶ *"The company gives back more than I can ever give."*

▶ LEADING "SCARED RABBITS" AND "ARROGANT JACKASSES": THE QUALITY LIVING STORY

Many successful leaders have a set of principles (what they believe) that they work to translate into practices (what they should do) with their employees. This is entirely in keeping with the generally accepted notion that success in leadership is best achieved by aligning actions with beliefs. Quality Living, Inc., a nonprofit provider of services to individuals with brain injuries, spinal cord injuries, or severe physical disabilities, takes this concept further than any other organization we know, and the result of its meticulous and passionate efforts is nothing short of astounding.

In its 20-plus years Quality Living (QLI), based in Omaha, Nebraska, has become the largest facility of its kind in the United States. The Pentagon sees QLI as a "model program," one where injured soldiers can secure the services they need and deserve. QLI is only as good as "quality staff," and maintaining that staff is something in which the organization excels. Its employee turnover rate is a quarter the national average in the industry.

We had the pleasure of interviewing Dr. Kim Hoogeveen, founder and CEO, and directors Alicia Elson, Jen Karolski, and Jon Pearson.

Q: When you started QLI you had no experience in this field. How did you go about establishing the leadership principles that QLI started with and has held closely to this day?

Hoogeveen: *A mentor of mine arranged a series of interviews with many of the finest business executives in our area. I listened carefully, and through those interviews I identified seven leadership principles that were common to those successful leaders. It was, if you will, a study of success.*

Q: How did this help you?

Hoogeveen: *In the beginning I didn't really know what I was doing; I was scared, to be honest. I certainly didn't feel like I was a natural leader, but I was willing to learn. As a psychologist, I had a lot of training in understanding how people behave. The leadership principles gave me a guide as to how I could help employees be successful by applying my training in a work setting.*

Q: So how did you take those principles and put them to work?

Hoogeveen: *That was where I was most concerned. The principles, in and of themselves, are abstract and open to interpretation. So I created a series of what we call "mindsets" around each of the leadership principles. These mindsets help our staff understand how to put each principle into action.*

Q: How many of these mindsets have you developed?

Hoogeveen: *To date, we have 260.*

Q: Did you say 260?! That's an amazing number. Can you give us an example of how one of the mindsets helps your managers and staff understand how to put a leadership principle into practice?

Hoogeveen: *Our second principle is about helping our team feel proud of QLI. We want them to feel a great passion for our work. So one of our mindsets is about when we can begin to help employees feel that sense of pride, and to us that begins in the preemployment process. Our employee interview, for example, is 60 percent about them and*

40 percent about selling QLI. Even if a person isn't hired, we want them to go away with a sense that this is a remarkable place to work, which in some way will come back to help us.

After someone has accepted an offer, we continue our efforts. We know after accepting the job a person can feel some cognitive dissonance about their decision. It's like when you buy a new car—you immediately begin to pay attention to any advertisements about that car on the television and tell friends how proud you are to have made that purchase to validate your decision. We want to reinforce to employees that they've made a great decision, so in that same spirit we send them home with a packet of information about QLI and what a great place this is. If a loved one—a grandmother, for example— stops by the home of our new employee, we want that employee to share with the loved one how excited they are to be coming to work here—that's how that pride can be built.

Finally, that old adage about having only one opportunity to make a first impression impacts how we conduct employee orientations. We don't have a person conduct those orientations just because they have a certain title or rank. We tap the best salesperson we have to share our history, our mission, the bumps in the road we've faced, and our successes. These acts help to develop a sense of pride about working for QLI.

Q: How do staff learn the 260 mindsets?

Elson: *We don't spring the whole thing on anyone at one time. For example, we just started working with a group that has several new employees. We chose 10 mindsets that are particularly important in their work. We'll use those to build on as they grow into their new roles.*

Pearson: *In football, the kicker doesn't need to know all the plays, just the ones that pertain to him. And most of what we do is on-the-job, that's where the teachable moments are anyway. Our job is to help them "live" these mindsets so they're not just words from a notebook.*

Karolski: *Exactly. The mindset book is really like a playbook. As leaders, it's our job to identify what's right for the team and the situation.*

Great leaders know how to think—the mindsets help us in that effort.

Q: Why is pride one of your key leadership principles?

Hoogeveen: *I think helping people to feel pride in their work is one of the greatest untapped assets in the workforce today. We want our associates to have a strong sense of pride in our company.*

We have a very specific understanding about pride. It's not pride, but bragging, if I tell you how wonderful my kids are. It's an act of kindness if I tell grandparents how wonderful their grandchildren are—that develops pride. We think it's an act of kindness to be associated with a great company, and we want our associates to be proud of that.

Q: How do you help find that kind of pride?

Hoogeveen: *It's impossible to feel pride in something you don't know about. So we spend a tremendous amount of time informing our staff about QLI. We constantly reinforce what the company is doing for them and for the people we serve. We tell our staff, frequently, I might add, "It's your company."*

We don't think, for example, that it's bragging to remind our staff that last year we spent more than $150,000 (nearly $500 per person) on special employee benefits. That's an act of kindness. And when a chain of e-mails goes around our company that shares a success that one of our staff has had with a resident in our program, that's a way we can all feel pride. A company "has no throat"—it can't talk. Leaders must do the talking for the company.

Q: You believe leaders must adapt to different people. Tell us more about that.

Hoogeveen: *I believe that exceptional leaders must modify their approach to the unique characteristics of each employee. I've always admired successful coaches, for example, who adjust their coaching style, including the plays they run, to bring out the best in their players.*

Q: Give us an example of how you work with your supervisors on this mindset.

Hoogeveen: *Different employees learn differently. There are some employees we call "scared rabbits." They lack confidence, are uncomfortable with authority figures, and are unlikely to challenge people in leadership. Employees with this profile are best taught by peers, not by someone like me. My role as a senior leader is to positively reinforce those employees when a particular success they achieve comes to my attention, and over time we hope to build their confidence so they can be more comfortable working with and confronting leader-types.*

There are other employees, when it comes to learning, that we call "arrogant jackasses." They have an attitude that prohibits them from being receptive to coaching from their supervisors. In those cases I intervene and tell the employee that we see great potential, but if they don't start listening to their supervisor, things may not go well for them, and the next time I have a chat with their supervisor, things had better be different.

Both scared rabbits and arrogant jackasses can eventually become successful employees, but how I lead them is very different. How each group might describe me to their coworkers or friends would sound like night and day. But understanding how each employee learns, and individualizing my approach to them, will make all the difference in the world.

Q: Building strong relationships is very important at QLI. Why so?

Pearson: *Our goal is to help people be successful in life. That requires us to know them and for them to know us. That takes a while, and there is always a risk in getting to know people too well, but we've seen the results of what happens when you are able to build a relationship where people know you truly care.*

Elson: *The more we learn about our associates, the better we are able to understand their unique strengths. Our supervisors have an eye for talent. As we observe, we're constantly asking: What went right? Who was involved in the success of the project? How did that person* *contribute to the success? What didn't go well that we could learn from? Only with a strong relationship in place can you really be a good judge of their character.*

Karolski: *We also know that when we have a strong relationship with an employee they'll be more open to advice and receiving feedback. We give and ask for a lot of feedback around here, so for people to be okay about that it's important that a strong relationship is in place.*

Q: When approaching leadership you are a self-described manipulator. How so?

Hoogeveen: *I think the term "manipulate" has gotten a bad rap in our society. For those of us who have children, we learn to become master manipulators—it's called parenting. The issue is not whether we're manipulating people as leaders. The more important question is, "What is our intent?" If our intent is to help a person grow, to help them discover and develop their talents, to be more effective at serving, then when it comes to manipulating, I stand guilty as charged.*

Q: You're not a group that tends to shy away from conflict. Tell us more.

Karolski: *As we mentioned before, we work very hard to develop strong relationships at QLI. If you have a strong relationship with someone, you can have a disagreement and the person you're disagreeing with doesn't feel that it's personal.*

Elson: *And with our culture it really isn't personal. Our culture is about doing what's right for QLI and the people we serve. Good people can have genuine disagreement on how to go about doing something—that's just part of being around a very talented team.*

Pearson: *Kim has a saying that we genuinely mean when it comes to conflict: "That's a stupid idea. Let's go have lunch." It's a great way of telling a person that your disagreement with someone really isn't personal.*

Q: How has your approach to leadership influenced your ability to develop future leaders?

Hoogeveen: *In the last 18 months, we lost four of our six senior leaders because of planned retirements or relocations. We were able to fill those positions internally along with the jobs those internal candidates previously held. In the midst of this we were going through our review from the Commission on Accreditation of Rehabilitation Facilities. Even though our leadership was in transition, we ended up receiving our highest rating ever.*

Q: We know the mindsets help you to create a great workplace. How does that effort translate into providing better care to the individuals with severe brain injuries whom you serve?

Elson: *I think that quite simply put, if employees are truly happy in their work environment, they want to ensure that everyone they work with shares in the attitude. Taking pride in working for a great company that makes a difference in the lives of others makes it easier to provide quality care to the residents. Our staff feel part of the bigger "whole," thus they take pride in building raving fans of the residents and the families, thus contributing positively to that bigger picture. They are also then positively reinforced for the exemplary job that they have done, hopefully creating the opposite of a vicious circle.*

Q: Our research tells us that companies with more engaged workforces are better able to deal with a crisis, whether that is an internal challenge or something like an economic recession.

Hoogeveen: *If you do a lot of this mindset stuff right, it's amazing how many crises you avert. Nobody ever gives the maintenance person credit for kicking the rag away from the furnace before he goes home at night so the place doesn't burn down, but that effort prevents the crisis. This place is littered with people who do that.*

Q: How do you support that behavior?

Hoogeveen: *One way is not second-guessing people. I think a lot of leaders beat this out of their staff by always looking over their backs. They wonder why nobody stomps out the little ember that led to the forest fire, but every time a crisis like that has happened in the past,* *employees were second-guessed; this behavior absolutely guts autonomous decision making. If we really believe "it's their company," we have to act that way, including when people make decisions.*

We've hired great people here. Most of them can do their jobs much better than I can. Why should I second-guess them? Many leaders make a fatal cognitive error that because a decision turned out badly, someone has to be at fault. We may spend time reviewing a decision so we can learn, but we trust people to make good decisions.

Q: Let's stay on the topic of decision making. You work very hard at helping your associates learn how to make good decisions on their own.

Karolski: *We recently had some of our cooks come to us with an idea they had about moving a door. This may not seem like a big deal for most companies—and financially it seemingly wasn't a great deal of money—but we took this as an opportunity to help our staff think about whether moving that door was a good investment of our money. We asked them to research their request, which actually required moving some electrical lines and making a structural change.*

Elson: *They learned a lot more about what goes into making a change like this, but more important, they learned how to research a problem and come up with a good decision. The end result of the process was the cooks decided not to move the door, but the skills they learned can be used in many ways in the future.*

Pearson: *I had an employee come to me recently and say, "I want to run something by you, but I don't want you to fix it," and most times I don't have to intervene. We encourage this kind of thinking, where we are acting more in a coaching capacity. In most situations like this we encourage our managers to role-play or shadow an employee rather than jumping in; that's the easy way, but not the way that develops people.*

Q: How do you know all this time and effort helping your associates embrace these 260 mindsets is paying off?

Hoogeveen: *This may sound like an odd example, but just recently, due to a reorganization, I had to terminate an employee who had* *been here 14 years. Her response was nothing short of classy. We spent 40 minutes together talking about her life, her kids and her goals. How she managed this stressful meeting was remarkable. She exhibited many of the qualities we teach with our mindsets—dealing with adversity, problem solving, and taking personal ownership for one's actions. She was scared, but still used the skills we teach. She told me that one of the mindset trainings helped her be better at work and at home and that she would always be grateful for that—I couldn't have received a greater compliment.*

Q: How has your work in developing these mindsets helped you?

Hoogeveen: *Developing the mindsets curriculum has forced me to look at each of the component parts that make up our leadership principles. Because I'm clearer about them, I'm better able to spot these talents in others. I've become a better talent scout.*

▶ SENIOR LEADERSHIP IN TURBULENT TIMES

As noted in Chapter 2, companies that increased their employee engagement scores during the months immediately following the economic implosion of 2008 scored significantly higher on five themes than companies whose scores declined during that same period. Two of those themes, which we call differentiators, are levers that senior leaders control.

Differentiator #1: Setting a Clear, Compelling Direction That Empowers Each Employee

Figure 4.1 presents how much some employers gained ground on this theme, even as the economy crumbled, contrasted with those that lost ground. The figure shows the dramatic differences for the first differentiator.

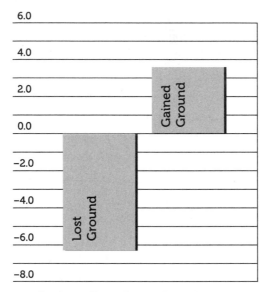

Setting a Clear, Compelling Direction
That Empowers Each Employee

Figure 4.1

Here are some representative survey comments from employees who remained engaged during the aftermath of economic collapse and from those who did not:

Voices of Engagement

▶ "Everyone knows what we need to do to accomplish company goals and are rewarded for doing so. Incentive is a big key to keeping everyone productive and [the company] has done an outstanding job implementing this."

▶ "This group has effective communication of goals and objectives and strategic initiatives to reach these goals."

Voices of Disengagement

▶ "We need more consistent feedback. I sometimes feel I don't know what is expected from day to day. Attitudes change and are hard to keep up with."

▶ "Stop telling about big company plans that never seem to happen.

▶ "Ask the people involved with a job for their input/comments before decisions are made."

Our studies tell us that in the best of times employees are more highly engaged when they see where the company is going and understand their roles in helping the company get there. This is largely a function of senior leaders and line managers clearly and frequently communicating where the company is headed and how each person makes a contribution. As a colleague of ours advises: *"Leaders need to make sure that the right employees are in the boat, know where it's going, have an oar in the water, and are pulling together!"* Indeed, we need to make sure we are helping our associates understand the strategy of the company, why this strategy makes sense, and how each person in the organization can make a positive and meaningful contribution to the success of that effort.

In difficult times, this responsibility becomes even more important. One supervisor at a company whose engagement score increased described how he felt about the direction of the company: *"Even in these uncertain times, I feel very good about working (here). They have made the right financial decisions to make the company strong, and I love the products we sell."*

What direction-setting practices should a company implement in difficult times? Our research shows that companies that survive and thrive in tough times do the following:

1. Develop a strategic plan for, and path to, success that will be compelling and confidence building for employees.

2. Clearly and consistently communicate the plan to employees at all levels and locations, using every available form of communication.

3. Seek and welcome every idea for making the plan a reality, e.g., streamlining of processes, innovation, new business, and cost cutting. Many companies are also using and leveraging Web 2.0 with company blogs and wikis to make it easier for employees to communicate their ideas. Best Buy, whose stock plunged 40 percent in one month in late 2008, received more than 900 cost-cutting ideas after starting its

Blue-Shirt Nation social networking site.[7] British Telecom was able to attract more than 16,000 employees worldwide to collaborate on its wiki.[8]

4. Talk to good clients and gain feedback about how your company has made a difference for them. Determine if this feedback could be used to develop new ideas that can be implemented quickly.

5. Examine every process that may be getting in the way of employees being productive; look at every step to see if things can be more streamlined.

Differentiator #2: Open and Honest Communication

Open and honest communication is important at all times, but particularly during uncertain times. Figure 4.2 shows the 10-plus per-

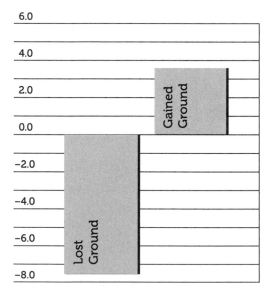

Open and Honest Communication

Figure 4.2

centage point swing in how employees at the gaining and losing firms perceived this practice.

Here are representative comments from employees that remained engaged as economic conditions changed for the worse and from those that did not:

Voices of Engagement
▶ *"Managers value your input and realize you're only human, so there is room for errors to learn and grow from them."*
▶ *"Communication is top-notch. It is never difficult to reach a manager or even the owner herself. There is an open dialog between all employees that breeds honesty and respect."*
▶ *"There's constant communication and openness about how the economy or recent mergers would impact the firm. We hold meetings regularly, which gives all employees an opportunity to voice our opinions or concerns about how the department can function more effectively."*

Voices of Disengagement
▶ *"We need better communication . . . more timely communication. There are a lot of good meetings at the corporate level that we do not always get to be a part of, so the more information that can be shared from these meetings, the better."*
▶ *"Don't ever again allow rumors to run wild over an extended period of time. Way too much time was spent on speculation."*
▶ *"Tough times call for lots of management visibility and encouragement."*
▶ *"Tell the truth, and keep people informed."*

Leaders who attained even higher levels of employee engagement in tough times were apparently doing a better job of keeping communication open and robust. Though leaders may be hesitant to keep lines of communication open when the future is uncertain or looks dire, the exact opposite is called for. One executive told us that in dealing with changes that affect employees, *"I communicate early and often. We even tell people when there is no news that 'there is no news.' They appreciate the candor."*

By December 2008, U.S. employers were stepping up their communication to workers about their financial performance and solvency to help alleviate growing levels of stress and anxiety caused by the recession. More than three-quarters of employer respondents to a survey by Watson Wyatt said they had already sent out, or were planning to send, updates to employees on the impact of the financial crisis. More than two-thirds (69 percent) of these employers cited "easing employee anxiety" as one of the top two goals of their crisis-related internal communication, while nearly one-third (32 percent) cited "earning employees' trust."[9]

Employees need a constant stream of information reinforced in different ways by different parties using different media. When a fast-food restaurant advertises a new menu item, it doesn't just run the ad once; it runs the ad again and again. Take a page from product marketing as you think about communicating with your employees. Opening an ongoing dialogue with employees can reap significant benefits.

> "Employees are anxious . . . and hungry for information. If the usual channels do not satisfy this hunger, the employees will decide for themselves what to expect based on rumors and innuendo . . ."
> — DAVID DELL

▶ HOW SENIOR LEADERS AT WINNING COMPANIES DRIVE ENGAGEMENT

When we interviewed the general manager of Gaylord Palms Resort and Spa, Kemp Gallineau, and Gaylord's vice president of corporate culture and training, Emily Ellis (both of whom we first introduced you to in Chapter 1), we wanted to find out how the Palms has attained and sustained its premier-employer status and especially how it has achieved such high survey scores in the area of senior leadership.

We asked Gallineau what impact the firm's CEO, Colin Reed, has had on building a culture of engagement:

Colin's leadership style makes a big difference. It's just who he is—exceptionally down-to-earth and approachable. If you ask him a question, he will answer it. He is honest, candid, and doesn't try to spin things.

Reed meets regularly with employees to let them know what the resort's business prospects look like. He is constantly reevaluating the company's business strategy. Gallineau went on to explain:

Nothing is sacred about how we execute. We are fortunate to have remained as successful as we are through hard times. We don't anticipate layoffs, but if we had to, Colin would give people the straight scoop. Our customers can change and sign on or off multiyear deals. Our staff knows that things can change, and if they do, we ask them to be a part of the change. The other thing about Colin—he truly wants to understand employees, and he cares about them and their families. He never penalizes leaders when someone below them in their unit calls with a complaint. He handles it in a constructive, noncritical way. We are not a "heads-are-going-to-roll" culture.

When asked to describe his own leadership style, Gallineau responded:

Open, human, and accessible . . . I don't want employees to be intimidated by me. I dine with them in our cyber cafe, park in no special place, sit in no special place. They know me as a human being, a fellow adult with a different role.

Ellis described the firm's approach to hiring and developing leaders:

At Gaylord, when new hires first meet our senior leaders, we tell them, "We are not going to treat you like a number." That means we have to hire leaders who treat people right. Employees in many other hotels don't ever even see their property managers. Leaders at Gaylord have to GET it—the way we do it here. We train our lead-

ers in what competent leaders do. Command and control isn't leadership. Those that don't walk the talk or treat people right don't last.

Gallineau elaborated on the company's leadership development philosophy:

I interview every candidate for a leadership position. They all have to be screened by the peer group with whom they would be working. We debrief interviews as a team. We need to know they are a fit. We use a competency assessment instrument to analyze competencies needed for each leadership role and situation, then validate those competencies and use the same tool to select the right person. We conduct behavioral interview questions based on competencies, not just for management roles but for all positions. We look for three key things in leaders and all in employees—high integrity, citizenship, and compassion. Honesty and integrity especially is a core value for us.

Finally, we asked Gallineau whether Gaylord tries to emulate the leadership practices of other successful hotels. His response:

Other great hotels have done the same thing, but we don't just look to emulate what other hotels do. We emulate great customer service practices wherever we see or hear about them. Lately, for example, we've looked at airlines for reservations best practices and new ideas, not just at what other hotels do.

Re-Engaging in Turbulent Times with Communication Practices

1. Ask employees for help. We recommend that management invite employees to get involved in generating new ideas. Most employees know ways to cut costs, improve quality, or increase sales. One sure way to jump-start employee engagement is to mine their viable ideas and get them involved in implementing them.

2. Allow employees their natural emotional reactions. Employees otherwise may release their feelings in nonproductive ways. We often recommend holding "50-50" meetings where employees are invited to speak and air their concerns for half the time while managers and executives listen.

3. Use periodic, systematic employee "pulse" surveys or listening sessions. This practice helps management keep abreast of the impact of the layoffs on day-to-day operations and demonstrates that employees are considered an important asset. Some employers, such as Gaylord Hotels and Resorts, hold regular listening and idea-generating meetings with employees.

4. Be open, visible, and vulnerable. John Chambers, CEO of Cisco Systems, hosts monthly breakfasts where employees who celebrate a birthday that month are invited and encouraged to ask him anything—no question is off-limits. There is risk in this, but the reward is magnified by the employee trust and respect that is gained. These sessions are videotaped and rebroadcast on the company's intranet. Chambers believes that employees want "unvarnished communication," reassurances, and transparency.[10] Don't sugarcoat the reality or challenge that lies ahead.

5. Proactively address the downside of fewer staff for the same amount of work. Involve employees in rethinking how tasks are going to be accomplished.

6. Make sure frontline supervisors get the focus and attention they need to sustain the day-to-day engagement of frontline employees. First-line managers have more direct contact with the majority of employees. What they think, say, and do matters even more. First-line supervisors often feel they are not targeted when it comes to open, two-way communication. Senior leaders need to make sure managers are given the information they need to answer tough questions from their teams during tough times. Minimize conflicting messages from different areas of a company, which signals disorganization and destroys confidence.

> **Engagement Declining among Senior Executives**
> Managers searching for signs of employee angst should look up the ladder instead of down. Employee engagement is falling faster among top executives than any other group, according to research from the Corporate Executive Board (CEB).
>
> Only 13 percent of senior executives at the vice presidential level or higher say they are "willing to go above and beyond what is expected of them"—a decline from 29 percent two years prior. In the December survey of the CEB's 79,000-member employees worldwide at 123 organizations, 20 percent of all respondents said they were disengaged, compared to 10 percent two years ago. (Employees are classified as either engaged, neutral, or disengaged.)[11]

▶ A CHECKLIST OF ENGAGEMENT PRACTICES FOR SENIOR LEADERS

Though leadership styles may differ and leadership practices may vary with business objectives and market conditions, below are some of the practices, based on our analysis, that *Best Places to Work* share in common. Check those that you believe your leadership team is currently doing well, and place an X next to those you believe your leaders should be doing or doing significantly better.

The best employers:

__ Communicate clear direction and realistic plans for continuing company success.

__ Work to build a culture of caring as well as a culture of high performance.

__ Select and promote managers who treat employees right and get results, and coach, develop, or remove those who cannot do both.

__ Train managers in the people management skills needed to keep employees aligned and engaged.

___ Hold managers truly accountable for treating people right.

___ Back up words with actions.

___ Demonstrate integrity in all business dealings.

___ Maintain visibility and personal contact with frontline employees.

___ Build and reward teamwork at every level, including the executive team.

___ Eliminate formal and informal "we-they" divisions between management and frontline workers.

___ Regularly communicate appreciation for specific employee contributions—made by both individuals and teams.

___ Regularly solicit employee input and ideas, and really listen.

___ Act in a timely fashion on workable employee ideas and suggestions, especially employee surveys; then let employees know what actions you took.

___ Allow managers and employees to experiment and fail.

___ Tolerate differences of opinion and healthy conflict.

___ Provide benefits and services that promote sustainable life-work balance.

___ Share information with employees whenever possible.

___ Forgo some traditional executive perks and disproportionate pay.

▶ FINAL THOUGHTS: WHAT'S IN YOUR LIVING ROOM?

We know of a large, multi-office firm that set a goal to become a "great place to work" and established a task force to research employee engagement best practices. The firm's goal was to significantly move the needle upward on the employee engagement scale, which, the firm felt, would give it an advantage in a highly competitive industry. The plan was to use employee engagement to build the "employment brand," which, in turn, would help the firm attract more employees.

The task force was well-intentioned. The members reached out to learn from employers that had received "*Best-Places*" designations. The task force conducted its own employee engagement survey, following up that effort with employee focus groups to gain a clearer understanding of the root causes of issues it could begin to address.

So far, so good.

The only problem was that much of this activity was being done while working around the CEO, whom the task force described as "old school" and highly autocratic. Her leadership approach was, shall we say, less than engaging. The engagement survey results revealed what many managers already knew: younger workers saw the firm's leaders as too hierarchical and command-and-control, accounting for a rising turnover rate and great difficulty recruiting new graduates. The CEO, although tolerant of the task force's efforts, had sent the not-so-subtle message that the task force could implement this "engagement program," but without including her as a participant or contributor.

She must have assumed she had been doing something right, or she would not have reached her high position—right? So why should she question her approach to leadership this late in her successful career? Perhaps because the forces of change had finally caught up to her and the firm.

The thwack from the elephant's tail, apparently in full view in the living room, will render many, if not most, of the task force's efforts for naught. How senior leaders get away with forfeiting, or in many cases ignoring, their responsibility to lead and engage employees is beyond our comprehension. They and all the organization's stakeholders will, in due course, pay a heavy price for the elephant that we call hubris.

CHAPTER FIVE

The *Real* Job of Managers

Keeping Employees Aligned and Engaged

It's not enough to do your best. You must know what to do and then do your best.

—W. Edwards Deming

If you truly believe your primary purpose as a manager is to do everything possible to help your employees succeed, you are acknowledging that each time an employee fails, it is one of your failures.

—Ferdinand Fournies

▶ CARRIE: LUCKY TO HAVE THE MANAGER I DO

> *I've been reporting to Gerard for five years now, and he's a big reason I'm still here.*
>
> *He gives me different ideas about how to do things, but he always gives me leeway to make my own decisions. He's a sounding board for me. We usually meet at least once a day to make sure I know what's expected. And I keep him informed so things run smoothly.*

Sometimes we are short-staffed and clerical work can get backed up. It's not just about delegating with him. Gerard is very hands-on. When he sees that his people are overloaded, he'll jump in, roll up his sleeves, and work alongside everyone else. That usually boosts morale. Our group works on two different floors, so he's always going up and down.

He keeps the doors of communication open. When I go to him, I usually get my answer, so I don't have to "answer shop." And he's very thoughtful when he gives you an answer. He has confidence about what to do because he has done the work himself.

During staff meetings Gerard goes over what needs doing better and what's going well. He usually starts off very positive. He gives specific feedback and concrete information. He praises and recognizes people right after things happen. He doesn't wait for meetings to do it. He also comes armed and documented when he has to reprimand. He's very firm. Many managers avoid confrontation. Gerard addresses performance problems immediately. There's no carrot and no stick. He'll just say "OK, I saw this—no more of that." Very direct. There's not a lot of tardiness or absenteeism here.

He is also extremely understanding. I have a two-year-old in day care, and he accepts that I have to take time off when she's sick. He also mans the phones over lunch while the staff goes out for a birthday party.

He's not perfect, but I hear some real horror stories about other managers, so I'm pretty fortunate to have Gerard as my manager.

▶ THE MANAGER AS DIRECT LINK TO EMPLOYEE ALIGNMENT *AND* ENGAGEMENT

In this chapter, we address the role that direct managers play in keeping employees both engaged and aligned with the organization's business goals and with their own performance expectations. As we have mentioned before, employee engagement isn't everything; the alignment of employee goals with organizational goals is at least as important as employee engagement to company success. Getting all employees to put their oars in the water at the same time and pull together toward the same goal is critical, but it's more difficult to accomplish than some may think.

Alignment means that the company's goals and the employees' goals are mutually reinforcing. This driver begins, of course, with senior leaders being clear about their goals and communicating them clearly, but it doesn't stop there. Direct managers must be held accountable for aligning those goals and linking them to employees' daily work objectives and professional growth aspirations. Senior leaders may communicate clear goals, but if managers do not clearly understand company goals and make them personally meaningful to their direct reports, employees' career and performance goals may remain misaligned. The following survey quote illustrates that capable senior leaders may have clear goals that are not cascading down to the level of the employee in a meaningful or effective way because of dysfunction at the manager level:

> *The executive level is highly competent and has clear goals and direction, while the management level is mired in constant infighting that lowers morale from the middle down. This makes it hard on a day-to-day basis at times to want to stay here. But once you look at the company direction you stay, because there are no better executives based on integrity and hard work anywhere.*

On the other side of the coin, if senior leaders fail to communicate clear goals, then managers certainly cannot reinforce them, and all employees are left guessing, as this comment reveals:

> *My department is a good example of one with a leader given too many directives from too many bosses, who, as a result, has no time for the people in the department and no idea what they're doing day to day. As a result we operate with virtually no leader.*

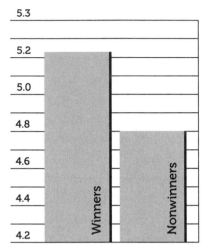

My Immediate Supervisor Gives
Me Constructive Feedback
on My Job Performance

Figure 5.1

▶ EVIDENCE OF THE DIFFERENCE GOOD MANAGERS MAKE

There were three additional manager-related survey items where we saw a significant difference between the scores of winning and non-winning employers, as Figures 5.1, 5.2, and 5.3 show and the selected survey comments echo.

"My immediate supervisor regularly gives me constructive feedback on my job performance" (Figure 5.1) was ranked #6 as a differentiating item.

Voices of Engagement

▶ *"Our managers' focus is more on process improvement than finger-pointing. The emphasis is not on who made a mistake, but on how can we all avoid making similar mistakes in the future."*

▶ *"We have weekly one-on-ones that provide great feedback and let me know what I need to do to perform my job 100 and effectively."*

Voices of Disengagement

▶ *"I have no idea if my manager is happy with me or not. I have come to assume, no news is good news."*

▶ *"The manager doesn't do well at telling you what you are do-ing good or bad until review time; it would be helpful to receive feedback as you go."*

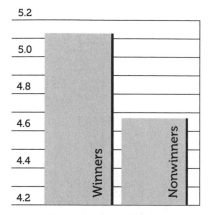

There Is Open, Honest
Communication between
Employees and Managers

Figure 5.2

Voices of Engagement

▶ *"Feedback is provided constructively and mistakes are not made, but learning opportunities are created."*

▶ *"I like being able to talk to management with concerns and questions without fear of being thought of as out of place or doing something wrong."*

▶ *"The supervisors and managers are simply SUPERB at being calm, giving direction and support, and encouragement."*

▶ *"There is open, honest communication between everyone with no fear of backlash."*

▶ *"They continue to keep their employees updated on the inside and outside things happening with the company."*

▶ *"Open communication is encouraged, even with supervisors."*

Voices of Disengagement

▶ *"She avoids anything confrontational and is even two to three months late in giving your annual evaluation."*

▶ *"Poor communications (and lack of) seem to be specific to my immediate area. Most of our local problems can be traced to one individual."*

▶ *"My supervisor doesn't speak to me, so I don't really know what's going on."*

▶ *"I don't hear a lot of information from my manager. I am not a manager, so I don't hear things directly at the management meetings. I think it is important to communicate in a clear manner the direction we should all get behind in order for people to be more energized and really committed to that goal."*

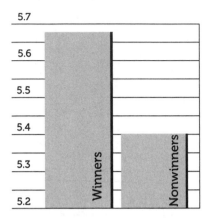

I Understand How My Job Helps
the Organization Achieve Success

Figure 5.3

Voices of Engagement

▶ *"I appreciate that I feel welcome to talk to any of my coworkers or superiors at any time that I feel is necessary."*

▶ *"My immediate supervisor meets with me weekly, informs me of the hospital's future plans, and asks for my opinion. The president and CEO regularly seek to be updated about all services and programs that directly serve our customers and clients . . . our patients. Work-related needs are thoroughly evaluated and supported."*

▶ *"I could make much more money in my position elsewhere, but there isn't anywhere else I would rather work. I feel like I am part of something, contributing to something on a larger scale."*

Voices of Disengagement

▶ *"My current supervisor needs some training in people skills . . . not a very good communicator, and I do not feel I can trust this person with personal issues."*

▶ *"It seems we almost have too many things that we are focusing on or too many goals. I wish we could really focus in on what we feel would give us the biggest competitive advantage and work really hard on that."*

> ▶ *"Everyone here knows they can make an impact and works toward a unified goal every day."*
> ▶ *"I always feel as though the work that I am doing is truly contributing to the company's success."*
> ▶ *"The upper-management team keeps the entire organization informed (atrium meetings at least quarterly) so that there is total alignment on corporate strategy, key performance indicators, shortfalls/risks, and new business opportunities. Objectives are well-defined. Progress is measured and reported. Successes are celebrated."*

> ▶ *"The call center people get praised on the number of calls they handle per hour. Yeah, they answer the phone and then pass the call on to another department or give them wrong information (instead of taking the time to ask for help) just to get the member off the phone and answer another call! Then people like me have to fix all of their mistakes, and it takes away from the possible time we could have to make our loan goals!!"*
> ▶ *"Though the company does an excellent job of communicating the overall company vision and goals, we could probably do better at relating those goals directly to what individuals do and how that contributes to our success."*

▶ EMPLOYEES VENT THEIR FEELINGS ABOUT BAD MANAGERS

If the continuing popularity of the *Dilbert* comic strip is any indication, employee cynicism about bad bosses has reached new depths. Workplace studies appear to confirm this. In one study, 24 percent of U.S. employees said they would fire their bosses if given the chance. *Only 6 percent of engaged workers said they would do so*, while 51 percent of actively disengaged workers said they would fire their bosses.[1] The CEO of the Gallup Organization has stated that "only one in 10 employees considers their managers capable."[2]

As usual, the words of employees provide insights deeper than numbers can reveal. The comments employees enter at the end of the *Best-Places-to-Work* survey are not prompted or categorized. They come "straight from the gut," revealing wellsprings of emotion, both positive and negative. Here are some of the survey comments from employees who are obviously disengaged and suffering the effects of working under poor direct managers:

▶ *"A lot of the managers have technical backgrounds and rose through the ranks, but they don't have managerial skills or common sense on how to treat people with respect. This is a daily problem."*

▶ *"The lower-level managers and supervisors need additional training in management. Unfortunately, numerous excellent employees leave after a short period of time due to a lack of motivation and recognition."*

▶ *"Some mid-level managers have been with the company a long time but are not very effective leaders. Too often individuals promoted to supervisory or mid-management positions are not skilled at managing people or programs and take a passive approach to dealing with problem employees or procedures."*

▶ *"The firm has a major problem with middle management. People are not trained in how to be effective managers and are not rewarded or reprimanded for good or bad management skills; therefore, the people who work for poor managers are often stuck in a bad position with no one to go to for help."*

▶ *"Having worked at other law firms before, the environment can be one where attorneys often view staff as second-class citizens. Ninety-nine percent of the attorneys are nice people to work with and show respect to all. No matter how much money an attorney brings to the firm, he or she is not allowed to be an a**hole—it just doesn't work like that here."*

As you may have noticed, in several of these comments employees are not so much pointing the finger of blame at managers themselves, but at company leaders who have made the decision to promote them into supervisory positions in the first place, or have failed to address their lack of management skills, either by confronting their ineffectiveness, by coaching them, or by providing management training.

Managers Behaving Badly—Classifying the Types

The varieties of bad management behavior we see reflected in the verbatim comments of survey respondents are not novel or surprising to most of us. Anyone who has spent time in organizational life has witnessed the dispiriting effects of the many breeds of bad managers on worker motivation and morale. We include the following categories of survey comments as testament to these toxic types and as plaintive evidence to the debilitating effects of tolerating such behavior:

Fostering distrust

▶ *"My manager does not win as a team and does not take responsibility for her job. Her motto is if 'I'm going down, I'm going to bring everybody with me' and doesn't know how to manage employees. She is really good about talking behind employees' backs."*

▶ *"The thing I find most amazing is the lack of integrity in my supervisor. He purposefully tries to create dissension among his employees. He will call someone in his office and tell them that 'so-and-so said this about you.'"*

Devaluing, discounting, failing to appreciate

(Also see Chapter 8 on valuing employees.)

▶ *"When opinions are given, they are ignored, only to be followed by the management's opinion."*

▶ *"Overall the firm has good people with good ideas. Managing client expectations while trying to maintain growth and increase overall profitability in an industry with increasing demands has resulted in neglecting the recognition and reward for employees of the firm."*

▶ *"I find it odd that a leading loyalty provider does little to incentivize the loyalty of their most productive employees, those creating the highest caliber of work, which is the marketed product and signature of the company. The frontline staff that enables this company to function 24 hours daily, 365, are greater both in various life experiences and scope of knowledge than the belittling communication received through middle management would have anyone believe."*

▶ *"The leaders of the organization do not value their employees. They do not recognize the good people. There is no appreciation for going the extra mile or a job well done."*

Lack of accountability and teamwork

▶ *"When employees fail it is because of management, but the employees get blamed."*

▶ *"This organization is all about internal politics. There are good departments and groups, but overall, working at this institution is—in the words of a former manager of mine whom I loved but who was forced out—like fighting in the Colosseum. We are gladiators defending a piece of ground. There is poor communication, little cooperation, and only occasional support, and woe be to the employee who has a bully for a manager."*

▶ *"Our department lacks the necessary leadership to ensure everyone is held accountable for their actions. Employees are allowed to pass the buck, which leaves other shifts accountable for getting the job done."*

Micromanaging and controlling

▶ *"The power trip of the local office manager is beyond belief! Favoritism is the name of the game, NOT what is best for the firm as a whole."*

▶ *"The betterment of the leadership comes way before the betterment of the community and staff. At this place of employment we experience a lot of 'superiorities' toward the staff, and there's no freedom or incentive to be open-minded, to express our thoughts, because of fear of retaliation from the leaders."*

▶ *"I really enjoy my department and my direct coworkers, but my manager is a micromanager with horrible communication skills, and she has managed to sour my work experience here."*

▶ *"My immediate supervisor is, unfortunately, to quote our office manager 'wound pretty tight and insecure,' which makes for a rather interesting challenge on a day-to-day basis."*

Bullying, abuse, disrespect (B-A-D)

▶ *"Many managers employ management by intimidation, and I personally don't share the same leadership style."*

▶ *"Coming from a company where I experienced value, good leadership, and employee development, it is sad for me to see that employees here are not respected by most managers. Promotions don't necessarily happen by merit and good work, and there is no employee development. We lack humanity."*

▶ *"The former manager made employees feel inferior, and she didn't trust our judgment. Her attitude toward some of the employees was extremely poor; it came to the point where she had to be reported to HR, but nothing was done about it. She discouraged us to the point that we are still feeling the effects, and it will take quite a while to recover from her demeaning attitude."*

▶ *"When I first started working for this company I thought it was going to be great. However, the doctor that I work for treats employees, as well as patients, like crap, and NO ONE seems to care to do anything about it."*

In the light of the comments in the previous category, consider a recent study that found the annual turnover costs traceable to manager bullying in a 1,000-employee organization to be $1.8 million (based on a conservative estimate of $20,000 replacement costs per turnover). Studies documented that 25 percent of those bullied left the organization, along with 20 percent of those who witnessed instances of bullying.[3]

Managers consumed by self-interest

▶ *"Managers manage to their personal incentive programs. They care very little about what is best for the business."*

▶ *"The region is managed by obnoxious pigs that don't care about anyone but themselves. The sooner I find another job away from here, the better off I'll be!"*

Weak and incompetent managers

▶ *"In a nutshell . . . we're a group who has become slightly jaded due to the fact that our supervisors commit to too much and can't say no, and, as a result, we're spread thin."*

▶ *"A majority of the frontline leadership know little about what is happening and have very little to offer when it comes to decision making. They are clueless on how to implement new technology to increase productivity."*

▶ *"My particular department has an ineffective management team who are uncaring to the hourly employees within the department. My immediate manager has poor managerial skills—she is unreliable and slow in responding to our needs/questions/concerns. She avoids anything confrontational and is even two to three months late in giving annual evaluations. She has poor follow-through with everything."*

GOOD EMPLOYER . . . BAD MANAGER

There were many comments indicating that employees are willing to overlook the negative effects of a direct manager if they have generally good feelings about the company and/or senior leaders. They seem to have decided to stay with their employers, not because of, but *in spite of,* their direct supervisors. One can only wonder how much more engaged they would be with more competent and caring immediate supervision.

▶ *"Company rocks; can't stand my supervisor. Getting promoted has been harder than I was first led to expect. I love the company. I do not like working for my direct supervisor."*

▶ *"My immediate supervisor will be changing after January 1. We are not a good match together. I respect most other people I have worked for/with."*

▶ *"I feel that the company is number one. However, I am not impressed with their choice in management for my branch. This individual does not represent the company's values, organization, or leadership; therefore, I feel cheated."*

▶ *"I don't agree with my supervisor's approach to management. But I do not think that the whole firm can be blamed for the incompetence of two or three people. I would still consider this place a great place to work!"*

▶ *"Great company to work for. Just sometimes you get a really bad manager. It's hard to stay focused on the job and the team when the manager is doing what he or she can to keep the team from working harmoniously."*

▶ *"Our department will not grow or be a pleasant place to work if the manager does not value his workers or coworkers, or if favoritism rather than individual ability is used to promote someone. We aren't recognized by our manager when things are done above and beyond our abilities. I think this department is very, very poorly run. I see lots of other departments grow by having a good manager who encourages team members to work together and have a good work ethic. I don't see it in my manager or department."*

▶ *"The executive leadership team (CEO and all others) is wonderful. There is a giant disconnect between their values and beliefs and those of middle management."*

▶ *"I feel the upper management does a terrific job, but I feel the supervisors lack respect for people."*

These comments clearly illustrate that a good workplace must be good on a daily, local level. That is, an employee may, in fact, work for a company he or she views and experiences as a good place to work, yet the employee's overall willingness to perform at his or her best is lessened by the toxic influence of a bad manager. Again, we can only lament that many otherwise capable senior leaders continue to tolerate these situations.

GOOD MANAGER . . . BAD EMPLOYER

It also happens that good managers compensate for the disengaging effects of the culture or decisions made by senior leaders. Here are some examples from the employees' perspective:

▶ *"This is a great place to work. The only area that lacks is the communication between upper-level management and staff."*

▶ *"As far as senior leaders are concerned, I have no trust for them. I trust my immediate manager wholeheartedly. I don't like the idea of senior leaders in their offices who have no idea of the stress we endure to keep the hospital running."*

▶ *"My immediate supervisor is very good and does his best with the power given to him. Senior leadership, on the other hand, needs to pull their heads out of their back end!"*

▶ *"I have been through many changes at this hospital, but I do not recommend it to my family and friends for anything but having a baby. Our department is among the best. Our directors are dedicated to their staff and go the extra mile to create a safe workplace in spite of the bottom line. This becomes more difficult every day, as they are pressured to reduce staffing and increase productivity. I see them despair, because their nurses are tired and worn, and still the company requires they cut back."*

Aligning and Engaging the Four Generations

We repeat: every person must be managed according to his or her uniqueness. With that firmly in mind, we offer the following general guidelines that experts on the generations consider to be valid for many, if not most, in each age group:

Traditionalists (born before 1946)

▶ Tap their experience.
▶ Give thorough orientations, and provide clear expectations.
▶ Say "please" and "thank you."
▶ Appeal to logic, sense of duty, the idea of leaving a legacy, and drive for results.
▶ Coach respectfully.
▶ Communicate face-to-face and in a more personal way.
▶ Reward with visual symbols of status.
▶ Train them in technology.

Boomers (born 1946–1964)

▶ Show interest in them personally.
▶ Ask . . . don't give orders.
▶ Tap their unique individual strengths.
▶ Challenge them to have an impact, leave their mark.
▶ Make the workplace warm, humane, democratic, harmonious, and casual.
▶ Explain the larger meaning of the work.
▶ Link their pay to performance.
▶ Provide growth and learning opportunities.
▶ Acknowledge their contributions.
▶ Help them keep pace with new technologies.
▶ Provide nontraditional work hours and phased retirement options.

Gen Xers (born 1965–1980)

▶ Challenge them early and often.
▶ Manage by objectives.
▶ Let them do it their way.

- ▶ Coach proactively, and provide frequent feedback.
- ▶ Evaluate their ideas on merit.
- ▶ Allow flexible work arrangements.
- ▶ Allow informality and fun.
- ▶ Minimize corporate politics.
- ▶ Bend the rules for them when you can.

Millennials (born 1981–1994)

- ▶ Budget plenty of time for on-boarding.
- ▶ Ask about their goals.
- ▶ Give frequent feedback.
- ▶ Provide strong team leadership and structure.
- ▶ Allow for bending of gender roles.
- ▶ Provide up-to-date technology.
- ▶ Provide lots of training and mentoring.
- ▶ Allow flexibility in regard to where the work gets done.

We discussed multigenerational issues with Kemp Gallineau, general manager of Gaylord Palms Hotel and Resort:

Q: Managers in some companies complain about motivating and managing the Millennial generation—those born since 1981 or so. Has this been an issue at Gaylord Palms?
Gallineau: *"No, not really. We use a lot of interns from the colleges, and we put a lot of effort in trying to understand them. I'm now in my 40s, and I realize things are changing.*

We grew up in a different time, when we communicated by memo and phone. They want things the way they want it because of the way they grew up—the Millennials grew up online and are comfortable using blogs. So, if we want two-way communication with them, we need to start using different media. Memos are passé—younger employees want to respond and give their two cents' worth. We have our own internal Web site where people can get photos of our last party. We need to embrace the techniques that engage that generation. They want more feedback, and that's good, because we think feedback is good for the business. Feedback to us means constantly communicating customer service scores and texting more. But you have to ask what feedback means to each employee. They're not all the same. It doesn't matter how—they all just need to get the message. I'm actually finding it fun to stretch and take the challenge of communicating differently with each generation and with each person. We can tap their creativity if we leverage how they like to communicate. We need a diverse group of people because that makes for the best teams. It's OK to debate and disagree and work through our differences, to have a healthy discussion. It's more work, but the outcome is better."

When Managers Are Not Engaged

We certainly cannot overlook what remains as a significant challenge for employers: many managers themselves are not engaged, and that being the case, we cannot realistically expect them to effectively engage those who report to them. Even though most managers are more engaged than the average worker, if only 25 percent of the workforce is engaged and if the percentage of engaged managers is double that number, that still leaves another 50 percent of managers who are not engaged.

Managers are employees too, of course, and they become disengaged for the same reasons as everyone else. Often, they are the worst critics of senior leaders because they are frequently caught between a rock and a hard place trying to manage their direct reports without the knowledge, direction, training, and resources they need to do so.

> If you are a manager and would like to evaluate your own level of engagement, we suggest you take the self-engagement inventory referenced in Chapter 10 by going to www. re-engagebook.com.

▶ DESPITE WHAT DILBERT SAYS, GOOD MANAGERS *DO* EXIST

Yes, good managers do exist. You may have been lucky enough to have had one or two yourself. It's just that there aren't enough of them to go around. Here is a sampling of the positive general comments about direct managers and supervisors that capture the kind of loyalty and commitment they can inspire:

- ▶ *"Our boss is an inspiration. I could not imagine working for anyone else, ever."*
- ▶ *"I know that I can always turn to my immediate supervisor if I ever have any problems, knowing that he will do what he can to make the company a better place to work. He will always go out of his way to make sure that we, as his employees, are happy."*
- ▶ *"My office manager is the best. She is a very caring person and genuinely concerned about her staff. She knows how to make me feel appreciated. She knows how to give constructive criticism. When I do extra things she asks, she always says thank you."*
- ▶ *"The only down side of working for such a great boss is that I'm afraid I won't like working for anyone after him."*

▶ WHAT MANAGERS DO TO ALIGN AND ENGAGE

Those survey respondents lucky enough to have good managers were not reluctant to express their gratitude. As you read the comments, notice the strong sense of appreciation. Would you agree that these employees are probably giving back to their managers their loyalty and best effort? The best managers create reciprocal commitment to employee and business goals. What behavior inspires such commitment? We analyzed survey comments and identified the following:

They coach and develop

▶ *"My manager was so supportive of my career goals."*
▶ *"My managers take an extremely proactive role in developing my skill set. I am learning every day."*
▶ *"I absolutely love where I work. I am often given new opportunities to challenge myself and grow as a young professional, and my immediate supervisor is always willing to provide feedback and professional development opportunities."*
▶ *"My direct manager is always helping me to achieve my potential, and he has fostered a great personal relationship between the two of us that makes him, in my eyes, not the typical boss, but more of a mentor."*
▶ *"I have had amazing opportunities for increased responsibilities over the last three years. I attribute that to my manager recognizing my strengths and aligning my work to maximize my contributions."*

They value their employees and show appreciation

▶ *"I really believe that my manager is a true example of what a director should be. She is always open for suggestions, and she makes everyone feel like they are important."*
▶ *"My boss is a great guy with a true open-door policy. I can walk into his office at any time and ask any question, and he takes the time to answer and teach."*

▶ *"We feel we are truly valued by the treatment we receive, and it makes us want to do the very best we can for the firm. The team concept includes the copy people right on up to the attorneys. I work for the most wonderful litigation partner, who is constantly complimenting me on the job I do—a little pat on the back goes a long way. I feel she genuinely cares about me as a person, not just someone who works for her. This is truly a great place to work, and I hope to finish out my working years here."*

They give employees the autonomy to use their own judgment

▶ *"I have worked at banks where every movement is monitored and no one has any authority. At ABC Bank, we have authority, and no one monitors every move. They merely monitor our successes and failures."*

▶ *"My supervisors trust my judgment, and no one is watching the clock."*

▶ *"I am treated as an adult who is responsible for my caseload. My supervisor does not look over my shoulder every minute to make sure that my work gets done. I am responsible for motivating myself to do a good job and setting my own standards. I've worked for a lot of other supervisors that have totally missed that whole concept."*

How Managers Can Overcome the Tipping Point of Company Size

A few years ago a company that had won *Best-Places-to-Work* competitions in its home city began to staff in remote locations, in part because of its success in capturing a significant share of the local market. As the company developed locations beyond the home office, engagement levels

---

began to decline. The difference between the home office and other locations was most strikingly evident on the very critical item related to perceptions of open and honest communication between employees and managers. The percentage of positive responses was 17 points lower in the remote offices on this item and 17 points higher on the percentage of negative responses. In fact, only 4 of the 37 items on the survey were higher in the remote offices than at the home office.

The verbatim urgings of one nonhome office employee solidified the point:

Get out of the office and into the field. All the programs in the world won't help an organization if you are out of touch with the most important resource a company has . . . people.

By contrast, here are comments of employees in companies with high scores on this item and on other items related to manager alignment and engagement:

▶ *"We are 20,000 strong and have very high engagement. It is hardwired into operations through management accountability and executive compensation targets."*
▶ *"If you keep in mind communicating your growth strategy and your ongoing projects to your coworkers, you will not have a communication problem. People want to know that you are TRYING to communicate as much as they want actual communication."*

The lesson here is that commitment to clear and constant communication at every level and site is the key to maintaining alignment and engagement as an organization grows in headcount and locations. Hardwiring manager accountability, measuring results, and building appropriate rewards into daily operations certainly all help to achieve the desired outcome.

▶ **BRINGING IT ALL TOGETHER: HOW MAKING MANAGERS BETTER MAKES THE DIFFERENCE AT WINCHESTER HOSPITAL**

In 2008 the *Boston Business Journal* announced that Winchester Hospital, in Winchester, Massachusetts, was, for the sixth year in a row, one of the *Best Places to Work* in the Boston area. The only difference that year was that the 230-bed, 2,600-employee hospital (16 sites) was more than just one of the best—it was number one, beating out the other 392 employers that applied. What made this achievement even more impressive was that Winchester Hospital was also selected—in the same year—as the number one employer in the *Boston Globe*'s Top-Places-to-Work competition based on employee opinions about company leadership, compensation and training, diversity and inclusion, career development, family-friendly flexibility and values, and ethics. The hospital ranks in the 90th percentile in the state in patient satisfaction (as rated by Press-Ganey, which specializes in measuring patient and employee satisfaction for the health-care industry) and enjoys an 87 percent occupancy rate, an 8 percent turnover rate, and a 2 percent nurse vacancy rate. There's more: in June of the same year, the American Nurses Credentialing Center awarded Winchester Hospital its highest honor—Magnet recognition for providing "the very best in nursing care and upholding the tradition within nursing of professional nursing practice."

In reviewing Winchester Hospital's winning *Best-Places-to-Work* survey results, we noted that scores on manager effectiveness were particularly outstanding—the highest of any participating U.S. employer. To uncover the story behind the scores, we interviewed Anne Lang, Winchester's vice president of human resources and legal services, and Kathleen Beyerman, director of staff development, clinical and nursing research. Beyerman also directs the hospital's unique Community Health Institute, whose mission is to serve the health-care needs of the surrounding community of 350,000.

Q: Why do you think Winchester Hospital received such high scores on the survey questions related to managing employees?

Lang: *We're a 230-bed hospital with limited financial resources. We don't have Ping-Pong tables and big lunchrooms. About 10 years ago, we asked ourselves, "What can we focus on for the most dramatic effect—to achieve great patient care and sustain a competitive advantage?" The CEO and I both had the same philosophy: it's all about leadership. We decided we had to focus on our leaders and do everything we could to make them better. Making our managers and supervisors better leaders became a key organizational priority.*

Q: So, how did you go about doing that?
Lang: *We built a leadership program designed to get every manager to see themselves as leaders and recognize that our success as a hospital is totally dependent on them. That meant that leaders needed to be more aware of how they could improve and the training necessary to be more effective at managing people. So, we started with our senior leadership team. We had them take a personality self-assessment and receive 360-degree feedback. But when we tried cascading the 360 process down to the next level of leaders, we found that they were just unloading years of pent-up negative feedback on each other and it was very destructive. We realized that many managers weren't giving honest feedback to each other because they just didn't feel comfortable doing it.*

Q: So, what did you do then?
Lang: *Well, about two years into our leader development process, we knew there were two reasons we weren't getting traction—1. leaders were still not as self-aware about their own leadership styles and behavior as they should be, and 2. if your leaders can't have difficult conversations with their direct reports, peers, and their own managers, all this is pointless. So we started making every kind of management training available, including a course called "Difficult Conversations" conducted by the Harvard Negotiation Project. This course had a big impact. Most of our current managers have attended 40 hours of leadership training and we plan to have them attend 8 hours of training each year. The training includes 2 hours on*

employee recognition because we identified that as an area where we needed improvement. We also train managers on generational differences.

Finally, because we weren't effective in selecting the right person for the job in some cases, we started training managers in behavioral interviewing techniques.

Q: How do you know all this training is working?

Lang: *We know because we can see every day that managers are doing a better job. We can see they are not avoiding confrontations. They come to me for coaching, knowing they have to have a difficult conversation and often they are dreading it. They ask if I will walk them through how to deal with a tough issue with an employee or sometimes with a peer, physician, or patient.*

Beyerman: *After attending training, I have managers who come in to see me for the same kinds of discussions to prepare for difficult meetings with employees. I have started suggesting that managers use the term "learning conversations" rather than "difficult conversations" because that's what they are really trying to do—explore and uncover the employee's perspective on why a performance or relationship problem exists. Usually, there's something both the manager and employee needs to know. I've been meeting with a manager recently who comes in and tells me about an employee she needs to confront. I think she already knows what she is supposed to do and say to this employee, but talking it over with me gives her a rehearsal opportunity. She worries about the risk involved—what the employee might think of her afterward and the risk that she might lose control of her own feelings. So we focus on keeping the discussion an interrogatory process, and on discussing the impact of the employee's behavior on colleagues and patients. We always try to get managers to end the discussion with a request that the employee change some specific behavior, so these discussions help managers get clear about what that request will be. So the training we do introduces the concepts, but these follow-on meetings let us know that managers have taken the ideas and methods to heart and are trying to make them work on a daily basis.*

Lang: *We also measure and monitor manager effectiveness by paying close attention to the results of our employee opinion survey. We have 2,500 employees in 16 locations and 60 different units, but we don't have any one function of more than 150 people. In smaller groups it is easier to see which units are scoring poorly and offer those managers additional training and coaching. We also have managerial effectiveness criteria built into our performance evaluations.*

Beyerman: *We are also just starting a more formal evaluation process where we schedule follow-up meetings to ask managers what they have learned in the training that they are using to manage people differently and better. We will also be e-mailing post-program evaluations.*

Q: What effect have the people management practices of your direct supervisors had on your ability to *retain* employees?

Lang: *A huge impact. We are 100 percent committed to managers playing the pivotal role in retaining employees. We have seen turnover rates in certain units change dramatically as a result of changes in management styles and behavior. We saw a difference in one area within six months. There was a manager who didn't listen well and didn't take feedback. We confronted the situation and helped the manager take a different approach. We constantly emphasize the Disney model, where leaders are evaluated not just based on the results they get but also on the behavior they exhibit in getting those results.*

Q: Have you noticed a reduction in your overall turnover rate?

Lang: *Definitely. Our voluntary turnover rate has dropped from 15 percent 10 years ago to 7 percent today. The change has been most dramatic with our nurses, which we track by vacancy rate. Ours is now down to 2 percent, which is unheard of. While most hospitals have nurse shortages, we actually have a waiting list of applicants. We believe it's because we have created a leadership culture that's all about continuous improvement, and a big part of that is treating everyone with respect.*

Q: How do you make sure you are selecting and promoting the right people into supervisory positions?

Lang: *We like to promote from within, but we try to get a good mix of inside and outside hires because we need new and fresh views. We make sure we conduct behavioral interviews with candidates for all management positions, both internal and external. We also have a development program for emerging leaders we call "Launching Leaders."*

Beyerman: *The emerging leader selection means so much to the people who are selected. For example, I just spoke to the charge nurse in maternity whose manager saw innate leadership ability in her and nominated her for the "Launching Leaders" training. She was telling me how much it meant to her to get to know other informal leaders from throughout the hospital during the classes, how it expanded her perspective, and how much pure fun it was for her to be learning and growing.*

Q: What do you do to make sure managers stay engaged as employees?

Lang: *We do a lot to develop them through training and conferences. We encourage their involvement in decisions that affect them and their people. We also have a human resources advisory board of 20 multidisciplinary leaders that serves as a means through which employees' concerns can be represented and voiced. No HR policy gets changed without going to the HR advisory board.*

Beyerman: *Some organizations talk about "pushing decision making down to the lowest level," which we think is the right idea, but we prefer to use the language "pushing the decision forward to the front line," where nurses and direct service workers can influence daily decisions. That way, we don't need to invoke the idea of a hierarchy with people on the bottom. Our staff know that if they have a worthy idea, they can run with it. We had a nurse who thought that patients were having to fast too long prior to surgery. She felt so strongly about this that she asked for permission to do some research and make a presentation to the anesthesiology department that included recommenda-*

tions for reduced fasting times. Her recommendations were accepted and implemented successfully. She had a very positive impact, and other employees know they can do the same.

Q: How have the values and practices of your senior leaders shaped your management culture?

Lang: *In health care it's easier because the values and the mission are clear to everyone. Our employees just want to know the organization is doing well, they have the equipment to do their job, and they can be involved in decision making. The visibility of our leaders is extremely important. Our senior leaders are out and about all the time, making rounds and letting all staff know they can be easily accessed. They are thanking employees, telling them "I heard you did a great job—thanks so much," and sending thank-you notes. It just comes instinctively to our senior leaders. They are nice people to begin with, and are sincerely interested in people's lives. We also have what we call "Chat and Snack" meetings once a quarter with the six VPs and the CEO, where they provide hospital updates and respond to questions from staff. These sessions have really helped to create trust.*

We also focus on fairness. We can't afford to be the highest-paying hospital, but we try hard to be fair with pay and benefits. We know other organizations make deals and exceptions on pay and benefits, but we rarely do. Where we do make exceptions is with employee recognition and development. Winchester has one of the most flexible workforces when compared to other hospitals, with many different shift options. We are open to making accommodations and working out arrangements with individual employees that make life and family responsibilities easier for them. We help nursing assistants pay for nursing school. All flexibility issues are job dependent and employees know that.

Q: If you were to create a headline that described how your company has developed a culture of strong management practices, what would it be?

Lang: *Leadership matters—that's the key. It's all about your leaders. Our Press-Ganey survey scores were extremely high on leadership.*

The biggest difference maker, I believe, is trust. When I came here 10 years ago as the VP of HR, a group of employees came in and told me a story of how a previous senior leader had denied that there would be layoffs just days before layoffs were announced. What struck me was that this had happened 20 years ago, and they had held on to their anger and sense of betrayal all those years. It was like it had happened the day before. My point is if you betray trust, it will stay with you forever.

Q: What advice would you offer to leaders at other companies regarding what they can do to create a culture where employees perceive managers as effective and caring?

Lang: *Educate all your leaders and hold them accountable for being effective and caring. Senior leaders know the 10 percent of managers who aren't operating optimally, but often do not hold them accountable and coach them to improve.*

Postscript

As this book was going to press, we contacted Lang again to get an update on how the hospital was surviving the continuing economic turbulence. She responded that patient volume was down, partly because many patients were putting off elective procedures. As a result, the hospital had decided to take some extraordinary measures, including suspending pension plan payments, reducing employee time off and allowable vacation days, forcing the use of some vacation, and sending employees home from time to time. *"These were difficult to announce,"* Lang admitted, *"but we announced them in such a way that employees knew we were doing what we had to do and that it was in the hospital's best interests and theirs. They understood that these actions were necessary in order to preserve their jobs. We believe we moved in to make these changes earlier than most hospitals in our area. We were straightforward and honest in the way we presented the situation."*

The hospital also reduced unnecessary spending, which included many niceties for employees, such as hospital-sponsored picnics, spot awards, parties, consulting services, and employee travel. To gauge employees' feelings about all these losses and to answer any questions, senior leaders became highly visible, managing by walking the floors and engaging employees in conversation. All this was going on just one month before Winchester staff were resurveyed for the latest *Best-Places-to-Work* competition. Lang worried that employee opinion might have been soured by all that had gone on. As it turned out, her fears were unfounded. Winchester employees once again rated the hospital as the *Best Place to Work* in its size category, the first time an employer in the greater Boston area had won the award two years in a row. *"Considering all that's gone on this last year,"* Lang said, *"this award meant more to us than the first one."*

▶ HOW ONE COMPANY DRIVES ENGAGEMENT BY ALIGNING ORGANIZATION AND EMPLOYEE GOALS

Just as for Winchester Hospital, we also see evidence that leaders and managers at other winning companies are going out of their way to make sure employees are engaged and aligned. Gaylord Palms Hotel and Resort, Orlando, Florida, which we have referred to in previous chapters, once again serves as a case in point.

We spoke with Kemp Gallineau, general manager of the property, and Emily Ellis, vice president of training and corporate culture, about dealing with poor managers to ensure corporate alignment:

> **Q:** Most organizations have managers that are less than effective or who violate company values of honesty or respect. How do you deal with those situations?
>
> **Gallineau:** *We are committed to honesty and integrity and have had to terminate managers for violating that value. We have to cut our losses if we get a bad leader . . . and do it quickly. We had to let a restaurant manager go who said he had scheduled an employee in a certain way and we found out it wasn't true. It was the second*

time he had been questioned for misrepresenting the facts of a situation. We have also had other kinds of bad leader behavior, such as yelling incidents. Our usual approach in these instances is to address the behavior directly, coach the individual, or get them into anger management classes, which has worked for us. Some have needed help with stress management, which is sometimes connected to getting better at planning and time management. Some of our people have had substance abuse issues, and for them we provide rehabilitation and counseling through our Employee Assistance Program.

Q: What steps have you taken to ensure that all your leaders are in alignment with key business objectives?

Gallineau: *We constantly communicate. We have a once-a-month "leader's loop" meeting where managers and senior leaders discuss objectives and key issues. It's always two-way. We hold stand-up meetings of all managers in the ballroom when needed. We have 187 nonexempts who are responsible for hiring and firing, so that's a big meeting.*

Ellis: *We try to keep everyone in alignment. We also hold Star rallies where we have giveaways and fun, and provide important information on what customers are saying, and twice a year we report the results of our employee surveys. People actually come in for these rallies on their days off.*

Aligning and Re-Engaging Employees in Turbulent Times

A survey by Accenture in November 2008 revealed that almost two-thirds of U.S. middle managers believed the economy was having a negative impact on their work environments.[4] The survey of more than 300 middle managers across the United States found that 6 in 10 felt that employees were concerned about losing their jobs or that morale was down. More than half the managers surveyed said they were dissatisfied or only somewhat satisfied with their own jobs. Fear of losing one's job pervades the workplace in turbulent times, and as negative economic news accumulates, it can be difficult to motivate staff. But this is when you most need them to step up. At times like these, much of the day-to-day responsibility for re-engaging employees rests on the shoulders of middle managers, whose words and actions have a magnified impact. That's why in tough times the best managers stand out even more.

With that in mind, we offer the following practices that managers, supervisors, and team leaders can take. Many of these tips apply to senior leaders as well. The focus here is mainly on the manager's role in maintaining trust, empathy, and two-way communication. We present tips on career growth, employee recognition, and promotion of health and wellness in later chapters.

▶ **Work to build or rebuild trust.** This is your most important mission. Be open and forthcoming with information, remembering that bad news is better than no news. Face-to-face communication is recommended for trust building. Don't hide behind e-mail communication. Act with integrity. Show courage in front of your team by asking for help or admitting you were wrong if you were.

▶ **Be credible and honest.** Don't say it's "business as usual." It isn't, so you might as well acknowledge that fact. Before giving out information, make sure it is accurate. If you don't know the answer to a question, say you'll find out and get back to your team as quickly as possible. If you can't tell as much as you know, simply say, "I'm not able to answer that right now." Never lie. If you're caught in a lie, no matter how small, you'll sabotage all your previous efforts to reach out, no matter how sincere they were.

▶ **Be a good listener,** allowing employees to vent and express their concerns. Seek feedback from direct reports. Know for sure how your team is feeling right now. Make no assumptions.

▶ **Partner with your employees** on goal setting and evaluation and in addressing the problems that your business faces. Sit down with each employee, discuss the current situation, and describe the strengths and results you expect in trying times, especially creativity, initiative, resourcefulness, and a positive attitude.

▶ **Hold group sessions** to talk through different economic issues impacting the business, and solicit employee ideas for cutting costs and creating new sources of revenue. Ask those who have experienced difficult times or survived wrenching change to share their wisdom with those who haven't.

▶ **Give people the personal touch.** Make a point of having one-on-one conversations with everyone on your team. Whatever shape your company is in, an uncertain economy affects everyone's ability to focus on the job at hand. Show people that you care about them and how they're feeling from one day to the next. Cultivating a sincere interest in just a few people's lives will do so much more than showing just a little interest about a whole lot of people.

▶ **Hold up the lantern.** In the darkest moments great leaders and managers show the team that there is a light at the end of the tunnel. This means that if you're not clear on the company's plan for surviving and succeeding, keep asking until someone higher up gives you a convincing response.

▶ **Make sure everybody is on the same page** when it comes to communicating messages to employees, including entry-level supervisors.

▶ **Squelch rumors quickly.** One miscommunication or tidbit of conversation taken out of context can wreak havoc on morale. Replace rumors, however small they may be, with real information as soon as you get wind of them and encourage employees to do the same.

▶ **Show respect and give people your full attention.** If you make an appointment or call a meeting, keep it. Show people you care by the little promises you make and keep. Leave the BlackBerry in your office. When in your office, keep your door open whenever you can. Turn off your computer screen when someone enters, and give each person your undivided attention.

▶ **Don't tell people that they should feel lucky to have a job.** That can be interpreted as a threat—one that is highly disengaging.

▶ **Continuously assess employee workload.** People are already stressed. Have enough people to get the work done instead of rewarding the best performers with increased workloads. Remember that there is a strong link between susceptibility to sickness and a stressful work environment. Ask your team to consider how things can be done differently or in a more cost-effective, streamlined way. It may be useful for your team to reexamine how work is being done and whether it should be done any longer.

▶ **Don't take the weight of the world on your own shoulders** and assume that your team is too burdened to help with the big issues you're working on. In fact, your team probably wants to help.

▶ **Consider setting goals on a quarterly basis instead of longer term.** This creates a stronger tie between employees' actions and the resulting accomplishment and allows you to change expectations quickly as the economic situation unfolds. Set easier-to-achieve goals if possible to create opportunities to experience and celebrate small successes.

▶ **Focus on retaining valued employees** in anticipation of the higher turnover rates expected as the economic recovery takes hold. Schedule one-on-one time with key people to remind them of their value to the team. Now more than ever, know what motivates each employee.

▶ **Strategically upgrade your staff.** Understand and plan for future staffing needs today, especially during recessions when many talented people are in the job market.

▶ **Challenge employees to step up.** Communicate that success or failure will be determined by how the team responds under pressure. Get employees to commit to what they will do each week to further the best interests of the business. Reward suggestions from employees who have ideas about making the business more efficient.

▶ **Use humor whenever possible.** One leader recently joked to his team, "The good news is that our building is up to the latest ADA standards and has complete wheelchair access. I figure it will be handy when we're still working here in our 90s."[5]

▶ A CHECKLIST OF MANAGER BEST PRACTICES FOR ALIGNING AND ENGAGING EMPLOYEES IN ALL TIMES

Though managers' styles may differ and priorities may vary with business objectives and market conditions, below are some of the practices, based on our analysis, that *Best Places to Work* have in common. Check those that you believe your organization is currently doing well, and place an X next to those you believe you should be doing or doing significantly better:

___ Communicate clearly and realistically the full range of challenges facing all those who aspire to management positions and the seriousness of their responsibility to build trusting relationships and keep their employees engaged.

___ Train managers in good people-management practices and reward them for taking the time to manage and coach their direct reports, not just for task completion.

___ Make treating people with respect and building trusting mutual relationships a living value within the company.

___ Require prospective managers to undergo a careful evaluation process to assess their suitability for the responsibility of managing people effectively before they are promoted into supervisory positions.

___ Create a technical career track as an alternative for those who continue to excel and add value but are not suited for or interested in line management.

___ Create a performance evaluation process that helps to identify and reassign, coach, or dismiss ineffective and abusive managers.

___ Provide 360-degree feedback and developmental coaching.

___ Recognize and reward the company's most effective people managers.

___ Work to assure that senior leaders are setting the right example for all managers.

▶ THE FOUR-LEGGED STOOL OF EMPLOYEE ENGAGEMENT

In the last two chapters we have focused on the roles of managers and senior leaders in engaging employees. But we must not lose sight of the self-engaging role of employees in an organization built on partnership and mutual commitment. As we read their many comments, we could not help wondering how many were written by employees who are habitual underperformers, chronic complainers, or "professional victims." Our survey research and consulting experience tells us that these categories constitute generally about 5 percent of the average workforce.

We have acknowledged that not everyone can be, or chooses to be, engaged and that even fewer can be fully engaged. The trick is for senior leaders, managers, and human resource professionals to make sure employees understand they are not dependent on management for motivation while at the same time taking their full share of responsibility for creating work cultures and conditions where engagement can thrive (see Chapter 10 on self-engagement).

For many leaders and managers, this will require a mindset change that they are not willing to make. The minority of leaders and managers who are focused on creating better places to work have long since adopted the right mindset and the right practices for aligning and engaging their workforces.

▶ FINAL THOUGHTS

A colleague of ours shared the following conversation she had with a client on the topic of employee engagement. The client, apparently frustrated by her admonitions about improving the culture at the company he owned, said, "Ann, it's not my job to make my employees happy!"

Ann's response? "Well Fred, it's not your job to make them miserable, either!"

There are still managers in this world who think they must cajole, intimidate, and threaten people in order to be productive. They worry that if they show any sense of concern or care for those whom they supervise, they'll be taken advantage of. They seem to be saying, "If you're not a pain in the ass, they'll think you're weak, right?" They ignore the advice we've given about what engages employees, yet continue to be stunned with less-than-expected productivity and a revolving door of employees.

Having said that, we also get the sense that there are many leaders who have an equally mistaken point of view when it comes to creating a great workplace, thinking that engagement is all about making employees happy. To them, employee engagement is about making things all sweet for employees so they, in turn, will love them right back. The overly schmaltzy image of everyone around the campfire singing "Kumbaya" comes to mind—let's just all be happy, right?

Wrong.

The pretzel logic behind these two mindsets is "either I must be really nice to employees or really mean." Managers at winning employers know there is a third path, which may include "nice" and avoid "mean" but, in truth, is about neither. It's about something completely different. It's about creating a relationship where employees feel their manager is genuinely interested in helping them be productive, giving them ongoing feedback that may include an occasional course correction, and celebrating employee success even when it might mean the employee will grow to be promoted into another job outside his or her current department.

Victor Frankl, writing in his remarkable book, *Man's Search for Meaning*, describes his response to the horror of the concentration camps: "An abnormal reaction to an abnormal situation is normal behavior." We aren't comparing poor workplaces to concentrations camps (although some of the employees we've met at low-engagement workplaces might), but it's reasonable to argue that the odd, unproductive behavior we see from some employees is their way of trying to make an "abnormal" situation more "normal."

If we, as leaders, start behaving in ways that are in the spirit of winning employers, we might be pleasantly surprised to see the response. We've known this, of course, for many years. Douglas McGregor, one of the first in our profession to challenge leaders about their assumptions and the way they manage people, said:

> I become steadily more persuaded that perhaps the greatest disparity between objective reality and managerial perceptions of it is an underestimation of the potentialities of human beings for contributions to organizational effectiveness. These potentialities are not merely for increased expenditure of effort on limited jobs, but for the exercise of ingenuity; creativity in problem solving; acceptance of responsibility; leadership in the relational sense; and development of knowledge, skill, and judgment. When opportunities are provided under appropriate conditions, managers are regularly astonished to discover how much more people contribute than they had believed.[6]

Professor McGregor wrote this in *The Professional Manager*, published more than 50 years ago. Sadly, many leaders still fail to see the simple genius. They hold onto the tired assumptions that commonly lead to employee disengagement. McGregor knew only too well why leaders could not embrace this new ideology—fear of a perceived loss of power and control, as witnessed by the "voices of disengagement" presented earlier in this chapter.

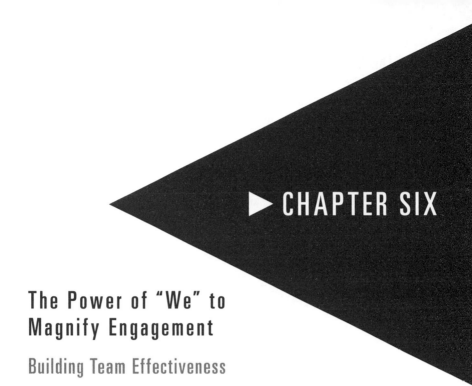

CHAPTER SIX

The Power of "We" to Magnify Engagement

Building Team Effectiveness

The leaders who work most effectively, it seems to me, never say "I." And that's not because they have trained themselves not to say "I." They don't think "I." They think "we"; they think "team." They understand their job to be to make the team function. They accept responsibility and don't side-step it, but "we" gets the credit. This is what creates trust, what enables you to get the task done.

—PETER DRUCKER

▶ THE $6 MILLION MISTAKE

Several years ago we worked with a leadership team at a successful business. As the organization grew, new leaders were brought into the executive committee, and the CEO asked us to facilitate a process of helping the expanded group better understand the new team's makeup and dynamics. We looked at personality and work styles, and how these leaders tended to make decisions, communicate, solve problems, and manage conflict.

◀143

Our analysis of their work styles suggested the team was quite effective at identifying novel ways of solving problems. The team was also able to act decisively and inspire people to action once decisions were made. But these strengths, we warned, may be masking a team blind spot—overlooking details related to how a decision might impact other parts of the organization "downstream."

Upon hearing this feedback the CEO leaned back in his chair, raised his arms in the air, and exclaimed: *"The consequences of the blind spot you described cost us $6 million! We made a very ill-advised acquisition a few years back. We did a terrible job of thinking through how the acquisition would impact other parts of our business, and it went so badly we eventually shut down the operation and wrote off the entire investment as a loss. How can we use what we have learned about ourselves today to avert bad decisions like that again?"*

Luckily, one of the new team members had an idea. Since one of her strengths was exercising caution and anticipating practical longer-term issues and problems, she believed she could help the re-formed team avoid similar disasters in the future. She was charged by the rest of the group to offer a healthy dose of skepticism to the decision-making process, one that has helped the team members more carefully vet decisions of all kinds. Having a more natural tendency toward details, she happily offers her counsel on those matters. She is also appreciative of other members of the team who help her see "the bigger picture," something that doesn't come as easily for her.

The CEO later remarked: *"It's great when we can better utilize the strengths of each team member to make decisions that serve the best interests of our firm."*

▶ TEAMWORK—MORE RELEVANT THAN EVER

The importance of teamwork has increased in recent years as many management hierarchies have been pared down, putting more pressure on companies to coordinate better horizontally to stay nimble, customer responsive, and competitive. As discussed in earlier chapters, another complicating factor is that workplaces are becoming more diverse, reflecting population changes and the emergence of new generations that bring different expectations into the workplace, creating new tensions and making smooth teamwork more difficult to achieve. Add to this the emergence of new communication technologies that enable employees to work more collaboratively in virtual teams of people throughout the nation and the world. For these and other reasons, there is unquestionably a new focus and premium on teamwork. At last check, we found more than 100,000 books on teamwork and team building on Amazon.com. That is why we were not surprised to see this theme rise to the top-most rung of employee engagement drivers.

▶ KEY DRIVER: TEAM EFFECTIVENESS

Two of the top ten survey statements that most distinguished *Best-Places-to-Work* winners from nonwinning competitors were team related (Figures 6.1 and 6.2): *"My team effectively collaborates, leveraging individual strengths"* was ranked #3 as a differentiating item, and *"I feel loyal to my immediate team or work group"* ranked #10.

To underscore the power of teamwork in driving engagement, we need only to point out that the statement that ranked #12 as a distinguishing item was also representative of this theme: *"The people I work with most closely are committed to producing top-quality work."*

We believe this aspect—the ability to depend on the performance of coworkers—as reflected in this last statement, represents an impor-

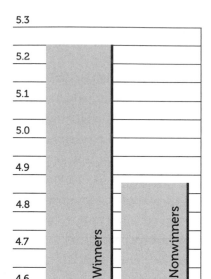

My Team Effectively Collaborates,
Leveraging Individual Strengths

Figure 6.1

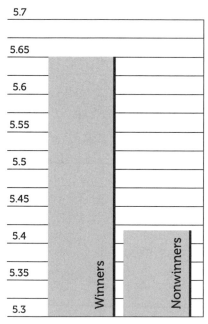

I Feel Loyal to My Immediate
Team or Work Group

Figure 6.2

tant additional dimension of teamwork and employee engagement. We depict the themes inherent in these three survey items as a triangle of teamwork (Figure 6.3) consisting of collaboration, loyalty, and dependability.

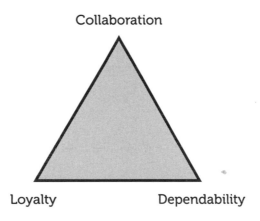

Collaboration

Loyalty   Dependability

Figure 6.3

▶ WHAT SURVEY RESPONDENTS HAD TO SAY ABOUT TEAMWORK

In the chart that follows, we present actual survey comments that illustrate a range of employee perspectives on the presence of this driver (in the "Voices of Engagement" column) and the absence of it (in the "Voices of Disengagement" column), organized according to three critical aspects of teamwork captured in survey items 3, 10, and 12— *loyalty (and trust) to other team members, coworker dependability,* and *collaboration:*

Voices of Engagement
Trust in and Loyalty to Coworkers

▶ "I have never had the opportunity to be teamed with such a wonderful group of individuals in my working life."

▶ "I feel committed to the organization and to my coworkers. I feel a part of a larger team that encompasses all of our many departments. We sometimes have opposing needs, but at the center, there is always the patient."

▶ "I love XYZ, they helped me through a tough time . . . I would not leave here for a million bucks. (Well, OK, maybe for a million, but it would have to be after taxes!)."

Dependable Coworkers

▶ "I am very proud to be surrounded by some of the best people I know. Each person here will go the distance for you, me, and anyone else."

▶ "Everyone is cross-trained, which promotes respect for each other's jobs. When you need to take a day off, there is no worrying that your job isn't being done when you're not in. There are always several people that help out any way they can. The teamwork here across all departments is incredible."

▶ "This is the most incredible place I have ever worked. The reason is the people. They are well trained, friendly, competent, welcoming of others, responsive to issues, and dead serious about satisfaction (employee, patient, and physician)."

Voices of Disengagement
Coworker Distrust and Disloyalty

▶ "I find there are quite a few trust issues in my department; you may get a smile, but watch your back."

▶ "It has good benefits and quality people; however, I feel that my immediate team doesn't demonstrate that it is a good team to work with. There is too much coworker gossip and interteam politics. We don't try to work out things openly, but we hide it and talk about it behind each other's backs. It is eroding our team's cohesiveness."

Undependable Coworkers

▶ "The teams I have to work with on the units are extremely wonderful and caring. . . . I don't find that with my own department, as several just sit around and just don't care; they don't interact with patients unless called."

▶ "The company needs to be more selective in their interviewing process."

▶ "Some of the employees are very motivated and want to excel, and some have been here for a while and feel they are entitled to just ride through."

▶ "I love my actual job, but there is no teamwork on my unit. The people I work with are very slack, and that leaves the select few of us to do their work plus ours."

▸ *"The reason this company is so excellent is not the benefits or pay. It's the OUTSTANDING coworkers upon whom I can depend to take full responsibility for anything put in front of them."*

Collaboration

▸ *"This has been the best place I have ever worked, and mainly it is due to my wonderful coworkers. My coworkers support each other and collaborate interdisciplinarily."*

▸ *"I love my team and my manager! We all work so well together. I can't wait to come to work in the morning."*

▸ *"I have seen many other businesses where employees are not happy. They never exchange pleasantries during the day, and I feel that is important to everyone getting along and wanting to be there. A person from across the hall said to me one day, 'You all get along so well. No one here (meaning their office) talks to one another!' That made such an impression on me about how well we all respect one another and enjoy being with one another."*

▸ *"I do feel that there are some employees that don't give their 100% to the company. If everyone gave their all, this company would be way ahead of the game."*

Lack of Collaboration

▸ *"Basically a good place to work, but communication is horrible. Nobody ever checks with others who may be working on a project, so there's lots of redundancy and lack of coordination."*

▸ *"I have noticed a change in working as a team; some individuals just do what they want regardless of how it affects others."*

▸ *"My coworkers are very negative. Most of them want to do a good job, but there is little encouragement from management or a consistent message about expectations . . . no clear procedures or initial job training. So, right from the beginning you feel like you are on your own. . . . No one knows what anyone else does. . . . There is no real team feeling here. . . . Some interactions have just become really unpleasant, and I don't have any interest in building relationships with my coworkers now."*

We had no trouble finding survey comments giving voice to these three themes. The comments capture the good, bad, and ugly of team dynamics that unpredictably occur when we hire and mix employees together. With some teams there is simply a serendipitous magic and team chemistry that develops. In other cases the blend of personalities and talents just isn't right. There will always be this unpredictable element to assembling a team of people.

▶ OBSTACLES TO EFFECTIVE TEAMWORK

We detected the following obstacles to effective teamwork among the less positive statements:

- ▶ **Failing to speak honestly** and directly with each other, indicating the absence of trust.
- ▶ **Team members are not willing to be genuinely open** with one another about their mistakes and weaknesses—in other words, not exhibiting the vulnerability required to build a foundation for trust to develop.
- ▶ **Covering ill will with surface amiability** indicates a fear of conflict. This fear can incapacitate teams from engaging in passionate debate of ideas. Instead, team members "make nice" and withhold their real opinions, preventing the team from moving through the conflict stage of natural team growth and development.
- ▶ **Lack of commitment to team goals** and objectives is apparent. True commitment to team goals and decisions is difficult to muster when team members cannot trust each other enough to speak openly and honestly.
- ▶ **Hiding personal and political agendas** to achieve one's selfish goals or gain advantage indicates that team members are not focused on achieving collective results.
- ▶ **A feeling of entitlement on the part of some team members to coast,** put forth less effort, and be indifferent to customers often results in resentment and possible burnout among the more productive and engaged team members. These symptoms signal that team members lack a sense of mutual accountability.

▶ **Tolerating in-groups, out-groups, and cliques** within the team is a sign of failure to communicate, collaborate, coordinate, and connect with other team members.

Leveraging Teamwork to Overcome the Tipping Point of 150

The "small company" atmosphere of the company is one of its greatest attributes. One knows just about everyone in the organization.
—SURVEY COMMENT

As organizations grow, they hire new employees and open new locations, and their leaders must take proactive steps to preserve team collaboration and stave off the loss of that family feeling. Here are some of the practices that are working for growing employers:

▶ Limit unit size where possible to promote better team building and relationship development. Create new locations or business units as the employee population grows beyond 150, where possible.

▶ When team size or remote office separation is an obstacle to teamwork, compensate by using technology (such as Cisco's TelePresence) to facilitate virtual communication, increasing the frequency of contact between team members, and building in face-to-face communication opportunities where feasible.

▶ Promote cross-divisional communication, project teams, and task forces.

▶ Identify people who have a network of relationships that form a natural bridge between two groups.

- ▶ Build "communities of practice," where employees separated by business unit or location with intense interest in a particular strategic issue or challenge are encouraged to share ideas and brainstorm solutions.
- ▶ Build teamwork through conferences where people from various locations meet to develop relationships and share ideas.
- ▶ Set up chat rooms, bulletin boards, blogs, wikis, and dedicated forums for the sharing of ideas and best practices.
- ▶ Increase planned social activities as the business unit size grows beyond 150 people per location.
- ▶ Increase the number and frequency of job rotations and lateral job moves to enhance employee familiarity with people in other units, and allow longer-term relationships to develop.
- ▶ When new hires come on board, make it common practice that they meet one-on-one with all team members and also with people outside their immediate team.

▶ CONDITIONS FOR EFFECTIVE TEAMWORK

Our personal experiences of working in teams and helping to build teams have led us to some conclusions about the factors that make teams effective. Other than just avoiding the negative factors cited above, we believe that much of what makes teams successful is about setting the right conditions for success up front. We have observed that teams function best when:

1. The mission and purpose of the team is clear and personally meaningful to all members.

2. Team members are willing to risk being open and honest with each other.

3. The team has the authority and freedom to get things done without interference.

4. Team members are accountable to each other for achieving results and know they can depend on each other.

5. The team leader operates as a facilitator-coach instead of a command-and-control or doer type. The best team leaders set clear goals and expectations, match players with tasks according to their talents, give positive and corrective feedback when necessary, allow the team to make decisions, and ask questions that stimulate learning and problem solving.

6. There is 100 percent agreement on ground rules for team behavior, including having trust in each other about confidentiality of certain information.

7. The team is not too big or too small. Though team size obviously depends on the team's task, we believe most task teams work best when there are enough members to produce diversity of thought, but not so many that the group becomes unmanageable. Team diversity, as we have indicated in our discussions of multigenerational workforces, can be an obstacle to overcome but, as winning workplaces have shown, can be turned into an advantage.

8. Team members are team players, have sufficient social skills, and are willing to submerge their egos and restrain their needs for attention or independence.

9. The team has the necessary information, resources, and cross-unit cooperation to get the job done right.

▶ HOW EMPLOYEES SEE LEADERS ENABLING OR UNDERMINING TEAMWORK

All the above conditions are within the control or influence of executives and managers. While having these conditions in place does not guarantee team effectiveness, we found strong evidence in the survey comments that leaders have great power to enable or undermine teamwork. We were interested in understanding how survey respondents view their leaders and managers. Do they see them as builders of teamwork who work to create these conditions or as destroyers of it? To that end, we scoured the survey comments to find and classify employee observations of leader behavior that promotes teamwork and also leader behavior that inhibits teamwork. We present these below, beginning with those that undermine team engagement.

Leader-Manager Behavior That Undermines Teamwork

We identified four categories of negative comments that employees referenced most frequently. Here is a sampling of comments by category or theme:

SENIOR LEADERS AND MANAGERS AS A SEPARATE AND SUPERIOR CLASS

The largest number of comments we gathered revealed a fundamental fault line that runs through many organizations—a "we-they" caste system in which superior-inferior, in-group–out-group relationships predominate instead of the partnership and mutual commitment that optimizes employee engagement:

▶ *"The workers who are not in management are not treated with respect."*
▶ *"The Controller and VP often refer to the accounting staff as kindergartners."*

▶ *"The hospital has a long way to go to upgrade its team effectiveness. The root of this problem seems to be a definite caste system within the hospital."*

▶ *"I think that senior management and HR underestimate the intelligence and common sense of those in lower positions. Just because we didn't all graduate from the same university does not mean we should be talked down to."*

▶ *"If you are coming into this organization at the mid-management level and higher, it probably is a great place to work. Below that, I would not recommend this organization to my friends. There is a very distinct line between salaried personnel and hourly personnel."*

▶ *"We may need more education, but that's no cause to treat us as a lower class."*

▶ *"This is a horrible place to work. Senior management is completely out of touch with the rest of the staff and there are several senior members who are only interested in their own agenda. Only people who are part of a certain clique gain advancement."*

▶ *"The clique known as senior management is wearing blinders. They preach teamwork/team unity, but all they really want are puppets! I cannot think of a single thing that the leadership of this organization does to create any unity among their employees. If you are not part of senior management, you are a nobody and your opinion absolutely does not count for a thing."*

▶ *"Different groups are treated almost like a system of social classes, with the white-collar and engineering positions receiving the lion's share of incentives and rewards while the blue-collar workers are effectively treated as cattle."*

▶ *"The company is a joke; if you are not in a management position, they frown on you. They offer this whole 'open and honest communication' policy, but they never honor it, not to the call center and support staff. I am currently in the process of looking for a new job, but while I am still here, I will gladly put my two cents in about how I feel about working here, because others should be warned as well."*

▶ *"I feel this organization cares nothing about its employees. Their only concern is making the numbers right. Management has their noses in the air and acts as if they are too good for the employees below them."*

LEADERS CONSUMED BY SELF-INTEREST TO THE DETRIMENT OF LARGER TEAM INTERESTS

Employee comments indicate that the employees are not just concerned that senior leaders are paid so much more, but that many senior leaders seem to be preoccupied with their own narrow interests at the expense of focusing on the overall well-being of the company and all employees. The following comments illustrate that perception:

▶ *"Senior management and the board of directors do not care about the workers, only about their stock options."*

▶ *"The executive team is simply interested in their own lifestyles. They are not interested (by action) in growing a talent pool and growing the business (although they speak like it)."*

▶ *"This formerly creative company is currently characterized by poor leadership exceeded only by its dedication to short-term self-enrichment at the expense of a valuable customer and client base."*

▶ *"The primary missing ingredient that leads to the root of all sins is that the top executives (President, CFO, and select few) are so overcompensated that they have no reason to try to change the organization or to be forward thinking. They operate in self-directed interests that serve only themselves to the disadvantage of ordinary employees and the shareholders."*

> ▸ *"Managers manage to their personal incentive programs. They care very little about what is best for the business."*

LEADERS AVOIDING ACCOUNTABILITY AND POINTING FINGERS

In many companies, executive team members do not play as a team. Instead, they compete for resources and engage in turf battles that distract from their focus on the bigger picture: engaging employees and customers. These comments indicate as much:

> ▸ *"There are far too many turf issues and too little accountability."*
> ▸ *"Employees fail because of management, but the employees get blamed."*
> ▸ *"Within teams, there is an excellent attitude. However, working with other teams is often like pulling teeth, for lack of a better phrase. This all starts with upper management's lack of account-ability; everything is always the fault of another department. This attitude has come to pervade the company at many levels and now negatively impacts daily production levels."*

SENIOR LEADERS SETTING A POOR EXAMPLE OF TEAMWORK

The avoidance of accountability and the prevalence of blaming behav-ior are often indicative of a larger issue—poor teamwork at the very top of the organization that creates fodder for further disengagement among employees who observe it:

> ▸ *"The biggest problem is accountability and a decided lack of high-level teamwork."*

▶ *"Members of the executive management team argue in front of other coworkers and do not demonstrate a positive role model to their employees."*

▶ *"The only organizations with leaders setting real examples and driving forward are engineering and sales. And these organizations are most crippled by the incredible weakness of the other teams. Executives are dysfunctional among themselves—they each go in their own direction."*

In one comment, we noted the beneficial effect that a new senior leadership team can have: *"A few years ago I would have answered the survey completely differently. The new management team seems to have solidified the direction that the company is heading, and that alone has made me more optimistic."*

Certainly, the lesson for leaders is to do the opposite of the above team-destroying sins: tear down the "we-they" barriers; suppress their own self-interest and do what is right for the whole team; not let a culture of blame get a foothold; and do everything they can to destroy silos and manage the ego issues that destroy executive teamwork. All this is much easier to say than to do, of course. If all or most of these issues are present, they are undoubtedly signs of more deeply embedded leadership problems.

Leader-Manager Behavior That *Builds* Teamwork

The good news is that great team leadership is alive and well in many organizations and units. Interestingly, employees' positive comments about team leaders divided themselves not into the same categories as the negative comments, but into two broad themes: (1) that their leaders were *on the team* as partners, not above it, and (2) that their leaders had worked to create a sense of community, fun, and camaraderie in the workplace.

Leaders and managers as partners (not a separate or superior class)

▶ *"They keep the staff aware of what is going on in the firm, not just the big cheeses."*

▶ *"This hospital does communication well—to their staff and employees and to the community. This is HUGE! There's very little politics. File clerks can talk to doctors. Directors of one department can go straight to any member of another department for inquiries or actions. It really is all about the patients here."*

▶ *"The management team is awesome; they actually communicate with their hourly employees and make me feel welcomed, appreciated, and glad to work."*

▶ *"The criterion that I value most is that the owners and management openly welcome feedback and opinion from anyone in any position. I don't just work with colleagues, I work with friends."*

▶ *"The executives and senior managers lead by example. They serve as team members when projects come up."*

▶ *"There is no hierarchy. If I have a problem, I feel confident going directly to one of the managing partners because I know they truly care. They know who I am and are always willing to help in any way."*

▶ *"In most of my previous places of employment there has always existed a division between management and associates. There is a great deal of social interaction between the two groups, which makes it a truly enjoyable place to work."*

Leaders promoting community, fun, and camaraderie

▶ *"We get treated every week to breakfast and once or more to lunch during a quarter. We have employee outings such as bowling."*

▶ *"We know how to mix fun with hard work. We have many events that enable the employees to really enjoy themselves and celebrate their successes. In addition, the company does little things, like serving free bagels on Fridays, that really make a difference."*

▶ *"The company is like a second family to me. . . . I am always amazed at how many people our company president knows personally—not just your name. She knows about your family, if you're working toward a degree, or just got married. People truly care about each other here. The sense of community is beyond words."*

▶ *"I came here a little over a year ago expecting a fast-paced corporate environment. I was pleasantly surprised by the friendly and social elements that came with high-energy, trusting coworkers. I have suggested the company to three friends, one of whom was hired. He loves it here just as much as I do."*

▶ *"I was shocked at the fact that when I came here, everyone was extremely kind and friendly. Working in a big company like this, you would think that there would be so many individuals that you cannot possibly get along with. Well, this company surely proves that wrong. Since day one I felt like I fit in. I remember people were introducing themselves to me almost that whole week. I was amazed how friendly everyone was."*

▶ *"The social atmosphere is also excellent. Again, I have been here three months and so far attended three company parties. Most bonding within the group, however, is done over the company foosball table. Yes, foosball is important."*

▶ *"I think the company has a unique way of fostering team building through fun events that at the same time benefit our community outreach initiatives. An example of this was a tie-dye event where employees got together and tie-dyed T-shirts that the team would wear while serving meals at a veterans' homeless shelter."*

▶ *"There is rarely a frown on someone's face. If and when one shows up, a coworker is always there to turn it upside down."*

▶ *"The company is more than a great place to work—it is family. I know that I can count on my coworkers, managers, and the organization to support me if I am ever in need, and I have seen the company do that on countless occasions for individuals who have faced personal crises. You just don't get that support anywhere else, and I can't imagine ever leaving here."*

Building Multigenerational Teamwork

Progressive employers aren't just letting teamwork "happen"; they are orchestrating it by breaking down generational/age barriers to communication and teamwork in a variety of ways. Here are some of the best practices we uncovered:

▸ Emphasize the importance of collaboration and teamwork to all staff regardless of their generation. Track and reward team accomplishments to make it credible.

▸ Staff teams with members of different generations whenever possible, to capitalize on complementary perspectives.

▸ Arrange two-way mentoring whenever possible, as when a Millennial trains a Boomer in Web 2.0 technologies and the Boomer coaches the Millennial in how to sell ideas to senior leaders.

▸ Facilitate in a variety of ways the development of relationships among generations. Hallmark Cards, for example, assigns members of different generations to meet monthly for an afternoon break and get to know one another. They are encouraged to ask each other questions, such as "Can you tell me a stereotype about your generation that you believe doesn't apply to you?"

▸ Set up office spaces in ways that facilitate openness, social interaction, and exchange of ideas among Millennials.

▸ When significant learning or mentoring needs to happen between a younger and more senior person, have them sit at desks so they face each other, or in the same office when appropriate.

▸ Ask senior staff to initiate more face-to-face communication with younger staff.

▶ Emphasize the importance of age-diverse teams working with other such teams and promoting virtual communication regionally, nationally, and internationally.

▶ Conduct multigenerational training in a fun and comfortable environment where employees discuss intergenerational misunderstandings and contemplate how they would respond to various intergenerational scenarios. Emphasize the leveraging of both differences and strengths to maximize team effectiveness and productivity.

▶ Coach younger workers not to drop more senior workers from critical informal communication networks. Some mature workers complain they are often shut out from watercooler banter and e-mail exchanges and are otherwise shunted to the sidelines.

▶ Make it clear that the most successful people in the organization will be the "Gen Mixers"—those who develop the most relationships with members of other generations so they can become more effective team players and team builders.

▶ OUR FINDINGS COMPARED WITH RECENT RESEARCH ON TEAMS

The November 2007 *Harvard Business Review* reported the results of a major research initiative cosponsored by the London School of Business and the Concours Institute, based on surveys of 1,543 employees representing 15 multinational companies and 55 teams in those companies ranging in size from 4 to 183. Although the teams in this study were geographically dispersed and many were virtual by necessity, we were interested in comparing their findings with ours. We noticed some remarkably similar findings.

Early on in their article, the authors, Lynda Gratton and Tamara J. Erickson, make this sobering observation: "Although teams that are large, virtual, diverse, and composed of highly educated specialists are increasingly crucial with challenging projects, those same four characteristics make it hard for them to get anything done."[1]

Many complex tasks in today's global business environment demand that teams of 100 or more geographically dispersed people collaborate on complex projects. Gratton and Erickson observe that "as the size of a team increases beyond 20 members, the tendency to collaborate naturally decreases." They also warn of increasing declines in team collaboration as the number of virtual members increases, as their views and backgrounds are less similar, as there is less mutual familiarity, and as the more highly educated and expert the team members are. The authors go on to report factors that enable companies to overcome the built-in obstacles to team effectiveness, including:

▶ *Executives making highly visible investments that contribute to collaboration, such as open floor plans or new communication technologies*

▶ *Creating a "gift culture" in which senior leaders give freely of their time to mentor and coach employees and new hires*

▶ *Making sure HR trains all employees in the requisite skills— effective communication, collaboration, and conflict resolution*

▶ *Building on "heritage" relationships by always having a few people on the team who know each other or have previously worked together on teams*

▶ OTHER TEAM FACTORS TO CONSIDER

In addition to the obstacles to team effectiveness already discussed, there are a few others that leaders and managers need to consider:

Team versus Individual Incentives

Many companies still haven't achieved the right balance between individual rewards and rewards for the achievement of team and organizational goals. As one *Best-Places-to-Work* respondent noted, *"I feel there needs to be more value placed on the team concept. The recognition is placed on individual basis, and some people need to be valued as team players."* Different business situations require different approaches, of course. Complicating this issue, many managers are not natural team leaders, but have been rewarded with promotion into management for being outstanding individual achievers. We suggest that leaders can correct this by implementing new processes for selecting managerial candidates with natural team leadership and coaching talent.

We thought it somewhat surprising that Gratton and Erickson in their study found that the type of reward system had "no discernable effect on complex teams' productivity and innovation" regardless of whether rewards were based on individual or team achievements.[2]

Undependable Team Members

As evidenced in some of the verbatim survey comments presented earlier in this chapter, employees held strong negative perceptions about coworkers they felt they could not depend on to do their jobs. The resentment many employees harbor about indifferent and unproductive coworkers is a common cause of employee disengagement. We recommend six ways to deal with the problem of nonperformers:

1. Implement a more careful and selective sourcing and hiring process so as to avoid hiring them in the first place.

2. Allow current team members to participate in the interviewing and selection of new team members.

3. Reevaluate and reassign employees who are mismatched in their current jobs.

4. Select and promote only those managers who are willing to confront poor performers without procrastinating.

5. Train all managers in successful performance management and feedback.

6. Hold all managers truly accountable for the performance of their direct reports.

When there is a serious commitment to these practices, we believe employees are more likely to comment as this employee did:

> *This is a great place to work. The senior management strives to make each individual in the company successful, not only professionally but personally as well. I have not met a person that would not stop whatever they are doing to help me out or answer questions. The company works hard at bringing out each employee's individual strengths. It is very true about the leadership principles they have about working with good staff. Everyone here is good staff. I have worked for the firm for several years and hope to do so for many, many more.*

Managers Still Believe Employees Are Interchangeable Parts

Unfortunately, too many managers still haven't grasped the concept that better teamwork comes about by recognizing and capitalizing on the individual differences and strengths of the various team members. It is the complementary nature of different strengths and talents that creates the magic, as any winning athletic coach knows. And yet some managers still persist in placing "warm bodies" in jobs just to fill available slots and then expect training to make them all equally competent. The best managers play chess with their people, not checkers.

Not Understanding the Elements of Great Teamwork

Most managers could benefit from a deeper understanding of team dynamics and the factors that undermine teamwork. Many leaders of the best employers instinctively understand the damage these dysfunctions can cause and build cultures in which they cannot take hold. As part of their overall team-culture-building efforts, many best-employer companies conduct management training to make sure all managers understand these elements of great teamwork; then they hold managers accountable for being effective team leaders.

▶ HOW TEAMWORK MAKES A DIFFERENCE AT NALLEY AUTOMOTIVE GROUP

There has to be a reason that one company continues to appear as number one or two among *Best Places to Work* in a large metropolitan area such as Atlanta for three years in a row. In fact, at Nalley Automotive Group there are several reasons, but the one that stands out is teamwork. In fact, no other U.S. company among participating *BPTW* employers in 2008 scored higher overall on the three team-related survey items.

Nalley Automotive Group (now the Southern Region of Asbury Automotive Group), has operated since 1919. It consists of 16 dealerships in the metro Atlanta area and includes Nalley Acura, Audi, BMW, Chrysler/Jeep, Honda, two Infiniti dealerships, Jaguar, two Lexus dealerships, Nissan, Toyota, Volvo, and three heavy truck stores. Nalley President and CEO, Henry Day, who has been with the company since 1975, has watched it double in size within the last 10 years to its current employee population of about 1,500. Day started as a service manager for Nalley Motor Trucks, and he worked for the firm's founder, Clarence "Jim" V. Nalley. Many of Nalley's dealer showrooms feature upscale lounges with wireless business centers and cafés offering complimentary coffee and soft drinks.

We spoke with Day, Service Director Domenick Colanero, and human resources Trainer/Recruiter Ryland Owen in December 2008 to gain insight into how Nalley has managed to maintain such consistently high levels of teamwork and overall employee engagement, even during down cycles in the economy and in the face of the auto industry crisis that had recently caused numerous dealerships to close their doors. Here are their answers to the questions we asked.

Q: What are the two or three most important things that you believe contributed to your high scores on teamwork?

Day: *We believe strongly that building trusting relationships and sharing information among the different managers at our dealerships is a key to our success. If a department head in one of our dealerships has a problem, he or she can quickly call up a counterpart at any one of our 16 locations for advice or assistance. We make it easier by releasing trend reports with a range of data about each dealership's performance to all other dealerships. So there are no secrets . . . there's total transparency. That kind of openness promotes communication and teamwork. Other auto dealerships may be too defensive or have too much ego to share this kind of information. We believe the more everyone sees the scorecard, the better the result. We trust our people with information that other companies might not, while still cautioning that it is confidential.*

Owen: *A lot of the teamwork that goes on is not seen by customers, and shouldn't be. Car dealerships are very compartmentalized, but we don't want the customer to even be aware of any departments. The departments should be invisible to the client. We call it the Nalley customized service experience. That means the customer is dealing with one person all the time, and that person is always in the forefront. But in the background there is a lot of teamwork going on.*

Day: *I like to compare it to going to a high-end restaurant, where one waiter takes care of everything. It ties the customer to an individual and builds loyalty. At some dealers, the customer ends up at the cashier's window trying to understand why there were extra charges after having their car serviced. We have no cashier. Our service advisors call and stay in touch with customers as we diagnose the issues with their cars and answer all their questions. The service advisor thoroughly walks the customer through the work that was done before* *taking any payment and then sets the next service appointment. Meanwhile, the customer's car has been washed and is ready to go.*

Q: What are some other examples of how teamwork happens at Nalley?

Owen: *We have mobile carts in the service area with laptops at each car that allow the service techs to communicate back and forth with the parts department. This allows parts requests to be handled quickly, and once the part is ready, a light will turn on notifying techs right away. This process speeds up our service to the customer. Also, if a service technician is at lunch, all the other service technicians know that they have to be ready to take care of the client. Every service desk is set up so that every client's service record is easy to pull up on the computer.*

Colanero: *Back in the '70s, we set up many of our shops in a team system so the techs all worked together in smaller teams, dispatched together, and were paid as a team. Most dealers have one dispatcher with around 10 service employees. The dispatcher will assign jobs based on the tech's skill level—A, B, C, etc. At Nalley, most teams have just three techs, each with a different skill level, and the group works together to determine who does which job. These smaller teams pool their hours. Individuals are paid at different hourly rates, of course, but the hours are divided equally.*

Owen: *This system allows C-skill techs to have more direct daily interaction with the A and B techs on their teams. It also creates more of an incentive for the senior techs to mentor and train new hires, because they need to be able to depend on them. So, it leads to more small-team bonding. This system also requires a service manager that is highly skilled, which Domenick is. It takes vision, discipline, and determination, plus the ability to read and know each person's abilities. The service manager needs to reinforce that the team is stronger than any one member.*

Q: How does your approach to building teamwork help make Nalley Automotive a *Best Place to Work*?

Day: *Well, I make a lot of mistakes because I'm always trying new and different things. I think people need to feel free to try new things and make mistakes. Most of us want to work in an environment like that, I believe. So, we encourage people to come up with answers. I involve our associates and ask how they would resolve a problem. When we implement a change, I ask for their ideas. That helps obtain their buy-in. When we expanded our hours and made the decision to be open seven days a week, I met with small groups of employees to explain the decision and get their input. Not everyone was happy about having to work some Sundays, but eventually they bought in to the idea that Nalley is in the retail business and we have to do what it takes to stay competitive. We also preach and practice delegation, which creates opportunity for everyone. When it comes to performance evaluations, we don't just set goals for people, we ask them what their 6-month, 12-month, and longer-term goals are. We also ask them what they would do to make the work environment better, and what can I do to be a better manager. It's about caring enough about employees to ask for their input. Teamwork begins with two-way communication.*

Colanero: *Henry doesn't want a cookie-cutter business operation, so each manager runs their department as if it were their own. We feel empowered to solve problems as a team. The term we use is to be a "lighthouse" to others at the same level who have experienced screw-ups. If we do that, we can solve anything.*

Q: High turnover can affect teamwork. How do you keep turnover down?

Owen: *We can't have teamwork if the players on the team keep changing, so we created a Nalley Guild in 1978 to give our elite technicians recognition and acknowledgment of the professional status they have reached. We now have 100 members—less than 10 percent of employees—in four separate guilds. We added guilds for sales, accounting, and parts/delivery. To be selected, an associate has to reach certain goals and standards, be here at least five years, have the appropriate certifications, meet specific performance and quality standards,* *and show leadership; only the most top-notch are selected. They are voted on by senior team members. Every dealership has a plaque on the wall showing all guild members companywide. You can also get voted out of the guild if you don't maintain the standards. Having these guilds shows new employees that there is something higher to strive for. Guild members also get distinctive uniforms and extra benefits, such as more time off, a tool allowance, and higher pay.*

Day: *There's a place for rookies as well. We identify high-potential candidates through a college recruitment program. When those candidates exhibit exceptional leadership skills, they're put on the fast track to a general manager position. We believe strongly in promoting from within; the average tenure of our 50 or so service and parts managers is nearly 20 years. Employees meet with their managers regularly and talk about the employee's personal and professional goals. It's an exchange of information that helps the employee see that there is a future here for them. Turnover bothers me. If an employee who has worked at Nalley for more than 5 years decides to leave, the first place I look is in the mirror.*

Q: How do you deal with poor performers and poor team players?

Day: *Our standards are so high that people who can't meet them don't stay. The bottom 10 percent know they don't fit. About 80 percent of our associates are strongly influenced by the work environment, our culture, and are generally more engaged because of it.*

Owen: *We are known as a place to learn the right way to do things, and not everyone can make it here. Not everyone can work at Nalley. Our teams will reject poor performers. They spit them out. They will report nonperformers to their managers.*

Q: Are team members involved in the hiring process?

Owen: *Yes. Team members sit in on interviews with job candidates and have input on who gets hired. Because they work so closely with their own team members, they have a strong vested interest in making sure the right person gets hired. We also pay $500 to employees who refer someone who is hired and stays for at least six months.*

Q: Have you done anything in particular to eliminate "silo-ing," or lack of teamwork among senior functional leaders?

Day: *We have had silo-ing in the past, generally between dealerships, and it has been a problem. It's something we have addressed by requiring previously unavailable information to be shared, which has encouraged more open and regular communication between dealerships. Sooner or later, every organization faces the problem of having to deal with pathological egos who can't work well in a strong team-based culture. We have not hesitated to let them go. We don't tolerate this behavior, even among top producers. You just have to cut out the cancer and move on.*

Q: Have you trained managers in effective team building?

Owen: *Yes, we emphasize team building in all our supervisory training. We have seen changes in many who have attended the training; they have become much more interactive than they were before the training.*

Q: Is there anything else you do that promotes and encourages teamwork?

Day: *One of the biggest things that serves to bond people together, and is often underestimated, is food. Everyone is running around and so busy all the time that we need to slow people down and create fun and relaxing moments here and there. Therefore, we encourage our managers to have cookouts. We will fire up the grills during the lunch hour and also encourage managers to interact with their people daily, especially to thank them for their good work.*

Q: How would you summarize your secret to being a *Best Place to Work?*

Day: *Many companies don't stay focused on what their goals are— they get off-track with changes in leadership and direction. We are consistent, accountable, and provide the opportunity for a career. We have car washers who move into the shop, then up into management. We are out-of-the-box thinkers leading change in the car business,* *and intensely focused on the customer experience. That's where our culture starts. It is our stated policy to treat every visitor as an honored guest in our home, every day, every time, without exception. Employees are challenged constantly to create a better experience for the customer. There are signs all over that say "10-foot rule," which means if a customer comes within 10 feet, they need to stop and take care of them.*

Making the customer happy is a whole lot easier when there are great people working to make it happen. When making decisions, we keep three questions in mind: Is it good for employees? Is it good for customers? And is it good for the company? If it doesn't benefit all three, it won't be a long-term deal. Our most precious asset is our people. We feel pretty fortunate to be in the position we're in. We have the best people in the business.

As one Nalley employee noted in the *Best-Places-to-Work* survey, "*I believe this company to be on the right track for future success. Its values and commitment to each employee are the reasons I love this company.*"

To get another perspective, we interviewed Jamey Lathem, team leader and technician at Nalley's Lexus dealership in Roswell, Georgia.

Q: When you first came to work at Nalley five years ago, what did you notice that was different than the other auto service centers where you had worked?
Lathem: *I immediately saw that technicians and all employees carried themselves in a certain way that seemed more professional. I noticed that everyone on the team felt pride in doing things the right way. It was a well-oiled machine with the focus being on taking care of the customer, not just putting money in our pocket.*

Q: What kinds of things do you do, for example, to take care of customers?
Lathem: *We go above and beyond. For example, a customer brought in his car because he was hearing a noise, and we listened and couldn't*

hear the noise. He said he would hear the noise most clearly when he was driving up the winding parking garage in the hotel where he worked. So our diagnostic specialist, Walter Neuman, and I drove his car to the hotel and drove it up into the hotel parking garage to see if we could hear what he was hearing. Sure enough, we did, and we were able to trace the noise and fix the problem.

Q: As a team leader, how do *you* build teamwork?
Lathem: *Mainly by teaching the new and less-experienced technicians. It's about more than just communicating technical knowledge. It's about instilling in them the idea that they need to have a team attitude and a customer-focused attitude and not just be thinking about their own concerns. Not everyone fits that profile, and if they didn't, they would stick out like a sore thumb at Nalley.*

We also spoke with Nalley customer Jim Strawinski, who purchased a new Lexus from a Nalley dealer in Atlanta in 1989. At the time we spoke, he was still driving the car, which was nearing 300,000 miles, and has had it serviced regularly over the years at the same Nalley dealership where he bought it.

Q: What makes Nalley different from other auto dealerships you've done business with?
Strawinski: *Well, I was a pilot in the Air Force, so I've always known how important regular maintenance is, but I had always taken my cars to independent mechanics, since I thought I could trust them more. But I decided to let Nalley service the Lexus because I just felt I could trust them, and they absolutely won my loyalty by providing phenomenal service.*

Q: What is it that they do specifically to make you so loyal?
Strawinski: *For one thing, the service manager makes you feel he is your teammate in dealing with the dealership as a whole. It's like he's on your side, like you're a family member, not just another customer. He'll give you his honest opinion about what he would do if it was*

his car being serviced. I never have the feeling that they are trying to talk me into having work done just so they could tack on some more charges. They will call up the mechanic working on your car to answer any questions you might have. One thing I've learned over the years is that an automobile is only as good as the mechanic that maintains it. I have had the same service rep now for 15 years; his name is Aaron Vuu. I know I can call him on the phone if I have a question. He's become my friend, actually. I knew when he was getting engaged, then getting married. I look forward to going in to see him.

Q: Have you noticed anything about the way Nalley staff work together as a team to create a positive customer experience?

Strawinski: *Yes. If I came in and Aaron wasn't there, another service rep would come up and take care of me. You can see there are no turf battles going on there. I have never sensed any tension between service and parts or between Aaron and other mechanics. Everyone seems happy there. Employees seem to be treated well, and they treat clients the way they want to be treated. They are just a first-class operation. People talk about car dealerships in the community—who's good and who's bad—and I have heard lots of bad stuff about other dealerships, but have only heard good things about Nalley.*

Postscript

We received the following update from Nalley Automotive in mid-2009 describing how the company had dealt with wrenching changes in the automotive industry:

> *Since our original thoughts were recorded last year, things have obviously changed in our industry. Survival and maintaining as much of our market position as possible have preceded outright growth.*
>
> *Recently, as a result of the Chrysler situation, we had to close one store that housed many valuable employees. We worked suc-*

cessfully to place all the staff either in our own dealerships or in neighboring stores.

On a broader plane, Asbury Automotive Group saw the need to reorganize by consolidating and centralizing much of the management of the corporation. A valuable result is that fixed operations, service, parts, and collision centers now have one executive responsible for the operations of the entire country. This has allowed us to break down the regional barriers and work as a single, large unit. Fixed operations senior, mid-level, and even local department managers travel, consult, observe, and generally communicate with all dealerships in different parts of the country. Associates at all levels see and feel the positive effects, and the possibilities they have by being part of a fluid environment.

It is difficult to assess success in our current market and economy. The last quarter of '08 was our worst, historically. However, we had begun to make strategic changes long before the main plunge in the economy took hold in the fall. As a result, our first quarter of '09 was much better, despite the economic conditions of the country. The painful cuts, and the much-needed consolidation, had produced the results that were required.

Practices That Maintain and Build Effective Teamwork in Turbulent Times

The following practices build on the ones presented in our last chapter, which also apply to the ongoing work of building strong teams in challenging times:

▶ **Maintain open and honest communication,** because trust and teamwork go hand in hand. Trust can be the first victim during uncertain times as employees become suspicious about impending layoffs. Keep the team informed, and keep meeting with team members one-on-one to clarify roles and expectations. Ask how they are feeling and respond to their questions.

▶ **Refocus the team on its mission,** which may have changed based on economic and market conditions and retooling of internal processes. Eliminate work that may no longer be necessary or critical.

▶ **Emphasize the setting and achievement of smaller, shorter-term team goals.**

▶ **Recognize and reward the achievement of team goals** as soon as they happen. Don't overlook the need to give special recognition to team members who are making disproportionate contributions.

▶ **Plan team off-site meetings or inexpensive team-building activities.** Consider starting new team customs, such has "pizza Thursdays" or brown-bag book reviews that contribute to team morale and capability.

▶ **Challenge the team** to consider a broader range of strategies for meeting customer needs, creating new revenue sources, and cutting costs.

▶ **Go to bat for your team** with more senior leaders, especially with regard to training and resources.

▶ **Reassess team members' talents** in the light of changing priorities.

▶ **Rethink team composition,** and add or remove staff where appropriate. Implement new proactive "guerilla recruiting" tactics if you haven't already, especially those involving social networking.

▶ **If team members have been laid off,** focus the team on ways to take up the slack, eliminate work that is not critical, or reinvent the way the work gets done.

▶ **Communicate emphatically how much you value** the talents and capabilities of remaining team members.

▶ A CHECKLIST OF TEAMWORK BEST PRACTICES FOR ENGAGING EMPLOYEES IN ALL TIMES

Though team structures may differ and priorities may vary with business objectives and market conditions, below are some of the practices used by successful employers. Check those that you believe your organization is currently doing well, and place an X next to those you believe you should be doing or doing significantly better:

___ Evaluate all teams on the criteria for team effectiveness described earlier in this chapter. Implement corrective measures as appropriate.

___ Conduct team-building training and facilitate team-building sessions.

___ Set company ground rules for communicating directly and openly instead of avoiding tough conversations and communicating in indirect ways.

___ Limit team and unit size where possible to maintain cohesion and communication.

___ Adopt business 2.0 technology that enables, supports, and facilitates collaboration.

___ Make it clear that gossip and behavior that undermines teamwork will not be tolerated.

___ Adjust the balance between individual and team rewards and recognition.

___ Look for appropriate ways to have more fun and morale-building team activities.

___ Plan and organize company-sponsored events (volunteer projects, etc.) that encourage social connectedness.

___ Review and refine screening techniques used to select team leaders.

___ Allow employees to participate in the interviewing and selection of new hires.

___ Celebrate company successes and milestones when reached.

___ Retool your new-hire on-boarding process to bring new team members to the level of contributing team member sooner.

___ Reorganize functions and assign goals so as to force cross-functional collaboration.

___ Use 360-degree feedback with team leaders or members.

___ Conduct team-building sessions for the senior executive team.

___ Initiate efforts that result in senior leaders becoming more visibly effective working together as a team.

___ Encourage senior leaders to spend more time interacting with frontline employees.

___ Eliminate artificial barriers between managerial and other employees.

▶ FINAL THOUGHTS

What an impressive exhibition of teamwork it was: 2,008 Chinese percussionists drumming in unison at the opening ceremonies for the 2008 Summer Olympics in Beijing. It was a dramatic demonstration of the power that Asian cultures place on coordinated group effort, and a reminder to Western television viewers that competing in a global economy will require all the teamwork we can muster.

There is, in fact, a strong tradition of teamwork in America—in team sports and the military, in particular. And yet there is also the opposite and no less treasured American tradition of the rugged individualist hero as personified by Charles Lindbergh or the Lone Ranger—the free-agent achiever. How we resolve these two seemingly conflicting traditions is a challenge in our current business climate. In many ways, business teamwork has failed recently. Corporate executives have disappointed us with their focus on self-enrichment at the expense of their companies and their customers. Executive teams in many businesses are in constant conflict over turf and scarce resources. Our senators and congressional representatives can barely maintain enough civility to get past their differences and pass constructive legislation for the good of the country.

Fortunately, there are a few positive examples, among them the *Best-Places-to-Work* winners that scored high on teamwork. They embody what is possible in most organizations—a transformation *from me to we.* We have noticed that employees at nonwinning companies tend to have more difficulty seeing engaging activity beyond the scope of their work and the work of their coworkers. They think they are doing a good job, they see some positive things happening with their coworkers, and as a result, they may have some hope that their employment will continue. But, sadly, their view tends to end there; they have less confidence that there is strength in areas beyond their own view.

Employees at winning companies don't just see the good things happening with what's within their "line of sight"—their work and the work of the coworkers. They somehow have gained a perspective beyond themselves and their coworkers in terms of what is working and what is successful in their organizations. They see strength in the quality of the supervisor. They see strength in the senior leadership of the company. They believe the entire organization is on the right track. These transformed employees see far beyond their own navels, and overall engagement is enhanced as a result.

In an age of technology and telecommuting, we now must accommodate new breeds of individualists—autonomous, mobile, results-only workers—the "nanobots" described in a recent *Wall Street Journal* article[3] and the Dwight Schrutes of TV's *The Office*, whose oddball and contrary perspectives may actually bring their teams into healthy conflict sooner.[4] Add to this mix all the other issues of difference—generational, racial, gender, political, class, and basic personality type—today's team leaders will be challenged as never before.

The good news: vertical hierarchies are gradually disappearing, and cross-functional teamwork appears to be on the rise. We think that companies like Cisco Systems are showing us a new way, creating an "open-source" culture and spreading the company's leadership and decision making into working groups that involve as many as 500 executives who compose a network of councils and boards and are encouraged by new financial incentives that reward social networking, innovation, empowerment, and team achievement.[5]

► CHAPTER SEVEN

Job Enrichment and
Professional Growth

The Present and Future Driver

Pleasure in the job puts perfection in the work.
—ARISTOTLE

▶ MARIA—ALL JOBS ARE REALLY THE SAME, RIGHT?

For most of Maria's life, a job was a job was a job.

It was a paycheck—never enough, but enough to get by. Jobs in her chosen profession of hotel customer service were simply a means to an end, helping Maria and her husband put food on the table, keep one step ahead of the mortgage company, and put a little away for retirement.

Friends and coworkers often told Maria "she had a gift" for making people feel welcome. The best parties were always at Maria's house—a fun theme, goofy games—everyone looked forward to an evening at her place. Hotel guests frequently commented on the little extras from Maria, such as remembering people's names or making an extra call to find tickets to the sold-out event. Yet Maria took these things for granted; she thought everyone was this way. She received no encouragement from her supervisors, who either didn't take much interest in her career or were scared of losing her talents if she got a promotion.

Then she received a call from Andrea, a former neighbor and friend, who had been working for another hotel. She kept prodding Maria to apply for open positions, telling her how terrific her boss was, what a wonderful group of people she was working with, and what good opportunities for advancement there were. This all sounded fine to Maria, but it would add another 10 minutes to her commute, which was already too long. Another 10 minutes for just another job? It didn't add up for Maria—no job could be worth that much more extra commuting time, could it?

Maria finally relented when her boss, who was never pleasant to work with, went on a tirade. Nothing Maria did was good enough for her boss, including her extraordinary efforts to assist guests. All her boss could focus on was the fact that the property was losing market share. Maria's boss gave her an ultimatum to "shape up or ship out." Maria decided she'd had enough and placed a call to Andrea.

As fate would have it, there was an opening, and Maria got hired on with the new property where Andrea was working. She immediately sensed a difference . . . everywhere! The staff were smiling, almost contagiously so, and the management team members were supportive, encouraging, and helpful. She was overwhelmed by the menu of training and development opportunities available, which her supervisor encouraged her to consider. Importantly, she found a real mentor in her new boss, who told her that "the sky is truly the limit" in terms of how far she could take her career.

Were there high expectations as well? You bet, but somehow she felt motivated to give her absolute best in this new work environment. The few extra minutes of commute time was an easy trade for a career where her talents are truly appreciated.

▶ "LUCKY TO BE DOING THIS WORK"

If we've learned anything from our studies of outstanding workplaces, it is this: they do a remarkable job of helping employees love not just the workplace but the work itself. In fact, one of the most common comments we heard from employees at *Best-Places-to-Work* employers was, *"I can't believe I have this job. I just love coming to work."*

These are more than just statements—they are exclamations of genuine gratitude mixed with surprise and confidence. Why do these ordinary, just-like-you-and-me employees love their jobs so much? The research led us to this clear conclusion:

> In many cases, their employers have carefully placed these employees into jobs that fit their talents and abilities and give them ongoing opportunities to grow and develop.

Let's look at what our statistical survey analysis tells us about the differences between winners and nonwinners on this driver—job enrichment and the opportunity for professional growth/learning. The results, as usual, show marked differences in levels of engagement.

▶ UNIVERSAL ENGAGEMENT DRIVER: JOB ENRICHMENT AND PROFESSIONAL GROWTH

This driver is rooted in the following three statements that were among the top survey items that most sharply differentiated winning from nonwinning employers, as Figures 7.1, 7.2, and 7.3 indicate: *"I know how I fit into the organization's future plans"* (ranked #2), *"I find my job interesting and challenging"* (ranked #6), and *"I see professional growth and career development opportunities for myself in this organization."* (ranked #14)

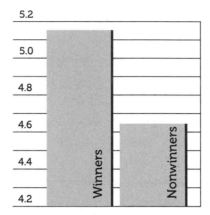

I Know How I Fit into the
Organization's Future Plans

Figure 7.1

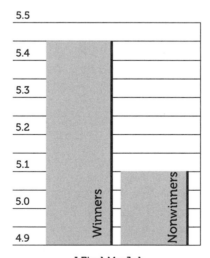

I Find My Job
Interesting and Challenging

Figure 7.2

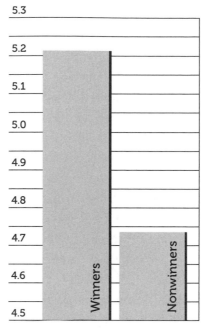

I See Professional Growth and Career
Development Opportunities for
Myself in This Organization

Figure 7.3

This universal driver speaks to fundamental needs that we all have—to receive intrinsic enjoyment from the job itself, and to feel that those who manage our work care about our continuing development and are helping us see a positive and meaningful future role for ourselves in the organization.

▶ MORE THAN JUST JOB SATISFACTION

As we discussed in Chapter 1, many business and academic researchers have studied the causes of job satisfaction and the conditions that increase it. Many had assumed that if employees were satisfied, they would also be more productive and stay longer.

Later research concluded, quite rightly, that enjoyment didn't necessarily equate to engagement, an outcome that we now know links directly to productivity and retention. Job enjoyment might be necessary for employee engagement, but is hardly sufficient. One dictionary defines enjoyment as "the state of being satisfied; contentment." Cows are contented. Contentment may be the feeling you have after a huge, carbohydrate-laden meal, but is that the kind of visceral emotion we want our employees to feel about their work? This is not to say that there is anything wrong with people being contented at work. Contentment is generally better than discontent. Our point is simply that we can't call it engagement. Some of the most engaged workers are actually discontented and thus all the more driven to serve and achieve.

We propose that this driver is about *job enrichment,* a higher standard than simple satisfaction or enjoyment. When workers' jobs are enriched, workers tend to work harder, achieve more, and feel deeper levels of commitment.

Overcoming the Tipping Point of 150: Job Enrichment and Professional Growth in Larger Organizations

Among the advantages that often come with being employed at larger organizations are more training, more advancement opportunities, and more mentors to choose from. However, as an organization grows larger, there may be disadvantages as well:

▶ An employee's job can become narrower, more specialized, and less satisfying.

Rx: Challenge employees to expand their jobs by identifying unmet needs, by creating job rotation programs, by providing skills and career interest assessment software or workshops to help the employee create new job goals, and by job sharing.

▶ Information about job opportunities at other locations or in other units is often not made available.

Rx: Create online job and talent banks with lists of all job descriptions including a resource and referral section with lists of books, professional associations, conferences, courses, articles, and other information recommended by coworkers.

▶ As more management layers are added, the distance between the average employees and senior leaders increases, and employees are not kept abreast of the changes in the company's plans, which makes planning their own futures more difficult.

Rx: Senior leaders and managers give open business briefings where they discuss strategic decisions and plans that may impact jobs, career paths, and skills that may be required in the future. These sessions can be recorded and made available on the company intranet.

▶ More management layers can mean more people to leapfrog on the way to one's ultimate career objective.

Rx: Emphasize strongly to employees that career growth is not defined as upward movement and that horizontal moves are sometimes the most enriching ones, as are "growing-in-place" options. This means the organization's leaders must endorse horizontal moves, remove barriers to lateral movement, and be willing to explore current changes in job assignments.

▶ It is often more difficult for employees to feel they can explore job opportunities outside their functional or business unit than within their unit.

Rx: Many managers are reluctant to "let go" of valued employees when those employees get restless and want to explore career growth options in other units. Senior leaders must make it absolutely clear that managers do not "own" the "talent" and that "talent hoarding" is unacceptable. By the same token, managers who do encourage employee growth and allow free movement must be recognized for doing so.

▶ As managers take on more direct reports, their spans of control increase, leaving them less time to meet with employees to discuss job enrichment and developmental issues.

Rx: Provide employees with career planning software and workshops so they can gain a better understanding of their strengths and interests, develop a list of realistic career options, and be more prepared for discussions with their managers; introduce (or expand current) mentoring programs; provide managers with a "tool kit" of worksheets and software for conducting career discussions along with supplemental training in how to use them.

▶ If the pace of company growth begins to slow, new job roles and opportunities may decrease.

Rx: Keep the emphasis on continually learning and using new skills in the current job role; explore job swapping where appropriate; keep employees up-to-date on company plans to spur new growth.

▶ WHO'S RESPONSIBLE FOR JOB ENRICHMENT AND PROFESSIONAL GROWTH?

Certainly the individual bears responsibility for performing well enough to deserve being developed, for making his or her career aspirations known, for seeking new challenges when the work becomes boring, and for knowing to avoid the wrong jobs. These are self-engagement prerequisites, among the many we present in Chapter 10.

But it is obvious that managers can and do play a powerful role in bringing out the best in the people they manage and in paving the way for their professional growth and advancement. In the thousands of survey comments we pored over, there were countless references to "management" and "leaders" and "the company" either choosing to make employee development a priority, or not doing so. Clearly, the responsibility for putting people in the right jobs and helping them grow is shared by three parties—the direct manager, senior leaders, and all employees. Human resources executives and professionals play a key partnering or supporting role as well, or should.

▶ ARE MANAGERS *EXPECTED* TO CHALLENGE AND DEVELOP EMPLOYEES?

For any number of the following reasons, many managers are not paying attention to people development:

- ▶ They were never coached themselves.
- ▶ They play favorites when it's time to promote or hand them the juiciest assignments.
- ▶ They rob employees of challenges by micromanaging or refusing to delegate.
- ▶ They just aren't "hardwired" to be coaches.
- ▶ They believe developing employees is more about fixing employees' weaknesses than leveraging their strengths.
- ▶ They are simply more interested in their own careers.
- ▶ They claim to be "too busy."
- ▶ They just don't care.

There are so many possible reasons that it's a wonder anyone gets developed at all. Fortunately, there are many managers who do care.

Many of them care because their leaders care. We see evidence that leaders at the *Best Places to Work* make sure managers care in several ways:

▶ By emphasizing the importance of employee development from the top down

▶ By making it clear that they expect managers to mentor and rewarding those who do

▶ By selecting and promoting managers who are naturally inclined to be people developers

▶ By making sure every manager knows that they do not "own" the employee and that there will be no hoarding of talent or blocking of lateral moves and reassignments if they serve the organization's needs and allow the employee to grow

▶ By stressing to managers the importance of anticipating employee restlessness and knowing which kinds of assignments will motivate which employees

▶ By knowing that training makes employees stay and keep learning more often than it makes them want to take what they've learned and go elsewhere[1]

▶ THE RACKERMOBILE, SUGAR BEAR, AND FANATICAL ENGAGEMENT: THE RACKSPACE HOSTING STORY

You may think that all the above practices are just common sense, but as we know, they are certainly not common practice. Our partners at Quantum Workplace informed us that Rackspace Hosting, a global provider of tailored hosting based in San Antonio, Texas, was the highest-scoring *Best-Places* employer on this driver. As we conducted our in-depth interviews for each of the six Universal Engagement Drivers, we contacted Rackspace leaders and employees to gain insight into how the company was getting such high marks from their employees in general and on this driver in particular. Here's the story:

▶ In its 10-year history, Rackspace has averaged more than 50 percent annual growth, with half of that growth attributed to referrals from satisfied customers. One of those customers remarked, *"If my other vendors just did 50 percent of what Rackspace does, I'd have a lot less gray hair."*[2]

▶ The company now hosts more than 45,000 servers for businesses of various sizes with almost 1 million e-mail addresses. Fully 1 percent of all World Wide Web traffic goes through a server that Rackspace hosts.

Chairman and cofounder, Graham Weston, shared with us how Rackspace has created a culture that is a significant advantage in a highly competitive marketplace—making sure employees (called "Rackers") are fanatical about doing their jobs well and taking care of Rackspace customers. For our Q & A, he was joined by project manager Robert Jackson, a Racker since 2000.

Q: Tell us a bit about Rackers.
Weston: *Our average Racker is comparatively quite young. We have tended to hire the Internet generation. This generation has lots of options. They expect something a bit different in their work experience. Loyalty, which many of them view as "working for the man," isn't as important to them as it may have been to other generations. They want to work where their values and the company values are compatible, where they can be themselves at work and at home. Naming our associates Rackers instead of employees helps gives us a real sense of identity.*

Q: When did you realize that keeping Rackers happy and engaged was a key to your business success?
Weston: *After a year or so into our start-up we realized that a lot of businesses, including ours, had what I call a "denial of service" model. In this model the business makes it very hard for customers to get great service, because great service seemingly costs too much to the business. So, instead of the business offering customers the opportunity*

to talk to a helpful person, it pushes them to an FAQ on a Web site or tells them to send an e-mail somewhere.

We realized there might be significant opportunity to turn 180 degrees away from the denial of service model to one of world-class service. But if we flipped our service delivery on its head, we needed to hire the right people and create an environment where they really wanted to work hard for us and our customers.

Jackson: *Even though we are a capital-intensive company, we are really a service company. When something goes wrong for a customer, technology doesn't matter . . . it's people that matter. We've never had a call system—push one for this department, two for that department. We invite customers to call us at four in the morning and see that a smart person will answer the phone within three rings. That's Rackspace.*

Q: Part of your approach to employees is to create what you call a "volunteer organization." What does that mean?

Weston: *We want Rackers to volunteer to work hard for us and for our customers. We want them to find great satisfaction serving our customers. We know it's impossible to have angry people doing great service for a sustained period of time. In the fall of 1999 we coined the term "fanatical support,"[3] which we initially used as an employee brand, but then turned into our market brand.*

Q: You've grown from a start-up to over 2,600 Rackers, including adding 1,000 in the last 18 months. How do you continue to maintain high levels of engagement as you've moved from that initial passionate group 10 years ago?

Weston: *I think it starts at the work-group level. That's the wellspring—that's the place to start. You can have a great corporate culture, but if a Racker has a bad boss, the corporate culture doesn't matter much. We also realized that senior leaders have a role to play in creating and maintaining a high-engagement workplace. Lots of permission is given to employees to be productive in ways they think best. This is a company that trusts people, and the senior leadership here has a lot to do with creating that culture of trust.*

Q: You work hard not to put Rackers into a position where they have to play "gotcha" with customers, which you believe hurts their job satisfaction. Tell us about that.

Weston: *I see so many businesses out there that have what I call a gotcha approach to their customers. They make customers pay for many additional, trivial things—they play gotcha in the hope of maximizing profits at the expense of the customer. They then put their employees in positions where they have to enforce these policies, which can be embarrassing and reduce job satisfaction. We never want our Rackers to be embarrassed about representing our company. Rather, we want them to feel empowered to serve.*

Jackson: *We don't have a rule book. If a customer has a problem, we don't say, "Sorry, I've never heard of that problem." Rackers are empowered to solve problems.*

Q: How do you find out what embarrasses Rackers?

Weston: *As our company grows it gets harder to get rid of "institutional gotchas." But we regularly ask them what puts them in a position where they feel embarrassed. We recently made a significant change in our approach to customers when we found out we were putting Rackers in a place where they were embarrassed to help. Although the policy seemed reasonable at first, every time a customer called about this particular matter they were embarrassed because they had to defend the policy.*

Q: Having incentives that align Rackers with customers is also important in building employee satisfaction. Has that been a challenge?

Weston: *We follow an approach where we want our customers to be "promoters" instead of "detractors,"[4] and have policies and a scorecard that creates promoters. We recently realized that one of our policies was creating a conflict between how Rackers were paid and what was in the best interests of our customers. There was an additional challenge that to do the right thing for the company meant that one group may need to refer a prospective customer to another group.*

We want to make sure incentives are not in the wrong place in terms of helping customers. So we changed that policy. We changed what success was. We made sure the best interests of the Rackers were the same as the customers' and that all Rackers would be motivated to get the customer into the right service. We always want our Rackers grounded in the ultimate good of developing promoters—that is our "true north."

Jackson: *Customer service isn't about a process. A process can make you better, but don't confuse customer service with the process. Customer service is about people. We had a customer whose offices in Florida were devastated by a hurricane. Thankfully, his servers were here in San Antonio. He asked us if there was anything we could do to help, and we had him come and work out of our offices for several months.*

Q: How did you get Rackers to embrace changes like the ones you've described?

Weston: *We get them involved in the change, gaining their feedback. We don't just inform Rackers of a change. We try to explain our thinking. We try to get them involved.*

Q: Does your culture allow Rackers to search for roles where they might fit?

Weston: *We're passionate about helping Rackers find their strengths, and we have a high tolerance for people changing roles.*

We have one Racker, who everybody calls Sugar Bear, who's been with us from the beginning. For the first five years Sugar Bear had several jobs in account management, sales, and purchasing. Although everyone loved Sugar Bear, he hadn't found his niche.

Because of our employee growth we needed to create an orientation process for new Rackers, which we now call "Rookie Orientation." Sugar Bear asked to give a presentation at our first orientation. The rookies really responded to Sugar Bear, and he came out of that talk high as a kite. Since then Sugar Bear has been the "Master of Ceremonies" for many companywide events and is also in charge of our weeklong orientation process, which we believe is the best in the country.

I'm really proud that we hung in with Sugar Bear. (Interviewer's note: Mr. Weston's colleague Rachel Ferry, a new Racker, was also present for the interview. She immediately chimed in that Sugar Bear's orientation *"was an awesome way to start my career as a Racker."*)

We believe strongly in helping Rackers develop their strengths. I teach a two-hour class on strengths. Helping Rackers appreciate their strengths allows people to say, "This is me." It's very liberating . . . very important for our management to emphasize.

Jackson: *We are all passionate about this company. Over time, like in my case and countless others, our natural strengths will bubble up. Our leaders allow people to explore where they fit best, and managers aren't protective of their people, keeping them from exploring other options inside Rackspace.*

Q: Because of your strong culture—what you describe as "culture thick"—do some people have difficulty fitting in?
Weston: *We have low empathy for people who come into Rackspace and believe they can and must immediately command respect because of their previous experience. We tell people if their experience helps you with your job, great. You command respect by participating, not pontificating.*

There's no business royalty at Rackspace. There are no trappings here. Our new office is made up of cubicles. With our growth and recently becoming a public company, we are challenged to find people who can adapt to our culture.

Jackson: *A flat hierarchy doesn't allow any place for senior management to hide. If senior management isn't paying attention to how Rackers are feeling about their jobs, others are and feel very capable of speaking up.*

Q: How important is recognition to employee satisfaction at Rackspace?
Weston: *We're very careful about our heroes. Our Rackers want to be in a company where the symbols of what is important to them are valued. We have several awards to honor our heroes. One is named after a Racker who courageously saved the life of a colleague in the*

ocean. When we recognize, we want them to not only know who the hero is, but why they are a hero.

One of my favorite recognitions is our Rackermobile, a BMW convertible that belongs to me. Managers get to nominate Rackers who have excelled, and they get to drive the car for a week. When someone asks the Racker about the nice car, they get to say, "This belongs to my boss, but he let me drive it for a week because I did a good job."

Q: Do you try to keep a pulse on how well your efforts are being received?

Weston: *We conduct an annual employee engagement survey. We also conduct frequent online "Happy Checks," which are mini-surveys we do to help us maintain an up-to-date sense of engagement.*

Jackson: *I'm a spoiled Racker. I hope new Rackers will feel the same way I do, that this is a once-in-a-lifetime opportunity. My wife and two kids are part of Rackspace. You can't take the Racker out of me.*

▶ THE VOICES OF JOB ENRICHMENT AND GROWTH OPPORTUNITIES

Let's listen in on what some of our 2 million–plus employees had to say about this engagement driver, or its absence, and how it contributes to or detracts from overall engagement in two key areas—one having to do with the intrinsic joys of the work itself and the other having to do with the individual's prospects for learning or advancement:

Positive Comments

Challenge and joy in the work itself

▶ *"The company is constantly seeking ways to improve my professional development through training, professional associations, and engaging work."*

▶ "I currently sit on a committee dedicated to enhancing the customer experience which gives me exposure to junior and senior players in other departments (which is great as it helps me grow and understand more of the big picture within the company as a whole)."

▶ "Excellent workplace from the standpoint of development—I and my coworkers are allowed to develop at our own pace, and our workloads are adjusted accordingly."

▶ "I commute, and I know I could get a boring job a lot closer to home, but instead I bought a better car for the daily drive. I'm not leaving!

▶ "Phenomenal place to work. The company values employees as individuals and is exceptionally committed to developing our strengths."

▶ "The thing that separates us in my mind is the level of empowerment the company gives to every employee in building the business and setting the direction of the company. If an employee wants to do a different type of work than the company currently does, all they have to do is make a case to the company management that shows how that different type of work will be beneficial to the company. If the employee can make that argument, the company will not just allow that employee the opportunity to pursue that type of work, but executives and other experienced employees will give their personal attention to support the employee's pursuit."

▶ "The reason I stay is that I like what I do most of the time."

▶ "I've worked a number of places, and this is the first that I feel truly cares about my professional growth and individual well-being."

▶ "I have worked at the company for just over a year and I have learned more than in college or graduate school. As a young person in the company, the management really takes you under their wing and they place a lot of trust and responsibility in you. They take a risk by giving you a lot of responsibility. They realize that the best way to learn is through challenges. The company is extremely focused on the development of their young staff. I love my job and I have grown to be extremely confident in my career. I have no plans to leave because I really feel that it is the best place for me."

Professional growth opportunities

▶ *"I started with the company right out of high school and since then I have had amazing managers who saw potential in me to move me up the ladder. I love my position and thank the great managers here for seeing something in me."*

▶ *"This is a great company to work for. There is a lot of room for growth and a lot of constructive criticism to keep you in line with your chosen career path."*

▶ *"This is a company that is dedicated to its people. It allows you to grow and develop and even change careers. There are plenty of opportunities within so that if you decide you don't like what you are doing, the firm will help you find something else internal that would suit your needs."*

▶ *"Anyone that I meet that needs a job I suggest they submit a resume . . . for any position. No matter how entry level or outside the box of what you want to do, the company will get you to where you want to be."*

▶ *"The leaders here take the time to teach, listen, and develop mentor relationships with younger staff."*

▶ *"Everything I have asked to learn or try, I have been given the opportunity."*

▶ *"One of the best things for me is that the company pays my tuition (in the Evening College program)! I am fully supported in this goal by a great manager and a flexible work schedule, and I have made tremendous progress toward my degree. I hope to finish within two years!"*

▶ *"My team lead pushes me to be the best that I can. She is guiding me through extra training."*

▶ *"I personally feel a strong level of support to grow professionally by taking courses (which the company pays for) and/or thanks to colleagues who give me new work responsibilities that gently expand my skills."*

▶ *"The company not only benefits me professionally but personally as well. Through work I have learned how to adapt to change, multitask, provide and receive difficult feedback, and, most of all, receive recognition for success."*

▶ *"The 100 percent tuition reimbursement program provides an unparalleled benefit that makes me recommend this as a place to work to all early career professionals who want to further their skills."*

▶ *"This firm gives you opportunities not found at other companies. Not every employee chooses to pursue those opportunities, but the opportunities are abundant to those that are willing to pursue them and willing to take the responsibility that comes with them."*

▶ *"I started working for this company a few years ago and have since been promoted twice from within. They are very good at recognizing people's strengths and helping develop their weaker areas. I would recommend, and have recommended, working here to several people."*

Alignment of employee and organizational needs

▶ *"My immediate supervisor meets with me weekly and informs me of the hospital's future plans and asks for my opinion."*

▶ *"The company does its best to meet the personal goals as well as business goals of its employees."*

Negative Comments

Now let's take a look at how employees describe the *absence* of those same practices:

Lack of challenge and joy in the work itself

▶ *"I feel that my talents and skills are not fully utilized in the current position I have. I have many talents and can be productive."*

▶ *"If the company put their employees into roles where the passions and talents were used, it would be a better atmosphere and morale would be higher."*

▶ *"My skills are beyond what this company needs on a day-to-day basis."*

▶ *"I just feel the company needs more room for growth. I understand that you may not be able to pay a lot more money, but at least give representatives responsibility for other projects so we will feel valued."*

▶ *"This has always been simply a job to me rather than a career. I got into it because it was convenient and fun as a part-time job. Full time it is not challenging. It is more and more about sales, which is not something I enjoy."*

Lack of professional growth opportunities

▶ *"In a small meeting the president of our company was asked why the admin staff wasn't ranked higher in pay. His response was, 'I don't know why anyone would want to be an admin; there's no career in it.' As an admin, I'm glad I don't work directly for him."*

▶ *"There are many managers, including senior-level executives, who place little or no emphasis on employee development."*

▶ *"What would make this company a GREAT place to work instead of a GOOD place to work is a greater opportunity for lower-level employees to be heard, recognized, and considered for advancement to levels above their immediate work group."*

▶ *"Opportunities for promotion and advancement for older workers are much less than for younger workers."*

▶ *"There is no promoting from within any more, just out-sourcing."*

▶ *"The growth opportunity here is just not an opportunity for EVERYONE. . . . You have to know certain people in order to get ahead. . . . I feel that the more you know, the less chances of advancing you have."*

▶ *"My position has no clear development path. It has been clearly stated that the next higher position is not an option for someone in my position who wants to move forward (too large of a step up and no way to get there)."*

▶ *"They do not seem to promote women."*

▶ *"Promotions seem to be based on the time put in rather than previous experience in the industry. The company rewards and promotes those who have been with the company the longest, although they may not be the best leaders or managers for the job. Also, there is not much room for growth or promotion in many departments."*

▶ *"I have been a top performer for over two years now. However, I have been overlooked for a promotion time and time again. I wouldn't normally complain, but the people who move up ahead of me are always a friend of the big boss or brother-in-law of a senior manager."*

Lack of alignment of employee and organizational needs

▶ *"I receive very little job satisfaction from my work here. I believe that is more of a reflection on my own goals and career path, which does not match well with the position I currently hold."*

▶ *"I have been employed with this organization for seven years. I feel undervalued and that there is not effective communication between management and employees. I feel that my job description is not aligned with my job performance matrix."*

▶ *"They need to put more emphasis on professional development and career goals. Find ways to match them with the goals of the company. I see the same people staying in the same positions for long periods of time, and I would not like to be one of them. Even if I like this company and would like to stay, I can't picture myself in the same position forever."*

▶ *"There is no democratic process in this company. Sometimes co-workers can choose their career path within the company, and they're allowed to do so. While at other times (especially with me) they do not allow us to change roles within the organization, and thus it does not align with my career goals or interests. The reason I have been given is that I have to prove myself. I have worked for this company for about three years, and I have worked as hard as anyone else, but I was neither rewarded nor allowed to change my role."*

Addressing Common Job Enrichment and Professional Growth Challenges in a Multigenerational Workforce

As we have emphasized before, each employee's challenges and needs are individual ones, not generational. Nevertheless, there may be value in presenting a few of the concerns that many employers are addressing in each of the four age groups:

Traditionalists (born before 1946)

▶ **Key concerns:** Tapping their experience and expertise, making sure they continue to feel valued, placing them in mentoring and knowledge-transfer roles to younger generations, giving them flexible and part-time options to contribute, giving them opportunities to leave a lasting legacy, and challenging them to learn new technologies.

Boomers (born 1946–1964)

▶ **Key concerns:** Reducing their stress levels and work hours, allowing more flexible scheduling and phased retirement options, encouraging them to delegate and empower younger generations, keeping them involved with younger workers on project teams and task forces, continuing to keep them challenged with tasks and projects where they can have an impact and leave a meaningful legacy, and challenging them to continue to learn and find opportunities for career renewal.

Gen Xers (born 1965–1980)

▶ **Key concerns:** Keeping them challenged and constantly learning (using a variety of media and learning methods) to keep them engaged despite limited opportunities for advancement caused by the postponed retirement of millions of Boomers, allowing them time off for personal and family life (and giving special recognition for sacrifices in these realms), not micromanaging them—trusting them with strong initial guidance and coaching to pursue results in their own way, and bending the rules and going to bat for them when you can.

Millennials (born 1981–1994)

▶ **Key concerns:** Providing them with the additional measure of feedback and coaching they need to take on the challenges they are eager to pursue, providing continual training and learning opportunities, encouraging them to work in teams and develop social skills, making them aware early on that they will be expected to take the initiative and make decisions independently and on the fly in unstructured situations, pairing them with older mentors, and taking a personal interest in their career goals and helping them develop the competencies they need to be successful.

▶ THE JOB ENRICHMENT FILTER

As we perused the comments of employees at *Best-Places-to-Work* winners, it occurred to us that there are several factors that go into creating an enriched job. We created the following table as a "filter" to use in assessing whether a job has the opportunity to be intrinsically rewarding to the individual employee.

This is different from a "job analysis" tool, where a human resources analyst tries to identify the key responsibilities and tasks for a job. Formal job analysis may be a necessary task in creating or modifying a job, but it may not get at the ideas presented below, which, according to our studies, lead to higher levels of employee engagement. The more you are able to answer yes to the items that follow, the greater the chances of that role having the potential for employees seeing their jobs as enriching:

Job Enrichment Filter Questions

Question	
▶ Do we have a method of selecting individuals who have a natural talent for the job or role, such as validated assessments and behavioral interviewing?	Yes/No
▶ Does the organization guard against putting employees in a position where the convenience and rules of the company and the needs of the customer unnecessarily clash, thereby putting the employee in an uncomfortable position?	Yes/No
▶ Is there a mechanism in place where employees get immediate and meaningful feedback on how they are doing?	Yes/No
▶ Do we allow good employees to explore new roles, acknowledging that their "failures" may at times be more a reflection of our having placed them in the wrong jobs, roles, or assignments?	Yes/No
▶ Do we help employees see how their work clearly contributes to the overall success or mission of the organization?	Yes/No
▶ Do we watch closely for those moments when an employee seems to be learning something very quickly, which may be a sign of untapped potential?	Yes/No

▶ Do we celebrate the small steps new   Yes/No
employees take as they gradually
become more effective?

▶ Do line managers modify a particular job   Yes/No
to better fit the unique skills or talents of
their direct reports?

▶ Do employees feel a sense of "comple-   Yes/No
tion" in their work, seeing a task through
from start to finish?

▶ Do we consider the possibility of task   Yes/No
swapping, recognizing that a task one
employee finds boring or unsatisfying
another employee may find challenging
and enjoyable?

▶ Are we asking employees directly,   Yes/No
"What are the strengths you most enjoy
using?" or "What was the most enjoyable job you ever had, and why?"

▶ Are we giving employees as much freedom   Yes/No
as possible to make their own judgments
and decisions about how to do the work,
achieve the result, or serve the customer?

If there is a particular employee whose level of engagement you would like to see increased, you may want to go back and consider each question with that person in mind.

Some may see the last filter question as the most controversial. We suspect talk about giving employees freedom makes some of you uncomfortable—are we asking you to cede your authority as leaders? Gaylord Hotels General Manager Kemp Gallineau had these thoughts on this very subject:

> We don't just say to our front desk agent "you're empowered to spend up to $200" to take care of a customer's concern. We let our

*associates, or "Stars" as we call them, make whatever decision they feel comfortable making and spending whatever amount it takes. We just let them know that they need to go to their manager if they don't feel comfortable making that decision. **Customers don't care about your rules** [emphasis ours].*

Mr. Gallineau brings us to the heart of the matter. Job enrichment is about providing an environment where the right person has been given the right support and the right tools so they wow your customers. You can't write a rule book thick enough to cover every crazy conceivable contingency your customers can throw at you—the folks at Gaylord and Rackspace know that. You've got to trust your employees to do the right thing. If you do, they'll likely find greater satisfaction in their work and amaze your customers, who will come back often and tell their friends.

▶ IDENTIFYING PROFESSIONAL GROWTH OPPORTUNITIES

Many senior leaders may say they are investing in the growth and development of their employees and managers, but leaders at winning employers appear to be doing a particularly effective job with their investments.

Where should you make your investments?

In the left-hand column of the following chart are five questions that organizations have traditionally asked when considering ways to help employees learn, grow, and develop professionally. In the right-hand column are a series of questions that we believe *Best-Places-to-Work* winning companies are asking; bear in mind that they are not intended to replace those on the left-hand side, but to complement them.

It's often been said that you cannot know the answer to a question you never ask. We encourage you to think deeply about these questions, as they may expand the options you consider about ways to help employees discover and develop their talents and interests.

Traditional Questions	*Best-Places-to-Work* Questions
Remedial	**Developmental**
What is the problem or challenge we need to address and fix with this employee?	How can we help this person build on what he or she already does well?
Broadcast	**Narrowcast**
How can we get everyone to learn this important content?	How can we offer opportunities that are tailored to a person's unique learning style, interests, and abilities?
Classroom Centered	**Experiential**
How can we make the time in the classroom as effective as we possibly can?	How can we create opportunities for people to "learn while doing"?
Content Driven	**Relationship Driven**
How can we help people learn this information?	How can we help people develop a better network of contacts, learn from each other, and collaborate better?
Linear Career Path	**Dual or Multiple Career Path**
How can we help people prepare for the next step on the organizational chart?	How can we help people prepare for the many career options that may be open to them?

Let us be clear: there is nothing wrong with training and development initiatives that support the implied objectives in the left-hand column. Smart leaders take a comprehensive approach by asking questions on both sides to make sure employees learn everything they need to know to be effective in their jobs. The questions on the right-hand side represent additional issues we must explore in a fast-changing business environment with flatter organizations, more tech-savvy generations with shorter attention spans, and reduced expectations of long-term employment.

▶ ANSWERING THE NONTRADITIONAL QUESTIONS

Let's examine some of the ways *Best-Places-to-Work* employers are answering the right-side questions in the chart above and implementing this engagement driver to facilitate the achievement of both individual and organizational goals.

Developmental: *How can we help a person build on what he or she already does well?*

We certainly want to do everything we can to help employees overcome any weaknesses or gaps in their skills, and so any training and
development efforts should incorporate programs to do this. But we
must take care not to overlook ways to help individuals build their
strengths—help them to do better what they already do well.

Arizona Spine and Joint Hospital (Phoenix) makes an attempt to
determine each person's strengths and then to develop and utilize
those strengths, Chief Executive Lloyd Scarrow explained. "We have
a pharmacist who is an excellent pastry chef, and so he contributes to
the hospital in both capacities. Our goal is not to be fair. We want
to treat people according to their uniqueness. To me, fair is an excuse to treat everyone equally bad."[5] At another winning company we
know, the HR executive supervises the maintenance staff because he
has a love for mechanical tinkering. Can you imagine trying to con-
struct a job description for a "pharmacist-chef" or "HR-maintenance"
position?

Getting people into positions where they're using their strengths
can have a significant impact on per-person productivity. Just think of
the potential a company could unleash if all employees were working
in roles that were suited to their strengths! At *Stryker Endoscopy*, in San
Francisco, the work environment is exacting. "At Stryker, you learn on
the job," Human Resources Director Jessica Winter said. "You develop
quickly and get rewarded with a promotion." It is not uncommon for
employees to have three promotions in their first four years. "We set
people up for success," added CEO Bill Enquist. "We understand their
strengths and put them in jobs that play to those strengths."[6]

Narrowcast: *How can we offer opportunities that are tailored to a person's unique learning style, interests, and abilities?*

Some of us learn best by reading the instruction manual; others learn
by watching someone who already knows, and still others learn in a
rap session with peers. Each of us has a preferred learning style.

This notion of different learning styles came home to us several years ago with a former colleague. Although we are voracious readers and are frequently recommending books and articles to each other, our colleague didn't embrace "book learning." This wasn't a matter of him being less intelligent; his preferred learning style was through experiential or small-group discussions. We found out that if he took a few notes about a topic in a roundtable discussion, he could retain every bit of what we needed to have him learn. So we stopped sending him books and tailored our learning approach to fit his style.

When it comes to motivating its employees, *Huntington Bank* is intent on not taking a cookie-cutter approach. Despite employing 450 individuals from all walks of life in offices scattered across the Ohio region, the bank's philosophy is to figure out what drives each individual. "Different things motivate individual employees," said Michael Prescott, Huntington's regional president. "A few of the most common motivators are recognition, success in their job or position, and compensation packages. At Huntington we take the time to understand what each associate's motivators are." Prescott's goal is to empower employees in "an atmosphere of success based on personal growth." He believes that's a primary reason employees enjoy working at the bank.[7]

Experiential: *How can we create opportunities for people to "learn while doing"?*

We have all had to sit through many training activities in the traditional classroom setting, and, alas, we will likely sit through more in the future. For some topic areas, the typical classroom format is acceptable for providing information to employees in a way that meets the learning requirements. In other cases, learning is best applied outside traditional settings. At *Enterprise Rent-A-Car*, all employees start as management trainees and learn how to run their own business from the ground up.[8] Doing this likely gives emerging leaders a far better perspective on the business, a learning outcome not likely found in a management training classroom.

Relationship Driven: *How can we help people develop a better network of contacts, learn from each other, and collaborate better?*

The old adage "It's not what you know, it's who you know" has application in our busy, complex workplaces. Often the way we get the right answer to a problem or learn something is by knowing whom to ask for support.

There are numerous examples of employers creating ways for employees to seek out individuals with similar interests with whom they may find mutual benefit and mutual learning. The professional services firm *Grant Thornton* has one such program, called "Women at Grant Thornton," a mentoring and networking program geared toward advancing women's careers at the firm.[9] Affinity and networking groups of all types are popping up in the workplace.

Dual or Multiple Career Path: *How can we help people prepare for the many career options that may be open to them?*

Although many of our employees will want to move up the traditional career ladder, this linear approach to learning has never met the needs of all employees, nor does it necessarily meet our HR planning needs. Because of increased spans of control, there often aren't as many opportunities to move up. Still, that doesn't mean we can't find ways to help our associates continue their growth.

At *St. Luke's Health* in Kansas City, the system's transfer policy allows employees to move laterally between institutions without losing seniority or benefits, and career ladder programs offer plenty of opportunities for advancement. Shauna Thompson, a quality system manager, has worked for St. Luke's Health System for 27 years. "I need a change of pace and new challenges every few years," she said, "and St. Luke's has been able to provide that."[10]

One of the nice perks for employees at *Barclay's Global Investors* is that the company offers opportunities for employees to try different jobs they're interested in. Chris McCrum, global head of human resources, for example, came from a financial background and now he's running HR. "We do that quite routinely," he said of Barclay's job flexibility.[11]

▶ ALIGNING EMPLOYEE AND ORGANIZATIONAL NEEDS AT GAYLORD HOTELS

We've suggested that it is in the best interest of employers to make sure their interests are in alignment with employee interests. When these interests are aligned, a natural consequence is higher engagement on this all-important driver.

But how far can you take this mindset? Surely there is a limit to such a lofty commitment? Gaylord Hotels is willing to take this commitment to great lengths and, in doing so, reaps tangible benefits. We again turned to Kemp Gallineau, the general manager of the Orlando property, to ask him about the firm's attitude toward employees who leave:

Q: Do people ever leave and come back?

Gallineau: *They sure do. We welcome people back if they leave and want to come back. There's an interesting story about that. Within the last year or so we have had three big, prestigious hotels open properties here in our market—right in our backyard. And we knew we would lose some people who wanted to go to work at these other hotels. We would be naïve if we thought we could offer the best fit and best opportunity for everyone when all these other outside options were there for them. So, believe it or not, we decided to offer a résumé-writing class to help them move on if that's what they wanted. To our amazement, only five who took the class left the hotel, and all five came back because the work experience at the new hotel wasn't what they thought it would be. The other hotels had either overpromised or misrepresented something.*

Q: That's remarkable that you would do something like that.

Gallineau: *The most interesting thing to us was that in the course of helping current employees with their résumés, we found talents we didn't know people had. We hire people who come from various backgrounds and from other countries. Many of them have received degrees or other training, and then, just based on economic reasons, they took whatever jobs they could get after that. We discovered some hidden talents.*

Q: So, you hire more for talent than experience?

Gallineau: *Yes, we truly believe in aligning talents. When we first opened the hotel, we were trying to fill 200 positions. There were only so many management positions to fill, and we knew that not everyone who applies for a manager's job is cut out to be a manager. They are often just tempted by higher pay or attracted by the status of the position. We always asked candidates for these jobs a question that really helped us determine who was a fit and who wasn't. The question was "What was the best job you ever had and why?" A lot of the candidates said they were actually happier when they were working in jobs one or two levels below where they were working at the time. So we moved some of them back into those positions, where they could do the work they enjoyed, and kept them at their same pay level. Some told us they felt relieved. One was a director of rooms who preferred her previous role being in charge of executive housekeeping. She missed the daily interaction with the housekeepers. So that was a surprise that so many candidates responded that way. It's not what we expected, but it worked out quite well. So many businesses promote people to failure.*

Such remarkable stories are commonplace among *Best-Places* employers. We said in our preface that these winning employers are a principled bunch, and there is no better example that Gaylord's commitment to aligning organizational and employee interests.

▶ WHO GAINS AND WHO LOSES IN TURBULENT TIMES

Although career goals and aspirations may wane in tough times, some employers—as Figure 7.4 shows—still achieve employee engagement gains, while others suffer a significant drop.

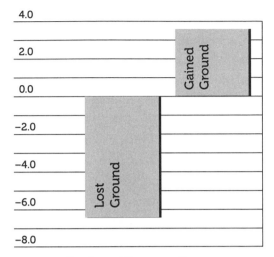

Continued Focus on Career
Growth and Development

Figure 7.4

Representative comments from employees who remained engaged in difficult times, and those who did not, include:

Voices of Engagement

▶ *"I love my job and enjoy the sales process. It's been the toughest year of my 26-year career in sales. I hope to continue as I know the economy will get to normal and we will succeed."*

▶ *"I also believe the opportunities to be promoted help create a great place to work and make everybody who wants to advance work hard for the company."*

▶ *"I have been impressed with the training they invest in workers, the money they spend to keep us up to date technologically so we are competitive, and the way they keep us informed."*

Voices of Disengagement

▶ *"There is little discussion about development, and when something is discussed, there is NEVER a follow-up."*

▶ *"Identify the best of the best on each team and work with them on their career path. These are the people you want to keep, but they are getting bored and feeling unappreciated and undervalued."*

▶ *"Put plans in place to continually help employees close their skills gaps. As the company and industry changes, employees too need ongoing development to be able to adapt to the changes."*

Job satisfaction is an important contributor to employee engagement in all times. We encourage employers to continue efforts to help associates stay positive and excited about their work and prospects for growth. Although some companies may choose to sever some employees as a cost-cutting measure, all employers must work to retain their most talented employees.

In times of uncertainty, employees worry not just about the status of their current jobs, but about whether there will be chances for them to grow. If employers can continue to make investments in the development of their employees, we believe that employees will respond in kind.

Job and Career Growth Practices in Difficult Times

1. Introduce stretch assignments, and increase frequency of career-related discussions.

2. Engage employees by providing opportunities where they can improve personal leadership skills. Leadership training gives employees who may be feeling stuck in their current positions an outlet to explore the next step and the ambition needed to move up in the company.

3. An employee mentoring program is one low-cost and effective leadership training idea that can help boost employee engagement. Partner employees with managers and executives, and have them shadow each other or work on a project together. Both partners will appreciate the change of pace, and the employee will pick up valuable,

hands-on leadership training that can't be found at any off-site workshop.

4. Focus employees on company growth as a key to personal growth. Challenge employees to create their own opportunities by identifying "unmet needs" in the organization. Welcome their proposals for new assignments or roles that could result in growth opportunities for them and the company, or even in the creation of new jobs.

5. Ask managers to hold "career checkups" where they ask employees how they feel about their current opportunities for career growth and learning, and paint a picture of possible bright scenarios for future growth as the company turns things around.

6. Encourage growth that doesn't require upward movement—horizontal moves, growing in place through new assignments, temporary job tryouts, job swapping, and skill-building rotations.

▶ A CHECKLIST OF MANAGER BEST PRACTICES TO ENHANCE JOB ENRICHMENT AND PROFESSIONAL GROWTH

What follows is a summary of some of the practices, based on our analysis, that *Best Places to Work* share. Check those that you believe your organization is currently doing well, and place an X next to those you believe you should be doing or doing significantly better:

___ Give new hires meaningful challenges right from the start.
___ Assure that managers are delegating challenging responsibilities and tasks.

___ Invite and encourage employees to propose and create new jobs within the company that fill unmet needs and that allow them to make better use of their talents.

___ When employees become disengaged (bored, restless, or stuck), find ways to help them grow in place and increase job challenge.

___ Provide prospective recruits and new hires with a vision of realistic potential career paths and opportunities.

___ Offer self-assessment and career self-management workshops to help employees take more control of their own career and professional growth and formulate both short- and long-term goals.

___ Hire on-staff or consulting "coaches" to provide confidential career advice to current employees.

___ Create and communicate competency definitions for all jobs (or projects as they change) so employees will know exactly what skills and strengths they need to have or develop.

___ Create an internal online site where employees can "test" themselves to see how their current competencies stack up to those listed for various positions, including recommended learning activities to close competency gaps.

___ Offer a wide range of job-specific and more general learning opportunities, including e-learning, podcasts, wikis, and other nonclassroom methods.

___ Provide cross-training in various jobs, functions, and technologies.

___ Create alternative career path progressions to provide for those demonstrating technical excellence and not aspiring to general management.

___ Grow the business! Nothing works better to provide more career growth opportunities.

___ Expand tuition reimbursement offerings.

___ Have employees complete individual development plans and keep them updated through discussions with their managers.

___ Train managers in career coaching and mentoring.

___ Recognize and reward managers who coach and develop their direct reports and allow them to move on to meet the growth needs of the employee and the business needs of the organization.

___ Encourage and facilitate lateral movement across functional areas.

___ Maintain a fair, consistent, and clearly understood internal job-posting system.

___ Allow employees to internally "post" their own jobs as a way of letting other employees know they would be open to "swapping" jobs.

___ Consider internal candidates for openings before interviewing outside candidates.

___ Create an internal "skills bank" using an IT system that can match employee skills and experience with current needs and opportunities.

___ Reduce months or years of tenure required to compete for internal job vacancies.

___ Allow good performers to move to new jobs without permission of their managers after serving in their current jobs for a specified period.

___ Have managers discuss employees' development periodically, and not just at appraisal time.

___ Base promotions on demonstrated talent, results, and true readiness, not tenure.

___ Build an effective organization-wide talent review and succession management process based on in-depth assessment of emerging leaders and key contributors.

▶ FINAL THOUGHTS

A few years ago we were engaged to conduct a series of focus groups where employees at a large bank were to give us insights into how the organization could better support their career advancement. We were told by several employees in different groups that if an employee wanted to gain promotion into another department, he or she would need to leave the bank for a year or two, gain experience outside the firm, and then come back. The organization's "stovepipes," as they called them, hindered employees from moving into other areas. Managers overtly told employees they would be penalized for their "disloyalty" to the department.

We found this attitude troubling, in large part because we were aware that most of the successful senior leaders at the bank had careers that took them through the major functions of the bank, allowing them to gain a perspective they might not otherwise have. Their internal management practices—both formal and informal—were getting in the way of what had been a successful leadership model of exposing their successful leaders to a variety of jobs in different departments. Their practices, then, were misaligned to the strategic needs of the bank, something we know winning *Best-Places* employers work like crazy to avoid.

The employees' comments shocked us, but since they had come from several sources, we felt an obligation to report them. Our internal sponsor agreed that, yes, this was "a problem that needed to be addressed." To this day the problem hasn't been solved, and, as a result, the bank has lost many talented employees who aren't coming back.

This "problem" seems to have legs, as we found it lurking in a large call center with whom we've also worked. In this case a flock of assistant managers, frustrated by an absence of any career support, regularly leave to work for various competitors. And when they're hired back a few years later, they are often under agreement with a search firm that, in essence, makes the retailer pay a big fee to get its former people back!

As leaders we must constantly ask ourselves whether our actions (what we are doing) are in alignment with our beliefs (what we value). Many organizations we encounter seem to go out of their way to put obstacles in front of the growth and development of their employees, often at the expense of what they say they value.

When it comes to job enrichment and development, it's time to start walking the talk.

► CHAPTER EIGHT

The Never-Ending Source
of Engagement

Valuing Employee Contributions

If you have some respect for people as they are, you can be more effective in helping them become better than they are.
—John Gardner

We are all motivated by a keen desire for praise.
—Cicero

► SHARON: A SHOCKING REALIZATION

Until that moment, it was just another day at the office park where we worked . . . the moment, that is, when the door to the hallway opened suddenly and Sharon came storming through. Her face was red, her eyes flashed with anger, and she slammed the door shut behind her with such vehemence that the office walls shook. She swept by the group of innocent bystanders who had been talking with one another, stepped quickly into her office, and slammed her door behind her. Again, the walls shook. We looked at each other and wondered aloud, "What was that all about!?!"

Only later did we find out. We had just witnessed the aftermath of a triggering event. Sharon had just learned that she was being paid significantly less than the men in the office doing the same job. She had reacted with understandable, but uncharacteristic, emotion. Phil, the firm's CEO, had just recently promoted Sharon from her job as office manager into the more prestigious role of professional consultant. She had spent most of her career in administrative roles and was at the top of her game, but the firm was growing so fast that new consultants were needed to handle the business. Phil knew Sharon could handle the promotion: she was extremely bright, service oriented, dedicated, empathetic, and professional. What he didn't know was that trying to buy her services cheap would result in the firm's losing a valued employee. Sharon went home early that afternoon and submitted her resignation the next morning.

Later that morning when Phil told us what had happened, we could see he was plainly upset and disappointed—with himself. "I really screwed up," he confessed. He hadn't slept much the night before. We suggested he call Sharon, ask her to reconsider her decision to quit, and offer to pay her the same as the other consultants, which is what he did. He actually did more than that; he apologized to Sharon, admitting he had been trying to save money wherever he could. Sharon thought about it overnight and decided to accept Phil's new offer. We were happy to have her back at work and told her so in no uncertain terms, but we wondered, "Would she ever really trust Phil after that?" We got our answer three months later when Sharon left to go to work for a competing firm.

▶ THE HUMAN NEED TO FEEL IMPORTANT AND BE RESPECTED

When Leigh asks audiences at his presentations to raise their hands if they receive *too much* recognition, he generally gets expressions of smiling bemusement, outright laughter, or responses of "Yeah, right!"

What he never sees are raised hands, except occasionally in jest. Does this mean employees are not getting *enough* recognition? We think so. One authority on work performance has reported that for every four accomplishments employees complete at work, only one of those accomplishments is acknowledged.[1]

Among the top 10 survey items that distinguished winning from nonwinning organizations was the statement *"If I contribute to the organization's success, I know I will be recognized,"* which was ranked #9 as a differentiator. As you can see in Figure 8.1, the engagement score gap was significant. And although not ranked among the top 10 most differentiating items, a related survey statement having to do with feeling paid fairly for one's contributions (Figure 8.2) also revealed an equally significant gap between winning and nonwinning employers.

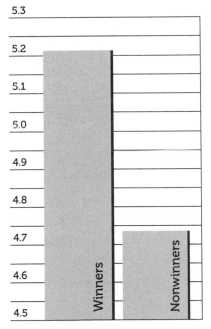

If I Contribute to the
Organization's Success,
I Know I Will Be Recognized

Figure 8.1

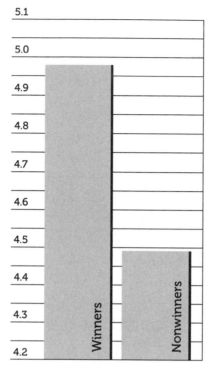

Considering the Value I Bring to
the Organization, I Feel
I Am Paid Fairly

Figure 8.2

Verbatim survey comments show a stark contrast between those who seem to be feeling recognized, valued, and fairly paid and those who unequivocally do not. Employees' comments reveal a larger universe of concerns than just having their contributions rewarded with praise or pay, although these appear to be the two most central. In actuality, valuing or not valuing employees encompasses a much broader range of issues, as you can see:

Voices of Engagement *Feeling Listened To*	Voices of Disengagement *Not Feeling Listened To*
▶ *"Management takes the time to listen to ideas and suggestions from the staff, which goes a long way."*	▶ *"Employee suggestions are ignored completely by management."*

▶ *"Our CEO meets with all employees and asks for ways that the company could be improved. He then compiles a list of all suggestions and notifies employees when action has been taken."*

▶ *"Management listens to you when you have an idea that could improve the quality of work for you or your team. They then allow you to move forward with that idea and support you and promote your idea along the way."*

▶ *"I would like to see management begin to ask the employees what they want and stop assuming they know what we want or need. They are so off-base."*

▶ *"Things have changed in the last year or so that have made many of the employees feel less important and that their input is not only not welcome, but not needed."*

Feeling Important or Valued

▶ *"A map was created with everyone's home address represented by a pin (so that consideration in terms of commuting could be given to all). Last week, HR sent us a top 10 list about the new space—it was really great, and everyone is buzzing with excitement!"*

▶ *"(1) Our leaders know everyone by name, and we have about 120 employees. I was called by name by almost everyone on my very first day, not just a generic greeting. I walked down the hall, and other staff I don't work with would greet me by name. I was absolutely amazed. (2) The CEO comes by periodically to ask how I am doing. (3) Achievements are recognized and people are thanked in our weekly community meeting."*

▶ *"I have worked as a room cleaner for 35 years and have never felt as valued as I do here at my hotel."*

Feeling Less Important or Valued

▶ *"For the most part I feel very underappreciated and underpaid. The management team here does not recognize employees enough. The director will not even speak to us at times; she just acts like we are not there."*

▶ *"We are underpaid, overworked, spit on by patients, cursed at by family, ignored by management. We can't get equipment that works or supplies to do our job."*

▶ *"Often we lack the supplies and resources needed to do our job adequately. Look at our retention level . . . there is no effort to keep loyal employees. In fact no one from management has met with employees to address what they feel they need or want to do their jobs or make them want to stay in this organization."*

Feeling That Contributions Are Recognized

▶ "Because we are a large company, in the past the company hasn't always effectively recognized its employees at every level. However, over the past couple of years they have really done a good job at correcting this problem. Recognition comes in many forms, and we have really begun to benefit from it in the trenches."

▶ "I've worked in various IT sectors before coming to the company. My current employer beats the pants off of these other places as a great place to work. Hard work is recognized, and because of that everyone is working hard, which in turn is making us very successful."

▶ "My current manager has a rare quality. He makes every individual feel important. I will do anything—work 80 hours, etc., if I know it is appreciated. Many days I go home exhausted, but feeling like I truly accomplished something. Money is good, but that feeling is so much better."

Linking Pay to Contributions

▶ "Employees are recognized for their accomplishments. We now receive gain-sharing checks when we meet our goals."

▶ "This company puts its money where its mouth is. The company continually affirms its appreciation for the workforce by distributing unannounced bonuses and

Feeling That Contributions Are Not Recognized

▶ "This place treats employees as completely disposable. There is no respect given for accomplishment."

▶ "I ALWAYS give 110%, and my supervisor never offers praise, thanks or even gratitude. My supervisor often passes off my ideas and my work as her own."

No Link between Pay and Contribution

▶ "The company has a wonderful bonus incentive program for upper management, and a very nice commission program for sales, marketing, etc. There is absolutely no incentive plan for corporate employees (who are not executive management)."

gifts as well as basing incentive compensation on personal growth and development."

▶ *"In my short tenure at the company, I have been rewarded, along with my colleagues, for a job well done with lunches as well as monetary rewards. Those of us who braved the snowstorms were paid full days' pay, regardless of the actual time worked those days. I felt my efforts were appreciated, and I didn't just feel like a number."*

Feeling "in the Loop"

▶ *"The company leadership is committed to communicating all information, not only the positive."*

▶ *"Posters are positioned throughout the buildings showing new projects, successful projects, and company achievements. The top officers of the company issue an e-mail each Friday that points out satisfied clients, new projects, and praises the people who led to those successes."*

Equitable Recognition

▶ *"When goals are reached you are recognized, regardless of what job you are in. Who could ask for more?"*

▶ *"The 'incentive' program has become more of a hindrance than a benefit. This incentive plan has caused employees to not work as a team for the good of the members. It is all about selling, and there is no commitment to help our customers unless there is a sale in it for the employee—right up to the VPs."*

▶ *"There is no incentive for better performance since the best workers get the same raises as the laziest workers."*

Not Feeling "in the Loop"

▶ *"Communication is only open among management. Non-management employees are informed of most organizational changes from the smoking crew and not directly from managers."*

▶ *"I've never really felt informed of the company's future goals or financial health going forward."*

▶ *"Staff often has to learn about company promotions/discounts/specials through customers."*

Perceived Inequity of Recognition

▶ *"Team recognition at the expense of individual recognition allows some people to fly under the radar while others work double time to get work done."*

▶ "The current CEO is making a real effort to make employees at all levels feel valued and included, and it seems to be working. The previous corporate culture recognized top management and upper engineering talent. Everybody else may as well have been invisible."

▶ "In all my years of employment, I have never worked for a company that tries so hard to be employee focused. Employees are recognized both publicly and monetarily. There are programs in place that continually allow the company opportunities to show how grateful they are for employees who go above and beyond the call of duty."

▶ "My team has been told that we chose a support role in the company and therefore forfeit any right to recognition."

▶ "During the year, nurses' week is ALWAYS recognized. However, social workers don't get recognition, secretaries don't get recognition. It makes for ill feelings when all disciplines work hard and deserve the same recognition."

▶ "The hourly people are the lowest priority in this company, whereas those who are exempt are more than taken care of—their high pay, their incentive pay, and much more."

▶ "The backbone departments that keep company losses in check are ignored."

There are many distinct subthemes expressed in these comments, not all of them focused specifically on recognition, but all revolving around one central issue: the employees' sensitivity about whether or not they—their ideas, opinions, contributions, and their presence—matter.

Engaging by Valuing the Contributions of All Four Generations

Though individual preferences vary widely, here are some rewards sought by members of the four age groups that experts on the generations consider to be valid for many:

Traditionalists (born before 1946)

▶ The satisfaction of a job well done
▶ Acknowledgment of loyalty, hard work, and sacrifice
▶ Praise for adapting to hard realities and change
▶ Appreciation for passing on knowledge, mentoring younger workers
▶ Face-to-face thanks, handwritten notes
▶ Traditional corporate status symbols

Boomers (born 1946–1964)

▶ Status based on experience and accomplishment
▶ Recognition for making a difference
▶ Thanks for going the extra mile
▶ Appreciation for being good team players
▶ Opportunities to mix in more flexible scheduling and time off
▶ Opportunities to leave a meaningful legacy

Gen Xers (born 1965–1980)

▶ Freedom to do work when and where they want
▶ Autonomy to do the job their own way
▶ Opportunity to socialize and have relaxed fun with coworkers
▶ Time off to pursue family and leisure interests
▶ Learning and growth opportunities that keep them marketable
▶ The latest technology
▶ Health-care coverage and convenience benefits

Millennials (born 1981–1994)

▶ Meaningful work
▶ Opportunity to develop relationships with others their age

▶ More responsibility, chances to prove themselves
▶ Time off to have a life outside work
▶ Appreciation for sacrificing time off
▶ Opportunities to be mentored and learn new things

For all four generations

▶ Recognition for collaboration and teamwork with members of other generations

▶ HOW EMPLOYEES GET THE MESSAGE "YOU'RE NOT IMPORTANT" IN BIG AND SMALL WAYS

In doing a microanalysis of employee survey comments, we cataloged some additional ways employees see the signs that may seem inconsequential and unintended to the leaders and managers who send them:

▶ The employee receives no eye contact or greeting from the manager when they pass each other in the hallway.
▶ The employee is not welcomed or is ignored entirely on the first day of employment.
▶ The manager allows phone calls to interrupt "important" meetings with employees.
▶ The employee has not received needed supplies, equipment, data, or assistance.
▶ There is a failure to respond to employee requests for information or meetings.
▶ Meetings are continually postponed, especially performance evaluations.
▶ The employee has to work in hot, cold, cramped, stuffy, disorganized, or run-down quarters; in noisy, smelly, or toxic surroundings; or in any other kind of unsanitary or unpleasant conditions.

- The employee receives delayed recognition for accomplishments, or none at all.
- Responses to administrative or HR requests are delayed or absent.
- Rules and bureaucracy stifle employee creativity and initiative.
- The employee is being paid less than entry-level workers or workers in similar jobs at other companies in the same market, or is paid less because of any factor other than performance, especially favoritism.
- The employee is recognized in a way he or she does not value or finds embarrassing, such as public recognition.
- Only team accomplishments are recognized, while the contributions of a key contributor on the team go unacknowledged.
- The employee is left off e-mail distribution lists.
- The employee is not invited to a meeting where he or she has knowledge that could provide valuable input into a decision affecting the employee or the team.
- A manager is not given the authority or budget in deciding how to reward employees.
- Employees do not receive any form of acknowledgment on their anniversary with the company.
- Remote office and evening shift workers receive less frequent attention.

The list is more illustrative than exhaustive. We could probably uncover dozens more ways leaders and managers reduce employee engagement through their lack of focus, empathy, and commitment.

While it is no doubt true that some employees have an exaggerated sense of their own value, we believe the failure of managers and senior leaders to acknowledge the daily contributions of their workers is usually the bigger problem. What many managers and leaders don't stop to consider is that missed opportunities to acknowledge, respond, invite, include, praise, remember, and reward are also missed opportunities to invest in and energize employees, which, as we know, leads directly to more enthusiastic customer service and better follow-on performance.

▶ WHY MANAGERS AND LEADERS FAIL TO RECOGNIZE EMPLOYEE CONTRIBUTIONS

Of all the ways of failing to value employees, there is one that probably accounts for the greatest number of missed opportunities to pump up engagement: recognizing an employee's accomplishment or contribution as soon as it occurs.

There are understandable, though unacceptable, explanations for why managers and leaders fail to do this:

- ▶ They believe they are too busy to take the time.
- ▶ They actually have the time, but are not paying enough attention to the employee's performance to notice the contribution.
- ▶ They believe "if you don't hear from me, it means you're doing a good job."
- ▶ They believe "employees shouldn't expect me to pat them on the back all the time for just doing their jobs . . . their paycheck should be enough."
- ▶ They are unsure about how best to recognize, so they do nothing.
- ▶ They never received much praise or recognition themselves, so they aren't inclined to give it to others.
- ▶ They believe employees will think they are phony and insincere if they suddenly start praising them.
- ▶ They are concerned that if they give special recognition to some, others will feel unfairly overlooked.
- ▶ They harbor a fundamental disrespect for some types of work or workers.

▶ They believe employees know they're replaceable and shouldn't expect to receive special treatment.

▶ They don't believe they should have to pay employees above market for sustained high performance or provide bonuses for special achievements.

▶ They believe that the employees they recognize will respond by asking for a raise.

▶ They don't know enough about the employees' jobs to distinguish between average and superior performance.

There you have it—a baker's dozen reasons. Having presented and discussed these at length with hundreds of managers in the training we do, we realize that many leaders and managers will remain firm in their resistance to "giving too much recognition" to employees whom they see as "already too entitled" or as "praise hounds who got trophies for just participating and expect more of the same at work." We do not advocate giving more recognition than people deserve. Those whose expectation of recognition exceeds the value they bring should receive the strong dose of reality they need—in the form of direct, fact-based feedback.

> **"We Can't Measure That Job"**
> One line of push back we inevitably get when talking about valuing employees is this tired old dodge: *"Sorry, we would love to do a better job of recognizing employees in this department. But the kinds of jobs they have just don't lend themselves to being measured. And if we can't measure them, then we sure can't figure out how to recognize who's doing a good job and who isn't."*
> Baloney.
> We've spent years working with employees and leaders in every imaginable industry and have yet to find a job that

couldn't be measured. When thinking about the tasks that are part of any job, ask the following questions:

▶ Can you count it?
▶ Can you rank it?
▶ Can you rate it?

You'll be pleasantly surprised at how easy it is, using answers from these three questions, to determine reasonable measures for a job—measures to which everyone can agree. And once that's done, you've just lost another reason not to celebrate the successes of those who are truly making a difference.

All employees deserve to have their contributions acknowledged, not constantly, but meaningfully and sincerely, especially when their contributions are above and beyond what is expected. When we notice moments of engagement and contribution, it takes only five seconds to approach the employee and say, "I saw what you did, and I just want you to know I appreciate it." All the above reasons that managers fail to recognize, combined, don't excuse us for not fully utilizing one of the most powerful motivational tools at our disposal: giving employees a challenge, helping them succeed, and then praising or rewarding them for doing so.

▶ HOW THE BEST MANAGERS PRACTICE DAILY RECOGNITION

Many managers have never been taught the right way to recognize and don't even realize that there is such a thing as a right way. But not knowing gives them pause and reason to fear they could appear awkward and come across as insincere. Here, in brief, are some easy-to-follow steps for effectively acknowledging an employee's contribution:

1. *Observe* the contribution. If you are too busy or preoccupied with your "own work" to observe and recognize your direct reports, then you are not fulfilling your responsibilities as a manager. Like the best athletic coaches, engaging managers spend time daily in directly observing employees' performance and in paying attention to indirect performance indicators so they are prepared to give informed feedback no later than it is needed.

2. *Thank* the employee for the *specific* contribution. Engaging managers never have to worry about coming across as insincere, because they express appreciation for something specific the employee has done. They don't just say, "Good job today." They say, "I noticed you stayed late two hours last night to get the proposal done, and I wanted you to know I appreciate that."

3. *Describe what the contribution meant* to the team and organization as a whole. In other words, how did the business benefit? Many employees fail to see the big picture about the daily value they contribute to the enterprise. Engaging managers "walk the employees downstream" to help them understand the full magnitude of their contributions. *Example:* "Because you offered to stay late and get the report done, we didn't have to call in a temp to do it or call the client to reschedule the presentation."

4. Acknowledge the employee's contribution *as soon as possible*. Engaging managers realize that the time to say thanks is right after the employee's contribution has occurred. With the passage of time the engaging power of the moment is lost or dissipated.

5. Get to know the employee well enough to *be able to tailor the acknowledgment* of the contribution. Engaging managers know that thanking employees for some specific contribution is the mainstay method for recognition. But they also know that personalizing the recognition adds even more engagement power. That's why the best managers go to the trouble to learn in advance how different employees like to be recognized. Some employees, for example, would rather have time off than a spot bonus. Some like the spotlight of public recognition, while others shy away from it.

6. Make an ongoing *commitment* to catching employees doing something right, and use those opportunities to magnify employee engagement.

▶ HOW DO YOU LIKE TO BE RECOGNIZED?

If you're not sure how to tailor recognition to the individual, use the chart that follows and check off all the ways you like to be recognized; then circle your top five. If you don't know how your direct reports would complete the activity, ask them to do it, and then meet to discuss it. You will probably be surprised by what you learn.

Simple appreciation	Salary increase	Public praise
More responsibility	More autonomy	Fun activity
More visibility	Time off	Serve on task force
More flexibility	Favorite work	Promotion
Inclusion in meetings	Trophy or plaque	Learning or training
Peer recognition	Special privilege	Taken to lunch
Face time with the boss	Praised to higher-ups	New assignment
Thoughtful gestures	Cash for great new ideas	Customer recognition

▶ WHAT WE HAVE LEARNED ABOUT PAY

The operative word used in the survey question related to pay is "fair." That seems like a concept that would be open to wide interpretation, but in practice only two themes resonate with employees, who are, in fact, quite clear about what "fair" means to them:

▶ **External equity.** Employees do want to know if their compensation with peers is *generally comparable to what other companies in the market offer.*

▶ **Internal equity.** Employees also want to know if their compensation is on par with what peers in the same job function in their organization receive and is *generally comparable where they currently work.*

Given the wide array of compensation experts and salary surveys on the market, external equity is an area that can be more easily addressed.

Internal equity, on the other hand, may be more difficult to address, often because salary bands tend to recognize tenure, leaving less-tenured employees on the short end of the stick. That, in and of itself, isn't bad except when the criterion of performance is thrown into the mix. We've heard grumbling from some lesser-tenured employees who are more productive—"I'm paid less while what's-his-name, who has been here forever, is sleeping on the job"; that's where internal inequities can generate bad blood.

▶ GETTING DOWN TO BASICS: TWO WAYS OF VIEWING EMPLOYEES

We believe that much of the engagement gap that exists between winning and nonwinning employers boils down to which of two predominating views of employees the leaders hold. While it's hard to say a company is "either-or" on these, and certainly each leader may hold views contrary to the general culture, most organizations tend to lean more one way than the other.

View of employees that predominates at winning employers: *"If we give, employees will give back."*

View of employees that predominates at nonwinning employers: *"If we give to employees, they will take advantage."*

Employee comments such as *"It's like we're guilty until proven innocent"* or *"Our leaders say that if we don't like it here, they can always find someone to take our place*" often betray a mindset that employees are mere commodities, entirely replaceable or expendable, and are constantly looking to avoid doing work. While it is certainly true that employers must continually evaluate whether employees are performing in a way that demonstrates their worth, and that a sense of overentitlement is an issue for many employees, maintaining the right balance between "expecting the best" and "inspecting the work" is the golden mean. We believe that most employers that inspire *"I'm lucky to work here"* exclamations in the *Best-Places-to-Work* survey comments section have managed to find the right balance.

Engaging by Valuing Contributions Despite the Tipping Point of 150

Company growth does not have to mean that employees stop getting the message that they are important and valued in a variety of ways. Here are some practices that allow successful growth companies to maintain a strong sense of family and community:

▶ Reward cross-functional and interoffice teaming and task forces.
▶ Reward group accomplishments with celebrations that create opportunities for socializing and relationship building.
▶ Solicit ideas from all employees regarding company strategies, work processes, and suggestions related to new revenues, innovations, and cost cutting. Reward those that are implemented.

▶ Incorporate extensive relationship-building opportunities into new-hire on-boarding.

▶ Senior leaders make extra efforts to visit all locations, be
visible, and get to know employees.

▶ Hold frequent leader listening sessions and employee
briefings.

▶ Give formal awards for special achievements to employees at all locations and in all divisions.

▶ Senior leaders and managers model a sense of caring
and family by showing personal interest and sensitivity
to employees in times of need.

▶ Be open with information, which serves to build a sense
of community and makes the organization feel smaller.
Leverage social media, such as blogs, wikis, chat rooms,
TelePresence, audioconferencing, and videoconferenc-
ing, to build and maintain a sense of community.

▶ Limit the employee population at all locations to 150
where possible.

▶ HOW VALUING EMPLOYEES MAKES A DIFFERENCE AT JOIE DE VIVRE HOSPITALITY

Started in San Francisco in 1987 by Chip Conley (while in his mid-
twenties) Joie de Vivre Hospitality has built a reputation for creating a unique collection of lifestyle businesses in the United States,
from luxury campgrounds to Japanese communal baths to boutique
motels. Joie de Vivre's brand personality has a lot in common with
the California lifestyle experience: fresh, inventive, casual, and grass-
roots oriented. Given the growth of Joie de Vivre Hotels throughout
the state, Joie de Vivre Hotels is California's largest boutique hotel
company, and it has become a hotel brand synonymous with the California travel experience.

Joie de Vivre Hospitality is the parent company of Joie de Vivre
Hotels and oversees all the other businesses beyond its 38 boutique

hotels, including restaurants, spas, and affiliate hotels. Joie de Vivre Hospitality is also the company that manages the various residential projects that have hotel-like services. In an interview with the *San Francisco Chronicle,* Conley recalled how he decided to name the business he started: "I'm going on this path because I'd better get some joy of life out of it, because I'm not going to make a lot of money. I made $24,000 a year my first two years, which is sort of embarrassing out of Stanford Business School." Joie de Vivre's collection of businesses now has annual revenues of just under $200 million per year.

Conley has said he defines success based on how much joy there is in his life and in other people's lives. That translates into building and sustaining an empowering business culture in spite of rapid growth. As Conley put it, "Most companies lose their culture as they grow. But what Southwest Airlines taught us is that it's all about empowering employees at the lowest level of the company as much as possible."

When JDV Hospitality bought the Kabuki Hot Springs and Spa in San Francisco's Japantown, employees got free communal bathing and 50 percent off on spa treatments. All employees get to stay in JDV hotels for free. Salaried employees receive one month paid sabbatical every three years, even during economic downturns. When the downturn of 2001–2002 hit the hotel industry, Conley didn't take a salary for four years. Senior leaders all took 10 percent pay cuts, and salaried staff accepted pay freezes to avoid mass layoffs. "It was what we needed to do," says Conley, "because we didn't want to kill our culture in the process of suffering through what was our Great Depression."

Conley's passion for building a premier workplace and inspiring others to do so is such that he has written two books, *Peak: How Great Companies Get Their Mojo from Maslow* (Jossey-Bass, 2007) and *The Rebel Rules: Daring to Be Yourself in Busines* (Fireside, 2001).

To learn more about Joie de Vivre's recipe for building a best workplace, we spoke with the company's chief people officer, Jane Howard.

Q: Why is employee recognition so important to Joie de Vivre from a business standpoint?

Howard: *It has been that way since Chip Conley started the company, before I joined almost 10 years ago. Valuing employees was never a conscious business decision. We are just conscious of our values, and one of them is valuing employees highly. We are a very people-centric business, and our people are not as highly paid as in other industries or even as highly as some in the hospitality business. Our philosophy has always been to at least pay at mid-range of what competitors are paying. We are vulnerable because boutique hotels are the first to be hurt by a declining economy. So we have to do something to keep a competitive advantage. For us, it is simple—we treat people so well that we don't have to be the highest paid. We believe in the concept of emotional bank accounts and the importance of making regular deposits. As human beings, we need appreciation, so recognizing people is something we are committed to do, and not just for business reasons.*

Q: How do you go about recognizing your employees?

Howard: *One thing we do is have an employee recognition week every June. We plan and hold more than 100 events up and down the state of California at or near our hotel properties, such as trips to Giants baseball games and, trips to theme parks, and each property has its own event, like ice cream socials. Some hotels do something different every day. For our big end-of-the-year holiday party, we give out lots of awards—for Rising Stars and for Extraordinary Service Providers (our biggest award includes an extra week of vacation plus an extra week's vacation at our domestic location of the employee's choice). We also have the Manuela Ramirez Back-of-the-House Service award, named for an former employee now deceased, and our Above-and-Beyond award.*

Q: What are some of the less formal ways you recognize employees?

Howard: *There are so many ways that I hardly know where to start. One thing we regularly do is, at the end of our weekly executive* *committee meetings, the CEO asks who wants to give recognition to an employee. Of the 18 people on the committee, at least 3 or 4 of them always seem to have a story to tell about an employee who has given extraordinary service. Recently, one of our executive chefs wanted a particular kind of turkey to be available at one of our high-end resorts. She knew she would have to get the turkeys there overnight and that there was no other way to do it except to drive them there herself. So she put 10 of them in the trunk of her car, and that evening she drove them down to our resort in Big Sur. That demonstrated incredible dedication. So, we sent her an e-mail expressing how much she cared and how much we appreciated her dedication to giving above-and-beyond service. She sent us an e-mail back the next day, saying, "Wow—you have no idea how well-timed that was. . . . I was having a really bad day." We have also started telling those kinds of stories at the end of our departmental meetings as well.*

Q: What impact has your approach to employee recognition had on your ability to attract and retain employees?

Howard: *The word has gotten out about us over the years. We continue to attract great people and it's because we are known as very fair, very culture-oriented, and as a company that cares about its employees. Our tagline is "People Matter Here." Since we hire great people, they are often sought out by our competitors and other employers. Sometimes one of our people will leave to accept an attractive offer elsewhere, but they often come back when they realize something important was missing in the new company. Eight months ago our current president, who was then vice president of operations, left to take a real estate job. After being there a while, she said it just wasn't the same, that the new company just didn't think of people, didn't value them, in the same way as we do. People don't often leave us and go to competitors. Usually, it's the other way around.*

Q: Besides recognition, what else do you do to engage and retain employees?

Howard: *We have a sabbatical program for managers. The managers of our properties work very hard—typically 50 or more hours a week—so we give them a month off with pay every three years in addition to regular vacation. We want to give them time to relax deeply. We think that has something to do with our 25 percent manager turnover rate, which is a third of the industry norm.*

Q: What else do you do that's creative or out of the ordinary?
Howard: *Chip Conley started something extraordinary years ago that has had an extremely positive impact, not just for Joie de Vivre, but for the entire hotel industry in the Bay Area. At the time the Bay Area economy was poor, and the lodging industry was particularly hard-hit. It was after the post 9/11 economic downturn. Hotels in the area couldn't pay as much as other industries, and people in the industry—from executives to frontline employees—were feeling demoralized. Great service comes from the heart—from the employee's heart to the guest's heart. Everyone was looking for a way to help people feel good about what they do without having to spend a lot of money. You can't force it to happen . . . it's discretionary. So, Chip had this idea: he would enlist other hotel CEOs in sponsoring a "Hotel Heroes" recognition program. Chip's idea was "let's appeal to their calling, which is to be of service." San Francisco is an expensive city to live in, but we can pay only so much, so we will help them see the value of what they do. So the participating hotels nominated employees they considered to be service heroes. We sold tables to the event, and the response from other hotels was overwhelming. We had a panel of independent judges decide the winners. We will be holding our fourth Hotel Heroes awards banquet next March. This has been very gratifying to see, because it has helped the entire industry and raised our profile in a very positive way as well.*

Q: What advice would you give other companies about creating a culture where employees are valued and recognized?
Howard: *I would suggest they invest in training new managers. We provide intensive training for new managers, emphasizing both the*

art of JDV—the culture and the science of JDV—the operational how-tos. We have JDV University, which offers 150 classes per quarter, and every class furthers the values of the company. We don't want our people to think we see them as just another cog in the wheel. We focus on enriching the whole person, which is why we offer art classes, sports classes, a class on how to be a first-time home buyer, an English-as-a-second-language program, personal financial management, and so many others. We train managers in how to treat their people, recognize them, keep them engaged, and make them want to stay with us. We offer a class that helps employees better understand who they are as a person and what they want to do. We also teach that organizational success is up to all of us and that we have to show initiative and be accountable. Valuing employees also means making sure all human resource processes are fair. So when making decisions that affect people, we make sure we listen to their views.

Q: Some managers don't like recognizing employees because they think the paycheck should be enough. How do you hold managers accountable for recognizing employees?

Howard: *For one thing, we have an item on recognition on our yearly climate survey—"I have been recognized by my supervisors in the last two weeks." We keep track of which managers score low on that statement, and we either coach them or come to a mutual decision that they are not a good fit for us. Managers who don't recognize their people usually don't last long here. When a culture is strong it spits out the people that don't fit. People either get on the bandwagon quickly or they get off quickly. The culture pushes them, plus it's the right thing to do. Some people need permission to be the kind of supervisor that recognizes employees, and we give them that permission. Instead of resisting, most of them say, "This is cool!"*

Q: What else is important for managers to know about recognizing employees?

Howard: *They need to understand that the people giving the most direct service to the customer need the most recognition. For us that* *means recognizing people at the lowest levels the most—those who clean the toilets and make the beds. We want them to know their jobs have meaning. Managers also need to understand that not everyone wants to be recognized publicly. That means they need to know each person individually. We tend to hire people who just naturally do that, who will remember the employees' names and their children's names.*

Q: Do you have bonus or incentive programs?
Howard: *Yes, we have an incentive program for employees who make their financial goals, but we leave the criteria and amounts up to the individual hotels. A room attendant might make an extra $50 if certain financial goals are met, such as efficient utilization of room supplies. Some hotels give gift certificates for Safeway or Starbucks. It's also important to know when to recognize teams as well as individuals. For example, we recognize teams when we open a new hotel property, which is a big production. The hotels that achieve highest customer-satisfaction ratings are recognized at our annual holiday party.*

Q: Valuing employees is about more than just recognition and incentives, isn't it?
Howard: *Absolutely. It's about employees having the right supplies, which is why we ask that question on our employee survey. It's about communicating openly, especially in a difficult economy. We practice open-book management, which sends the message that we respect employees enough to think they deserve to know as much as possible about the business.*

Q: If you were to create a headline that described the approach or philosophy your company takes to recognizing and rewarding employees, what would it be?
Howard: *Help them see the meaning in their work. It's like Chip wrote about in his book,* Peak: How Great Companies Get Their Mojo from Maslow. *Maslow's pyramid of human needs begins with the*

most basic—survival, or money, then moves up to recognition, then up to meaning and mission at the highest point. We try to satisfy all the rungs on the pyramid.

Re-Engaging in Turbulent Times by Valuing Employee Contributions

Against a tide of negativity, uncertainty, rumors, and worry, one of your most powerful weapons is the time and effort you spend letting employees know how much they are valued, especially those who are stepping up their efforts to meet the threats and challenges the organization is facing. Here are some specific ways to send that message:

▶ Listen more than ever to employees' ideas and concerns. Then take action to demonstrate that you weren't just pretending to care.

▶ Show how much you value your employees by continuing to invest in them with training and mentoring, so they will be able to capitalize on new opportunities as difficult times pass.

▶ Recognize and reward employees who go above and beyond and make sacrifices for the good of the company.

▶ Challenge all supervisors to notice and appreciate all employee contributions. This may require that you first step up your efforts to recognize the supervisors themselves. Spread the word about customer success stories. In times when bad news spreads like wildfire, good news is the only way to really fight it.

▶ Advocate strongly for fixing the pay system if it's broken. Perceptions of internal pay inequity and lack of competitiveness with the outside market are only heightened in uncertain times. If people don't know how pay increases and bonuses are determined, start informing them. If pay is perceived as not linked to performance, do everything in your power to establish that link.

▶ Celebrate team accomplishments to reinforce the need for the group cohesion and teamwork that are required in times of intense challenge.

▶ Confront poor performers. In hard times, good performers lose motivation when they see poor performers tolerated. "Why should I work so hard," some ask themselves, "when there's no consequence for being a slacker?"

▶ Resist the temptation to "crank up the negative consequences." Leaders at all levels feel the pressure in difficult times, and the natural impulse for some will be to "motivate" with threats and fear. This may produce compliance, but it won't inspire commitment.

▶ A CHECKLIST OF TEAMWORK BEST PRACTICES FOR VALUING EMPLOYEE CONTRIBUTIONS IN ALL TIMES

Though recognition philosophies and practices may vary from firm to firm, what follows are some of the practices used by successful employers. Check those that you believe your organization is currently doing well, and place an X next to those you believe you should be doing or doing significantly better:

__ Train managers intensively in the basics of effective informal recognition.

__ Supplement manager training with employee recognition "tool kits" containing sample recognition letters, thank-you cards, electronic tips and reminders, merchandise and service coupons, and an electronic inventory of ways employees like to be recognized.

__ Selectively supplement informal recognition processes with more formal awards and recognition programs that build support for the culture, values, and business objectives.

___ Use committees, not individuals, to increase fairness in evaluating winners of formal awards.

___ Create opportunities for both team and individual recognition and awards.

___ Make sure employees are well-informed about the formal award nomination-and-selection process and the criteria for selecting winners.

___ Do not allow formal programs to dilute the focus on managers' daily delivery of informal recognition.

___ Look for opportunities to acknowledge contributions with sincere appreciation.

___ Encourage peer recognition by introducing new and more formal processes such as bravo cards, pass-around trophies, peer-nominated awards, and redeemable-points programs.

___ Solicit and facilitate customer recognition of employees who exceed their expectations.

___ Make new hires feel welcome and important.

___ Ask for employee input, then listen, and then respond.

___ Keep employees "in the loop."

___ Reward results with variable pay aligned with business goals.

___ Reward results with pay increases or bonuses big enough to motivate higher performance.

___ Monitor the pay system to ensure fairness, efficiency, consistency, accuracy, and openness.

___ Look for ways to increase on-the-spot recognition using cash.

___ Involve employees in designing new pay systems.

___ Provide the right tools, equipment, data, resources, and staff assistance.

___ Keep the physical environment fit to work in.

▶ FINAL THOUGHTS

A young doctoral student, after the birth of his first child, penned a doctoral dissertation titled "Ten Perfect Ideas for Successful Parenting." A few years later, after he and his wife had a second child, his new circumstances and experiences with the second of his offspring led him to change the dissertation content to "Ten Decent Good Ideas for Successful Parenting."

And what happened to the dissertation after he had his third child? He threw it away.

We know how each child is valued can be as different as the number in the flock. The same is true for our employees. Each employee with whom we work also has very different needs, goals, and a "definition of success" unlike any other.

We've gotten used to the old industrial model of management, one that came out of the manufacturing plants of titans like Henry Ford and Alfred Sloan. In this model of factory production it was important that each employee worked as a cog in the wheel of industry. Although that model of management worked well in the Industrial Age, this cookie-cutter approach should end up on the scrap heap with the Atari Computer and leisure suits.

Medical science is furiously working toward the development of drugs and therapies that would be unique to each person—customized, if you will—to each person's particular immune response. Cancer vaccines, for example, are being developed that use part of the patient's own cells to create a therapy designed just for that person—a targeted versus a shotgun approach. We need to take the same attitude to valuing employees. Each person we have the privilege to lead has different interests, desires, talents, and needs. Once we truly attempt to understand individual employees, we can be in a much better position to create the environment that is conducive to each person's success.

Call it "designer engagement."

▶ CHAPTER NINE

Employee Well-Being

The Ultimate Benefit

An ounce of prevention is worth a pound of cure.
—BENJAMIN FRANKLIN

▶ KIM'S STORY: "LIE DOWN UNTIL IT PASSES"

Kim really hates to exercise.

She hates everything about it—the time, the sweat, the pain. Consequently, she doesn't work out much. In fact, Kim has a catchy one-liner ready when it comes to discussing the topic with family or friends: *"Every time I get the feeling to exercise, I lie down until it passes."*

In her heart of hearts, Kim knew she should be working out more often. She had a closet full of clothes that didn't fit. She found herself getting easily fatigued, even on short walks with her dogs in the park. Then Kim faced some difficult news—her blood pressure was up, and her triglycerides were elevated. Kim knew her days of double cheeseburgers and chili dogs as a basic food group in the company lunchroom were limited.

By the way, did we mention that Kim is the human resources director where she works? Kim found her health condition and attitude toward well care ironic, because, as the HR leader, she knew she should be leading the charge in employee health and well-being. She should be the one getting programs in place that help employees (including those like her) take more responsibility for their health and well-being.

The bad news kept coming: the health benefits broker informed her that the company premium for the next year would be increasing . . . dramatically. The increase was in large part due to significant claim activity for employees with heart and diabetes problems, two conditions that she knew can often be managed more effectively by making lifestyle changes than dousing them with medications.

Kim considered her situation: was it time to put away the glib jokes and change her personal and professional point of view? She decided that if she was going to be the leader of wellness where she worked, she should start this movement, literally and figuratively, herself. Her doctor cleared her for moderate exercise and suggested a diet that included more fresh fruit and vegetables and fewer chili dogs—no big surprise there.

Several of her friends exercised in the mornings, but that didn't fit Kim's work schedule. She found that a couple of friends took an exercise class three times a week right after work. That made some sense. Her doctor told her to commit to the new regimen for 30 days. The first week or so was miserable; she felt embarrassed to be so out of shape, but she kept going in spite of her feelings. She also found some low-calorie recipes on the Internet that sounded—and, as she found out later, tasted—pretty good.

At the end of the month Kim noticed several positive changes: a little weight loss and more sound sleep, and most important, she felt better about herself. She still doesn't love to work out, but she loves the benefits.

Kim had also been doing her homework about a worksite wellness program, and what she had discovered was exciting. It looked like many employers who were making an investment in wellness were seeing positive results for themselves and their employees.

The company president, an avid runner and tennis player, took quickly to Kim's proposal for an employer-supported wellness initiative. Kim told her that the program did require some investment and commitment from senior leadership, but it would pay many dividends, including a reduction in claims for incidences that could be prevented or lessened with changes in lifestyle.

The early results are beyond Kim's expectations: more employees participating in the wellness programs than hoped for, including a very successful on-site health fair. The company now has plans to expand its diabetes and cardio well-care programs, has partnered with a local fitness consultant to provide some on-site classes, and has dramatically changed the cafeteria menu—more salads and, yes, fewer chili dogs. It's too early to see if claim activity will be significantly impacted, but the initial results are promising.

▶ THE CHANGING LANDSCAPE OF BENEFITS IN THE ENGAGEMENT EQUATION

Ten or fifteen years ago, many who studied and wrote about employee engagement focused very little attention on the role of employee benefits (health insurance, pensions, and the like) as an engagement driver. Most placed far more emphasis on the ongoing daily feeling that an employee has about her or his work experience or quality of supervision. The conventional wisdom seemed to be that employee benefits were not necessary and essential for employee engagement in the same way as quality of leadership or good teamwork was.

The prevailing opinion seemed to be that employee benefits were really important at two times in the life of an employee: *when the employee changed jobs* ("How do my benefits at my new employer compare with those of my old company?") and *when there was a need to use the benefits* ("My son just broke his four front teeth; what are my dental benefits?" or "I'm retiring soon; what's the state of my pension?"). In

ployee benefits were important intermittently, but not
asis.

mployee benefits are, and always will be, an important component of an overall compensation and benefits package. If
an employer is too far "below market" in terms of available overall
benefits and "workforce-friendly" services, there might be negative
repercussions in the employer's ability to recruit and retain employees.
But until recently, there has not been much discussion about whether
employee benefits—both the benefits themselves and the perception
of how competitive they are in the marketplace—actually have an impact on employee engagement.

As we mentioned in Chapter 3, employee benefits were important,
showing some relationship to overall employee engagement when we
began these studies in 2004, but were no better than middle of the
pack when it came to explaining the variance of employee engagement scores between winning and nonwinning *Best-Places-to-Work*
employers.

That was then, and this is now.

The more recent data are quite clear; 2 of the 10 survey items
that best predicted overall employee engagement scores are the two
employee benefits statements included in the *Best-Places-to-Work*
survey:

> *"My benefits meet my (and my family's) needs well."*
> *"We have benefits not typically available at other organizations."*

The differences on these items between winning companies and
nonwinners are graphically represented in Figure 9.1.

We are not, by the way, the only researchers to come to this conclusion. A study carried out by Hewitt Associates determined that
"highly engaged employees experience better health and overall well-
being." As Hewitt's Neil Crawford noted:

> The 115,000 employees surveyed as part of the 2009 study clearly
> revealed that high engagement goes hand in hand with better

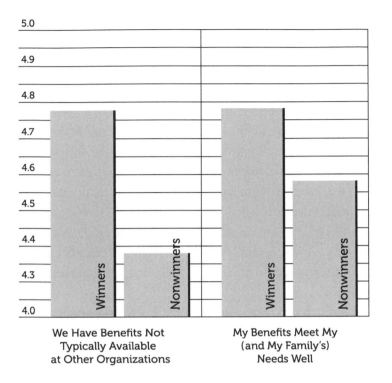

Figure 9.1

health and well-being. . . . Employees at organizations with high engagement reported better physical health, lower job stress and work overload, and greater financial security. In addition, they also believe that their employer's benefits plan contributes to their overall well-being, although there is room for improvement with respect to retirement savings programs.[1]

Our analysis of the anecdotal comments shows an expanded definition of benefits, a broader characterization that goes beyond health care and retirement. Employees and employers alike now talk about "work-life balance," a term less known in the business world 20 years ago, but now accepted more widely as something an employer must consider when thinking about this engagement driver, especially for younger workers.

▶ IGNORE THIS TODAY AND RISK YOUR CORPORATE HEALTH

We recall a conversation with a corporate client who had participated in a *Best-Places* event in 2005. The overall results for this client were solid—good, with room to grow. We were facilitating a planning session with the company's senior leaders, looking at a few issues that seemed worthy of action planning related to management, career development, and benefits. The company's results for the two benefits items on the survey were mediocre. Employees' anecdotal comments indicated their concerns about the quality of health-care benefits, including the portion employees were required to pay. There were also complaints about the retirement plan, which, in this case, didn't match up well with those of the company's competitors.

As the discussion continued, the CEO, after digesting all the data, remarked: "I'm not happy about the concerns about our employee benefits. But I don't think we're losing any employees, nor having difficulty recruiting employees because of this. I think we can prioritize our efforts elsewhere." The members of the executive group discussed the matter and agreed that their energies could be best served addressing other recruiting and retention drivers.

At the time we didn't offer much resistance to their reasoning, agreeing with the CEO about the potential impact of the survey results for employee benefits and their impact on employee engagement. With the passage of time and changing circumstances, the sands of employee engagement have shifted under us. Consider the following news items that have graced our media outlets in the ensuing years,

▶ HEALTH-CARE SPENDING

According to a study published by Reuters, health-care spending will hit $2.5 trillion in 2009, devouring 17.6 percent of the economy. The study reported: "That would mark the biggest one-year increase recorded since the government began tracking the data in 1960."[2]

▶ UNPAID MEDICAL BILLS

More and more Americans are struggling to avert a significant crisis—unpaid medical bills. The *New York Times* cites two studies by the Kaiser Family Foundation and the Center for Studying Health System Change, which were completed in 2008 before the financial markets reached a state of crisis. Policy analysts said the findings underscored the additional strain that medical care had placed on working Americans.[3]

▶ SOARING PREMIUM COSTS

In Omaha, Nebraska, the city's health care costs increased 17 percent from 2007 to 2008—a staggering burden for the 3,800 employees and retirees.[4] Sad to say, this increase is common for many employers.

▶ RETIREMENT WORRIES

In March of 2009 only one in three Americans believed they would be able to fully retire as huge losses in home and stock prices dented their confidence in the future. Just 32 percent of Americans thought they could someday stop working altogether, down from 39 percent from the 2008 survey. That represented an 18 percent decrease in just one year, and a 22 percent decline from the 2007 survey. "Americans anticipate having to work longer, as their nest eggs have been shrinking and the economy has made it harder to save," said Chris Moloney, chief marketing officer at Scottrade.[5]

Some diseases, which many would consider highly preventable, are skyrocketing in claim activity.

▶ THE COST OF DISEASE MISMANAGEMENT—DIABETES

As diabetes is rapidly becoming one of the world's most common diseases, its financial cost has been mounting—to well over $200 billion a year in the United States alone. One recent study put the total at $218 billion in 2007.[6]

> ▶ THE CONSEQUENCES OF DISEASE MISMANAGEMENT—KIDNEY DISEASE
> An analysis of federal health data published in November 2008 in
> the *Journal of the American Medical Association* found that 13 percent
> of American adults—about 26 million people—had chronic kidney
> disease, up from 10 percent, or about 20 million people, a decade
> earlier. "We've had a marked increase in chronic kidney disease in
> the last 10 years, and that continues with the baby boomers coming
> into retirement age," said Dr. Frederick J. Kaskel, director of pe-
> diatric nephrology at the Children's Hospital at Montefiore in the
> Bronx. "The burden on the health care system is enormous, and it's
> going to get worse.[7]

An intriguing article in the *New York Times* revealed that some actually make decisions about marriage based on health-care benefits.

> ▶ AFFECTING FAMILIES
> In a 2008 Kaiser Family Foundation poll, 7 percent of adults said
> someone in their household had married in the past year to gain
> access to insurance. The foundation cautioned that the number
> should not be taken literally, but rather as an intriguing indicator
> that some Americans "are making major life decisions on the basis
> of health care concerns."[8]

Whether we agree with the moral implications of these results,
it is clear that the availability of benefits is becoming an increasingly
important aspect of our lives, which strongly equates to the perceived
quality of our overall work experience.

Regardless of the causes, employers must now seriously consider
whether their employee benefits package is impacting their overall
employee engagement. We understand there can be considerable expense in such an undertaking, but our data strongly suggest that employees, whether they even realize it or not, have a strong need for
quality employee benefits; and if they don't have them, they are not as
likely to give more discretionary effort in their jobs.

We recently worked with a CEO who wanted to conduct a series of
employee focus groups after receiving the organization's *Best-Places-to-*

Work survey results. A common employee complaint was having to give back most of their salary increase from the previous year because of an increase in their share of the health-care premium. One employee remarked: "Twice a month I look at my paycheck and realize that I'm just working to pay for my health insurance." To this employee and many others, employee benefits are no longer an "intermittent" need, but one that hits home with every paycheck. Because of the reasons already stated, the quality of benefits, or lack thereof, is now "top of mind" for employees. It is no longer an episodic driver—important when we change jobs or when we have claim activity. It is now a full-fledged driver that most employees see and feel at the same level of importance as the other five drivers we outlined in the previous chapters.

▶ EMPLOYEES WEIGH IN ABOUT BENEFITS

Although the above comments speak volumes, here are additional comments selected from both the engaged and disengaged who participated in *Best-Places-to-Work* events over the last several years:

Voices of Engagement

▶ "I have worked for two other large corporations in the past, and the benefits I receive now are head and shoulders above any former place of employment."

▶ "I came on with an agreement that I would work part-time, and the firm has been tremendously accommodating. I accrue benefits at a part-time rate (vacation and sick time) and get employer-provided life insurance and long-term disability insurance. My hourly rate is extremely fair, and I have the flexibility that I need because I want to have time with my family."

Voices of Disengagement

▶ "They need to keep a close eye on employee benefits. It seems the coverage continues to decline, yet the cost continues to rise. This is a problem nationwide as I understand it. But that doesn't mean our company has to follow suit with the rest of the pack."

▶ "We need better benefits . . . vacation, holiday, and sick leave are horrible."

▶ "The company should provide benefits without punishing those who use them."

▶ *"The company takes care of their employees and makes sure that we have amazing benefits. They are constantly going above and beyond and creating fun days for the employees. They reach out to the community in a big way each year."*

▶ *"My family really enjoys the benefit of me working for such a large company that cares about its people. My health insurance and benefits coverage is outstanding, but it is the 'goes the extra mile' things that the company does to make working here so much fun. Besides department team-building activities, we also have fun family activities. This past year I've enjoyed going to baseball and hockey games, participating in the corporate cup run, and other various activities all provided. Having free bagels and donuts on Fridays, having occasional celebrations like the pancake feast, and having kids make the artwork for our new building—all great benefits that no one else provides for their employees."*

▶ *"They are sensitive to, and place value on, the employee's family life."*

▶ *"I think that with the company having mostly women working for them, they should have paid maternity leave. That would benefit more than half of the staff."*

▶ *"There needs to be an IRA match program established. There are no benefits—insurance or dental— for part-time employees."*

▶ *"There's too long of a wait period for benefits to start for new employees."*

▶ *"Offer more health insurance benefit choices."*

▶ *"We have a number of part-time staff (less than 30 hours/week) that we have trouble keeping more than a year because we can't offer them benefits. It would be nice to do so."*

▶ *"Provide additional benefits, such as flexible hours, casual dress, and work-from-home opportunities."*

▶ *"Pay more of our benefits so that some employees do not have to apply for state aid for their insurance benefits. Raises barely cover the increased costs of insurance benefits each year. Thus salaries stay rather flat."*

▶ *"Child-care benefit would help ease many employees' burden in this area so that they can be even more focused at work not having this issue to cope with."*

▶ *"We can improve our benefits offerings to make them more flexible so that employees feel their personal needs are being taken care of and they can concentrate more on their work."*

▶ *"The flextime, 401(k) match, and paid individual medical benefits keep me here. My pay is low compared with similar positions in my field, so if any of these benefits disappeared, I would seek another job. But as long as those three things remain, and the people in my department remain of the same caliber of professionalism, I will stay. I am able to be a single mother who supports her family with just one job and about 30% from my parents, instead of more, thanks to the flextime that allows me to juggle doctor trips, parent-teacher meetings, and family emergencies. The 401(k) match allows me to provide a half-way decent retirement plan. I'm grateful for what the firm provides."*

▶ *"This company cares; my wife became very ill and eventually passed away. They provided assurance, compassion, and support. They gave me the greatest gift of all—time to be with my wife during her illness. This is highly unusual as I had been with the company only months when we discovered the illness. God bless this company."*

▶ *"Overall, I like my job, and it fits into my current schedule. The one thing I have trouble with is getting time off. I feel they could be more flexible. For instance, I once had a doctor's appointment that I had to schedule far in advance. I gave notice that I would be unable to work that afternoon, about a month and a half in advance. I was given a form e-mail response saying that it couldn't be guaranteed, and that it would depend on the call volume that day. I ended up being scheduled that day and had to talk to someone to switch my schedule. It made a stressful situation worse. With situations like this it is hard to say that I really feel valued as a person."*

▶ TWO VERY DIFFERENT MINDSETS EMERGE

As we review the difficult news about employee benefits and look at the gaps between the haves and have-nots, several important themes begin to emerge. They tell a story of companies that are taking very different approaches to the well-being of their employees. It reminds us of those conversations one hears about "different world views" on a particular topic—two perspectives that vary greatly in how they regard the subject. Let's look at these mindsets and then review their implications.

Old Mindset

▶ Some employers are just trying to "get by," offering only the bare minimum of resources . . .

▶ Some employers see their workforce only in the context of what happens during work hours . . .

▶ Some employers are making it the "problem of the employee" by directing all additional costs to the employee side of the balance sheet . . .

▶ Some employers blindly continue paying more claims related to diseases largely seen as driven by poor lifestyle . . .

▶ Some employers see benefits as an expense that drains resources from the bottom line . . .

▶ Some employers see benefits as a "one-size-fits-all" proposition, harking to the words of Henry Ford, who told buyers they could have their car any color they want as long as it was black . . .

New Mindset

▶ . . . while others are making genuine efforts to meet the needs of their employees.

▶ . . . while others realize that employees have lives outside of work that must be understood and appreciated.

▶ . . . while others work to collaborate in partnership with the employee.

▶ . . . while others want to "fix the problem before it starts" by emphasizing prevention and well-care practices.

▶ . . . while others see it as a long-term investment that can reap generous returns by making employees more productive.

▶ . . . while others look to tailor their offerings to meet the needs of various constituent groups of employees who may have different needs.

We find it interesting that companies are going in such divergent directions when it comes to thinking about the health and well-being of their employees. As we were trying to articulate what *Best-Places* employers are doing to build overall employee engagement through this driver, we came across a Hewitt survey report on employer-sponsored health benefits in which 4 percent of companies reported they are taking steps today that will enable them to discontinue offering health-care benefits, while 19 percent indicated that they are moving away from directly providing health-care benefits—up from 4 percent in 2008. Hewitt surveyed more than 340 employers, representing more than 5 million workers. "In today's environment, employers are under pressure to cut health-care expenses, but they realize that short-term cost-management tactics do not address the underlying drivers of health-care costs," says Jim Winkler, head of Hewitt's North American health management consulting practice. "This leaves them with two options: making a long-term commitment to improving the health of employees and their families, or exiting health care altogether," he adds.[9]

We note that the mindset of many employers is to distance themselves from employee health and well-being benefits. However, winning *Best-Places-to-Work* employers are, in fact, going in the other direction.

One CEO at a *Best-Places* employer said to us: "Any time budget cutting is mentioned in the employee benefit section, it is dismissed as an option by our team. Our company finds other areas to adjust so that employee benefits can remain as a meaningful part of the value proposition for employees." Another stated: "Senior management regularly evaluates associates' benefits with the intent of maintaining, or enhancing, the value of our benefits package in a manner that does not increase their financial burden. Over the past several years we have as a corporation absorbed more and more of the burden of increased costs in order to invest in our long-term relationship with our associates."

There were times when these CEOs doubted the wisdom of their stands, they confessed. Acting on this new mindset isn't always the easiest thing to do, and in difficult times might be seen as folly. But the employee engagement results that so many of these winning employers have achieved prove what is possible and give cause for aspiring *Best-Places* employers to stand firm as well. Here's a snapshot of how Gaylord Hotels, one of our featured employers, has taken up this commitment. General manager of the Orlando property, Kemp Gallineau:

We have fitness centers just for our Stars [their term for employees], *and cafeterias that are second to none and on par with what we offer guests. We serve our Stars healthy menu items, not leftovers from banquets. We know we have to give something to employees for them to want to give back to us. Over St. Patrick's Day, we held a day of classes to teach employees about personal finance, how and when, and whether to refinance their houses, how to manage their 401(k) investments, and many other topics. Because of the declining economy, some employees were pulling money out of their 401(k)s out of sheer panic, so we decided to educate them about alternatives that wouldn't deplete their savings. We have family movie nights where employees can bring their significant others and kids and get to know other families. We have health and wellness fairs. We also provide mobile mechanic service at a discount where employees can have their cars serviced right in our own auto garage. If they need more serious repair work, we provide a shuttle to take them back and forth to their dealership or mechanic.*

Gallineau continued with this touching, powerful story:

We have a group of leaders that cared enough about an employee who was about to lose his house through foreclosure that they stepped in and helped him save it. They chipped in and made his house payment. The employee's father in Haiti had died around that same time, and the employee didn't have enough money to go to the funeral, so they stepped in and paid for that, too. They took it upon themselves to do something about it. We have had other employees this year who almost lost their houses, and their coworkers pitched in to keep it from happening—not just managers, but line-level Stars as well. They weren't looking for recognition, just the satisfaction of helping a fellow human being. I think it also says something about our culture that employees can feel comfortable enough here to make themselves vulnerable, to open up with their coworkers and trust them enough tell them what's going on in their lives, knowing they will be compassionate.

With a clear and determined mindset, Gaylord Hotels embodies the spirit of this universal engagement driver. This caring mindset guides the organization's actions, and these actions have led to remarkably low employee turnover and high guest satisfaction in perhaps the most competitive hospitality market in the world.

Engaging and Re-Engaging the Four Generations with a Focus on Well-Being

Each employee's challenges and needs are individual ones, not generational, as we have emphasized before. Nevertheless, there may be value in presenting a few suggestions for enhancing employee well-being that commonly arise among various age groups and may be applicable to all. Our intent is to alert you to needs that more frequently occur and should be addressed, not to reinforce assumptions and stereotypes that may not necessarily apply to any given employee within these generations.

Traditionalists (born before 1946) and Boomers (born 1946–1964)

▶ Anticipate early retirement and plan for succession.
▶ Allow phased retirement, part-time work, and consulting opportunities.
▶ Encourage flexible work arrangements you do for other generations.
▶ Focus them on preventative health and wellness practices, such as better diet and more exercise.

▶ Consider providing new benefits, such as grandchild care.

▶ Don't make assumptions, such as "They won't care about tuition reimbursement."

▶ Include them in relationship-building activities with younger employees.

Gen Xers (born 1965–1980)

▶ Provide benefits for those building new families, such as home loan assistance, child-care subsidies, vacation, and time off.

▶ Offer tuition reimbursement to promote continuous learning.

▶ Allow flexible schedules and a telecommuting option when possible.

▶ Provide elder care and child care.

▶ Allow and create opportunities for fun at work.

Millennials (born 1981–1994)

Same as above, plus:

▶ Create opportunities for internal social activities and social networking.

▶ Encourage community involvement and volunteer activities.

All four generations

▶ Ask employees what benefits and services they most want and need, making sure that all age groups are represented in focus groups and on benefits committees.

▶ Offer a broad array of choices so employees can pick and choose the benefits that meet their individual or family needs.

▶ Maintain sufficient staffing to guard against employee burnout.

▶ *BEST-PLACES-TO-WORK* PROFILE: CREATING A CULTURE OF WELL-BEING AT VERTEX PHARMACEUTICALS

We believe that new mindsets can lead to new approaches that can address pressing health-care needs and rising costs. We illustrate this by telling the story of a winning *Best-Places-to-Work* company that is sorting these priorities in such a way that both employees and employers are winning:

Vertex Pharmaceuticals Incorporated, Cambridge, Massachusetts, is a global biotechnology company committed to the discovery and development of breakthrough small-molecule drugs for serious diseases. The company's strategy is to commercialize its products both independently and in collaboration with major pharmaceutical companies.

With 1,400 employees, including 200 in San Diego and 100 in the United Kingdom, Vertex added 300 new employees last year, including many top scientists, who are attracted to the company's mission—"innovate to redefine health and transform lives with new medicines." The company's recruiting brochure pledges a workplace "where each day feels more like an experience than a job. . . . Where quality of life is a way of life, and passion is always tangible." The company's high scores on the *Best-Places-to-Work* survey are evidence that Vertex has indeed built a special culture; it received one of the highest scores in the United States on employee well-being.

The company, which has a self-insured medical plan, chose benefits that provide employees with choice, flexibility, financial protection against catastrophic loss or hardship, and health and financial wellness. The basic benefits platform divides offerings into standard, nonstandard, and voluntary, which are 100 percent employee-paid, and two more: unique benefits and wellness. Here is the full list:

Standard (designed to protect)

▶ Medical
▶ Prescription

- Dental
- Life and accidental death and disability
- Short- and long-term disability
- Flexible spending
- Employee assistance program
- 401(k) (contributes up to 60 percent of pay with 100 percent employer match of first 3 percent contributed to plan and 50 percent of next 3 percent with 100 percent immediate vesting)
- Relocation assistance

Nonstandard (designed to attract)

- Investment education
- Back-up child care
- Elder-care services
- Twelve weeks paid maternity leave
- Two weeks paid paternity leave
- Two weeks paid adoption leave
- Service awards
- Employee stock purchase plan
- Educational assistance

Voluntary benefits (designed to support)

- Supplemental life and accidental death and disability
- Spousal life and child life
- Vision plan
- Long-term care
- Prepaid legal plan
- Discount home and auto insurance
- Discount banking program
- Discount entertainment tickets program
- Discount pet insurance

Unique Benefits (designed to retain)

▶ Four weeks paid vacation
▶ Child-care subsidy
▶ Generous transit pass subsidy
▶ Free on-site parking
▶ Annual financial and health fairs
▶ On-site mammogram
▶ Meeting-free days
▶ Education advisory services

Sample wellness programs (designed for care)

▶ On site: fitness center, chair massage, yoga, Weight Watchers, flu shots, lactation rooms
▶ Educational seminars, first aid, CPR training
▶ Lunchtime walking programs
▶ Healthy food options in vending machines and cafeteria
▶ Wellness weeks with on-site annual screenings
▶ Discount and reimbursement program—gym memberships, weight loss, nutrition, and more
▶ Online personal health assessments

Vertex holds three core values dear, expressed as follows: Fearless Pursuit of Excellence, Innovation is our Lifeblood, and "We" Wins, meaning success through teamwork. We spoke with Lisa Kelly-Croswell, senior vice president of human resources, and Marie Noel, associate director of employee benefits, to find out more about the firm's employee benefits, the philosophy behind those benefits, and how they serve the business strategy.

Q: Of all the benefits you offer, which ones do you think account for the high scores you received on that factor?
Kelly-Croswell: *Well, it's really the whole range of benefits and our overall approach to employee well-being. But if you're asking me to*

identify the benefits that most distinguish Vertex, I would say first it's the four weeks of vacation every employee gets from day one, and next would be our child-care subsidy. The subsidy is available to Dependent care FSA Plan participants and is delivered in the form of an employer match, which is up to $1,000 per year. We are the only company in the Boston area or in our industry I know of that does that. After those two, I would say our generous paid maternity and paternity leaves, our Employee Stock Purchase Plan, and our medical and dental plans, where we rank in the 100th percentile of low employee contribution rate.

Q: How would you describe your overall approach and philosophy about benefits and employee well-being?
Kelly-Croswell: *We want our employees to be focused on their work and the very important mission that brought them here, so our approach is to remove any obstacles that may stand in the way of us delivering on our mission to transform lives with new medicines. The other part of our philosophy is tied to our core value of innovation—we want employees to be innovative and we as a company want to set the example by offering innovative benefits.*

Q: In most companies it's not easy to put new benefits in place. Are you continuing to introduce new benefits?
Kelly-Croswell: *Absolutely. We try to keep our fingers on the pulse of what employees need. We have introduced several new benefits just in the last three years. More than 50 percent of our workforce is in their 20s and 30s, and we know younger people value time off to have a life outside work. All our employees work very hard and deserve some discretionary time. We used to offer three weeks vacation and four weeks after five years. In an executive meeting a couple of years ago I suggested we go to four weeks from day one of employment, and our CEO said, "Sure . . . let's do it!" It was surprisingly easy to get the policy changed. We had a focus group to gauge employee reaction, which was extremely positive, then announced the new policy two*

weeks later at an all-employee meeting. We even added another week for employees who hit the five-year mark.

Q: Do most employees take the full four weeks vacation each year?

Noel: *Yes, most do because the vacation days do not carry over into the next year, except for California. We also remind employees that in order to deliver the high level of productivity expected, we need everyone to be refreshed, energized, and productive. Still, many don't take the time they have coming to them because they are so committed to our mission.*

Q: I would think the generous vacation time would be a great attraction for new recruits.

Noel: *It definitely is. That was part of the reason for doing it; it helps us stand out as an employer of choice. Many of our new hires come from larger pharmaceutical companies and yet are very impressed with our benefit offerings. Our HR generalists conduct "90-day check-ins" with new hires to get their evaluation of the on-boarding process and employee benefits always gets the highest rating.*

Q: Do you try to provide benefits to appeal to all age groups and life stages?

Noel: *Yes, we do, in fact. It's important to offer meaningful benefits to all employees. When we communicate our benefits to employees, we show examples of benefits that tend to be used by people in their age group. For example, employees in their 20s tend to be concerned about career development, therefore they may take advantage of the tuition reimbursement program and our on-site training and mentoring programs. Employees in their 30s may be thinking about starting a family or concerned about child care, saving to buy a home, or paying off credit card debts, therefore they may take advantage of the child-care subsidy, backup child-care services, investment education seminars, and the banking and discount mortgage programs. Employees in their 40s may be facing elder-care issues and/or concerned about paying* *for their children's college education. They may take advantage of educational advisory services through College Coach, backup elder-care services through Parents in a Pinch, or utilizing Worklife EAP services. Employees in their 50s and 60s they may be thinking about retirement, and may start to reevaluate their 401(k), long-term care insurance, and take advantage of our investment education sessions.*

Q: What preventative measures have you taken in your benefit programs?

Noel: *About three years ago, we initiated an employee health and financial wellness program. Our goal was to educate in leading healthy life styles in a fun and informative manner. We recognize that healthy, happy employees have a direct impact on overall pro-ductivity, creativity and the sustained success of our company.*

Q: What are some other unique aspects of the Vertex approach to wellness?

Kelly-Croswell: *We have a very active (20-member) Employee Wellness committee that represents all areas of the company as well as the different sites. Committee members meet once or twice a month to help research and plan wellness activities, such as Wii bowling tournaments, wear-red-to-work day, and lunchtime walking com-petitions. The program is also unique because the committee sponsors a one-week-long health and wellness fair in the Spring and a one-week-long financial wellness fair in the Fall. Most companies offer a one-day health fair per year and do not include a financial wellness component. At Vertex, we spread the activities, such as seated chair massage and cholesterol/vision/hearing testing, over several days to give all employees an opportunity to participate.*

Another unique component to our wellness program is the part-nership we have with the Dana Farber Cancer Institute–Boston Mammography Van to deliver mammogram screening at our facili-ties. Friends and family members are invited to participate. We work closely with our medical insurance administrator to identify the top claims categories that could have been potentially prevented with an aggressive wellness initiative. For a couple of years, breast cancer was in the top five "potentially preventable" category.

We also offer quarterly educational seminars on various health topics. We have an on-site fitness center that is well used, yoga and Weight-Watchers groups, nutritional counseling, flu shots, lunchtime walking programs, healthy food options in our vending machines and cafeteria, and much more.

For financial wellness week in the fall, we highlight all our financial protection programs, including our group legal plan, life insurance, long-term care, and 401(k). We also offer a series of Investment Education workshops every quarter—from the basics to the more advanced.

Q: Have any employees actually been diagnosed with illnesses as a result of a wellness initiative?

Noel: *One of our female employees, a scientist, was diagnosed with breast cancer. She was not diagnosed during one of the on-site mammogram screenings, but she was definitely one of the reasons why we decided to provide on-site annual screenings for the convenience of the employee. The female scientist was able to receive treatment under our health plan with virtually no out-of-pocket costs. She also received 12 weeks short-term disability benefits at 100 percent pay. She recovered fully and returned to work with praise for the company. She was appreciative because she didn't have to worry about the financial aspect and could just focus on getting well.*

So far, out of 280 eligible women, 30 have had their annual mammograms on site. At least 2 women this year have been identified as having abnormal results and needed follow up with their primary care provider.

Q: Do you have evidence that these wellness initiatives are working?

Noel: *Yes, we do. One piece of evidence is the fact that absenteeism is very low. Over 90 percent of our leaves of absence are related to either maternity or paternity leave. We have about 50 to 60 babies* *born under our health plan each year. All of the mothers are returning after taking the three months of paid maternity leave. Other evidence is that our overall health-care costs are usually at or below market trends.*

Q: Are your employees sharing more of the costs of health care, like at most companies?

Noel: *Yes, even before the downturn of 2008 we were moving in the direction of transferring cost sharing to employees in concert with our prevention initiatives. About three years ago employees paid zero to 10 percent of health-care costs. Today employees are paying about 13 percent and, by the start of next year, most will be paying 14 percent. We have no plans to go higher than that. There has been no backlash from employees over cost sharing because employees do compare the actual dollar amount they pay for health care versus what their friends and family pay, and they realize that what Vertex charges is still much lower than what other companies charge their employees.*

Q: Are there other new benefits you'd like to comment on?

Noel: *Yes, it's interesting that we were thinking about emphasizing financial wellness even before the financial crisis. We were already planning to hold our first annual financial wellness week. We have 401(k) and Employee Stock Purchase Plan providers come and do seminars. We also instituted College Coach recently, where we provide counseling and support for parents to help their kids get ready for college. It has been a big hit; we had standing room only at our last session. The group legal plan and discounted pet insurance were also new this year, and employees were surprisingly appreciative.*

Q: Do you put a lot of emphasis on communicating benefits to employees?

Noel: *Yes, especially during open enrollment time. We're always trying to come up with new and creative ways to communicate. We have a diverse population who like to receive information via different delivery systems. Some employees prefer the highlights, some want more* *detail than others, some prefer e-mail communication, others prefer face-to-face. To deliver our messages effectively, we use the weekly company newsletter to announce changes and promote wellness. We also send information to employees' homes so family members can see what's new. We also offer live workshops as well as recorded sessions (video on demand). New this year, we offered short podcasts, and of course the benefits fair where employees can speak to someone and get an individualized look at their situation. We also publish an annual benefit statement summary showing how much we spend on benefits so employees can appreciate how much value they are getting.*

Q: Beyond benefits, what does Vertex do that promotes employee well-being?

Kelly-Croswell: *The benefits are simply an expression of our culture. We have created a very open work environment designed to support innovation, which means people have to feel free to try and fail. We value teamwork, so we encourage and get lots of cross-functional communication. We also came to realize that meetings were getting in the way of having the time we need to do important work, so we instituted meeting-free days, every third Wednesday of the month, when we all have time to catch up on work or even take a few moments to pause and think. Now our researchers have more time to do research. This has been very well received. We are also very flexible about adjusting schedules. We just have a very supportive culture and our benefits prove it. We got a comment from an employee who attended our College Coach program that says it all: "This solidifies that Vertex Pharmaceuticals has a real understanding of employees' well-being, and it shows commitment."*

▶ **THE "PAY-ME-NOW-OR-PAY-ME-LATER" PROPOSITION**

If we continue to allow employees to live less-than-healthy lifestyles, we should not be shocked that our health-care costs go through the roof. In Chapter 1 we mentioned Greater Omaha Packing (GOP) of Omaha, Nebraska, a *Best-Places-to-Work* employer. GOP is one of those employers that you might not immediately identify as a candidate for such recognition or one that would be a leader in well care. The company is ranked fifth in beef processing nationally, with annual sales of nearly $1 billion. GOP received recognition in the press for implementing a program, designed by a company called Simply-Well, to address employee health problems while, at the same time, improving employee engagement. The program has a participation rate that approaches 90 percent of staff, and according to SimplyWell in an article about the program:

> Repeat participants over the past five years have experienced a 27% improvement in normal blood pressure readings while 16.7% fewer participants have elevated total cholesterol and 41.3% of participants have decreased elevated glucose levels. Since 2001 this group has experienced an average health care cost increase of only 2.4%, far below the national average.[10]

Many employers are enjoying similar benefits by providing resources to employees so they can take greater responsibility for their own health. SimplyWell also reported the results of a study showing a positive correlation between reducing employees' health risks and enhancing their productivity. The study of more than 770,000 employees from 106 companies found that those with none of the eight assessed health risks had a productivity loss of 3 percent, while those with all eight health risks had a 24 percent loss, or eight times more. The research included data from employees' health risk assessments.[11] Researchers at StayWell Health Management and wellness expert John Riedel conducted the study:

> Intuitively, we know that keeping employees healthy is the best way to reduce health care costs, and there's a large body of research in the industry demonstrating this is true," says Riedel. "But until now, we haven't had as much data showing that people who have

healthy lifestyles with few risk factors are significantly more productive in the workplace than people with high numbers of health risk factors."[12]

Think Your Business Is Too Small to Get into Wellness? Think Again.

As we've stated frequently, being a large employer doesn't necessarily hinder the ability of an employer to create programs that support the development of an engaged workforce. We tip our hats to a handful of resourceful employers in the south-central Michigan town of Jackson, who, in spite of the auto industry decline and a more generally unhealthy population, are pressing ahead with a well-care effort focused on small businesses. An article in the *New York Times* summarizes their unique approach, one that doesn't require governmental support, allows policy-making flexibility among participating employers, and has attracted a number of small businesses that may not have otherwise gotten involved in a well-care effort:

> With fewer employees to rely on, small businesses are particularly vulnerable when workers take sick days or function poorly on the job. "If our employees are not healthy and alert, they can't do things like designing projects," said Mike Shirkey, owner of Orbitform Group, a machine tool company in Jackson with 55 employees.
>
> An engineering graduate of the University of Michigan, Mr. Shirkey compares the wellness program with the "measure and improve" approach that he applies to manufacturing. Two years ago, Mr. Shirkey helped persuade other business owners in Jackson to join a CEO Roundtable, a forum and self-help group for top executives that is trying to ad-

dress employees' health as a crucial part of corporate strategy, rather than as simply a cost-management problem.

Kirk Mercer, president of R. W. Mercer, a Jackson-based contractor that builds small factories, doctors' offices and other commercial buildings in the Midwest, said he was so taken with this approach that he was urging his small subcontractors, each with a handful of employees, to join the wellness roundtable.[13]

▶ EMPLOYEE BENEFITS IN DIFFICULT TIMES

In difficult times we know employers will be challenged to maintain their commitment to employee well-being. As reflected in Figure 9.2,

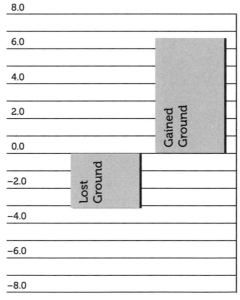

Employee Benefits That Demonstrate
a Strong Commitment to
Employee Well-Being

Figure 9.2

our research clearly shows that some employers are susceptible to losing ground on this key engagement driver, while others surge ahead, in spite of the more challenging conditions.

Here are some representative survey comments both from employees who remained engaged in difficult times and from those who did not:

Voices of Engagement

▶ *"The company offers competitive benefits and salary. Provides a great wellness program to assist employees."*

▶ *"My employer values health and wellness, ensuring each employee has the opportunity and tools needed to lead a healthy lifestyle."*

▶ *"In the last three years our company has made vast improvements in employee benefits and company culture."*

▶ *"I don't know of another company where employees come first. . . . We have benefits unlike any big company I have ever worked for, such as massages during company time, and an above-average 401(k) match, even during hard economic times."*

Voices of Disengagement

▶ *"The current economic times are stressful. This is when the company's true colors show. Our education benefits are reduced, and we didn't get a raise."*

▶ *"Need to be more flexible for leave when family emergency occurs."*

▶ *"1. Easier scheduling. 2. Easier scheduling. 3. Easier scheduling."*

▶ *"The benefits are expensive, and we need more holidays."*

▶ *"The benefits aren't great, health insurance is expensive, no maternity leave, and not great paid leave."*

▶ *"There are benefits given to other groups that are not afforded to all employees."*

▶ *"There needs to be more understanding for sick children through schedule changes."*

Companies that enjoyed higher engagement scores in the fourth quarter of 2008 did markedly better on items related to employee perceptions about benefits. In difficult economic times, employees need to feel that their "security" needs are being met. Having quality, affordable benefits is certainly one of those needs that, when addressed, positively impacts overall employee engagement.

Employees are naturally concerned about benefits, particularly given that many are paying an ever-increasing burden of health insurance premiums. We encourage employers to communicate regularly with employees about the value of the benefits they have. Many employees are either totally unaware of certain benefits or uninformed of their true value. At a minimum, employers should continue to communicate what benefits are available and how employees can easily access them. From an article posted on the Society for Human Resources Management (SHRM) Web site: "Companies spend upwards of 30 percent in benefit programs; what employees hear about is their medical premiums are up this year," Mel Stark, vice president and director of the reward practice for Hay Group's Metro New York office, stated. Someone earning $75,000, for example, likely is receiving another $25,000 worth of benefits, he said.[14]

Practices That Promote Employee Well-Being in Difficult Times

1. Communicate the availability and value of *all* benefits.

2. Conduct surveys or focus groups to find out what new benefits are truly needed.

3. Hold meetings where employees can put their life-work responsibilities on the table and work out ways to give and take so that both personal and work commitments can be met.

4. Make employees more alert to signs that coworkers may be burning out over becoming overstressed. We know of one company that asks employees to report situations where employees are in the "red zone"—putting in several consecutive weeks of 60-plus hours or long periods without time off. The company has "interventions" with these employees, insists that they take time off, and finds ways to assure the employees' work gets done during their absence.

5. Educate employees about stress and time management, healthy diet, exercise, and lifestyle. Hold on-site health fairs and screenings, help subsidize health club memberships, etc.

6. If "takeaways" must happen, such as suspending the employer retirement match, clearly communicate the decision and the reasons behind it, and try to restore as soon as possible.

7. Encourage fun activities and employee get-togethers to build cohesion and relieve stress.

▶ PLANNING YOUR WELL-CARE STRATEGY

In a recent survey of employers, Quantum Workplace asked winning companies how they approach their employee health and benefits efforts. After reviewing these entries, we identified an approach that we believe can help your organization in your planning efforts:

1. It has to start from the top. You've read the stories from Vertex and Gaylord, which show senior leadership doing what senior leaders should be doing—leading. If employees see that leaders from all quarters support well-care efforts, they will likely value them more and pay appropriate attention. Chapter 1's feature employer, Quality Living, initiated a financial literacy program a few years ago. It has been a resounding success, mentioned frequently as a highlight for employees, many of whom did not know how to manage their personal finances. The program was strongly advocated by CEO Kim Hoogeveen in words and in deeds.

2. Communicate early and often. Winning employers seem to go out of their way to make sure employees understand what's going on related to their benefits. They work to gain feedback about offerings and talk through "takeaways," where benefits must be reduced or eliminated. A few representative comments about what's working for these employers:

Communicating directly, openly, and honestly about these issues. Quantifying the commitment the company has to its employee program through a four-year communications and education program around Total Rewards. Producing an annual total rewards summary mailed to employee homes outlining the investment the company makes to employees and highlighting all that is offered.

This is a struggle every year, because we are experiencing rising costs each year like most companies. I think the one thing that I try to do is to tell employees the facts. I have open meetings with them and I show them the numbers and share what the firm is paying, and compare it to what they are paying so they see we are still contributing the greater percentage of the cost. We are also trying to educate them to be better consumers in purchasing health care and make better decisions in drug selection, physician visits, etc. We have recently introduced a high-deductible health plan, which is helping them to make better choices.

3. Communication goes both ways. Winning employers actively listen, so employees feel the communication is two-way:

We utilized the same surveys that we use with our customers to identify what employees really want/need. Then we tailored our benefits programs to meet their needs and wallet. Most of our team members are looking for learning and development opportunities as well as challenging work assignments. Things like health and disability insurance were secondary.

Since we are employee owned, we ask our employees to help make decisions on what benefits are important to them. Do they want to invest more in the health and dental plans, qualified plans, or education and training? If the employees are helping to make those decisions, they are much happier with the outcome.

4. Communicate face-to-face, even if the news is bad. There may well be a time when you will need to cut back on benefits or put more of the payment burden onto employees. Winning employers *do not* do this by e-mail; they stand and deliver the news in an open and honest manner:

> *We have had to cut benefits to maintain a profitable organization. Many times when these decisions have occurred, we have met with our employee committee, explained the reasons for the decision, and have allowed for open suggestions and communications on how to manage the situation. In the event that we have no other choice but to cut a benefit, it is explained to the entire organization in our quarterly meetings.*

5. Lose the cookie cutter. Winning employers realize that one size doesn't fit all when it comes to benefits:

> *We are not cutting employees' benefits, but are offering alternatives to our employees. We offer several different levels of health insurance to ensure everyone can afford health care. In addition, we contribute 50 percent (which is good for a business of our size). Employees are also given seven paid days off (not including holidays) in their first year. We believe that everyone needs to have time off. Another alternative we offer is if someone misses a day, instead of deducting time they are able to make that up by staying late or coming in early. These couple of things have been positively accepted by our employees.*

> *We have been fortunate in keeping benefit costs low through increased employee education (healthy living) and an excellent benefits broker to help us through the renewal processes. Although the overall dollars have increased slightly to employees over the past few years, the percentage that employees pay has remained the same. We have increased our offerings to employees so that they have a choice of plans, and instituted a more comprehensive vision plan.*

Employee Well-Being and Company Size

We noted in Chapter 2 that employer size has a negative effect on perceptions of employee benefits: the larger the employer, the dimmer the view of employees when reflecting on the two survey items in this chapter. Larger employers will need to address this perception and work harder to overcome this apparent barrier. The admonitions stated previously should be "biggie sized" to ensure messages about employee benefits make it to all corners of a large enterprise:

▶ The frequency of messages may need to increase by an exponential factor.
▶ More varied forms of media should be used.
▶ Messages about benefits should be ongoing, instead of "just at enrollment time."
▶ Additional training directed at supervisory staff may be helpful if employees feel less connected to staff functions such as human resources.

As one executive told us, "Just about the time I think we're overcommunicating about benefits is the time we may have it about right."

▶ A CHECKLIST OF BEST PRACTICES FOR ENGAGING AND RE-ENGAGING EMPLOYEES WITH BENEFITS AND A FOCUS ON WELL-BEING IN ALL TIMES

What follows is a summary of some of the practices, based on our analysis, that *Best Places to Work* have in common. Check only those that you honestly believe your leaders and managers are performing well:

___ Frequently monitor the wellness needs of all employees through surveys, focus groups, or standing benefits committees.

___ Select the benefits and services that meet the needs of employees, especially the organization most needs to be successful to achieve its strategic objectives.

___ Target areas of greatest need, and provide benefits and services that meet these needs in ways that exceed those provided by other competing employers.

___ Before implementing new benefits, practices, and services, take time to meet with a cross-section of employees to identify potential pitfalls in the practical administration and equitable application of the benefits and discuss how they can be avoided.

___ As much as possible, provide a cafeteria of benefits and services that allow the differing needs of employees to be met.

___ Build appreciation for the cost and value of all benefits provided by periodically communicating their value to all employees.

___ Accelerate and upgrade efforts to educate employees in preventative health practices, and reward those who follow these practices.

___ Implement both formal and informal recognition practices that demonstrate that caring for the health and wellness of employees is highly valued in the organization.

___ Guard against cultural norms that create disincentives for healthy behavior, such as excessive work hours and discouragement of taking vacation time.

___ Introduce and sustain financial wellness education initiatives.

___ Plan and sponsor a variety of social, recreational, celebratory, and fun activities that help to build a healthy sense of community, cohesion, and esprit de corps.

___ Promote a "give-and-get-back" mindset among leaders and managers that views the enhancement of employee well-being as a vital piece of corporate strategy rather than as benefit costs to be cut.

▶ FINAL THOUGHTS

One of our favorite management books is *The March of Folly*, written by Pulitzer Prize–winning historian Barbara Tuchman. Through four historical case studies, she explores the concept of folly. For something to qualify as folly for her book, Tuchman explains, it must:

▶ Be clearly contrary to the self-interest of the organization or group pursuing them

▶ Be conducted over a period of time, not just in a single burst of irrational behavior

▶ Be conducted by a number of individuals, not just one deranged maniac

▶ Have had people alive at the time who pointed out correctly why the act in question was folly (no 20-20 hindsight allowed)

Is there no greater folly than the health-care crisis that is before us today? We know many of the answers, particularly when it comes to changing the incentives within the health-care system, that promote disease care and ignore prevention. We know, as we discussed before, that many of the medical conditions we face are "discretionary"— brought on by poor lifestyle changes.

One executive we know has started a diabetes prevention program that is showing great promise. The program bathes the employee in support: additional nursing care, stress management, and dietary programs, even payment for using a local gym. Interest in the program is high, and early results are showing a significant improvement in the health of program participants. Through efforts like this, our friend has been able to maintain premium rates at the same level, and there are not many employers out there making that claim.

As the cost-benefit calculus for this program becomes clearer, our friend eventually wants to take the program a step further—to the point that if employees don't make reasonable lifestyle changes that are funded and supported by the employer for conditions that are clearly related to lifestyle (type two diabetes, for example), the payment for diabetes drugs may fall completely onto the employee. Bravo, we say.

We hope that health care in the United States will continue to change in ways, we hope, that both provide better services at a reasonable cost to consumers and offer health-care providers fair pay. Whatever approach ends up being adopted, let us create a health-care system where we support employees to take greater responsibility for their own health, making the right and fair investments as employers that are in our best interest to do so *and* provide meaningful consequences if they don't.

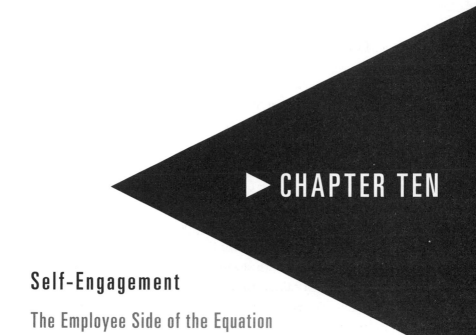

► CHAPTER TEN

Self-Engagement

The Employee Side of the Equation

I always remember an epitaph which is in the cemetery at Tombstone, Arizona. It says: "Here lies Jack Williams. He done his damnedest." I think that is the greatest epitaph a man can have—when he gives every thing that is in him to the job he has before him. That is all you can ask of him and that is what I have tried to do.

—HARRY S. TRUMAN

▶ STEVEN'S STORY: WEATHERING THE PERFECT STORM

Steven wondered how he'd gotten himself into this mess. There he was, rolling along nicely in his career, when, according to friends and colleagues, his *"ship began to take on water."*

Steven always loved computers, even before computers were "cool." He fondly remembered long nights at the university computer lab in the late 1970s, readying boxes of punch cards he'd carefully programmed, so he could haul them around campus. Steven just knew the effort would pay off, and for the first 20 years of his career he could not have been on a faster track—great company, lots of promotions, and frequent calls from headhunters wanting him to jump ship for better-paying gigs. His life as a technology project manager could not have been better.

Then came a series of unfortunate events that proved to be his perfect storm: the bursting of the dot-com bubble, computer jobs moving offshore, and the introduction of new technology platforms with which he had less competence. This typhoon left his employer no choice; Steven and a group of fellow middle managers were let go.

Steven received a six-month severance package from his employer in 2001, but instead of taking time to update his skills, he frittered away the window of opportunity. He took a programming job just to pay the mortgage, but felt bitter about this "demotion"—something his new employer sensed. That job lasted barely a year.

For the next five years Steven floundered, slogging from one dead-end job to another. A reunion with an old college pal got him thinking about his course. Steven's friend could sense his anger, disappointment, and lack of enthusiasm about work. His friend gave him it to him straight: *"My friend, you need an attitude adjustment. You are your biggest enemy. If I were a manager, I wouldn't hire you."*

From Drowning to Sailing

After several years of drowning in his own pity, Steven decided to take a hard look at his life and his attitude about work. Could he sail himself out of this perfect storm?

The job he held at that time was far below his skills, and he found himself working for a supervisor a dozen years his junior.

Steven decided to reach out to his old college friend for help. His friend reminded him of the way he felt about his profession in the early days of his career: *"Do you remember how excited you used to be? Do you remember how those long hours paid off for you? I know you still have that in you. You just have to find it."*

His friend was right. He did love this work, but he'd let his anger get in his way. Steven pledged to turn his career around by heading straight into the tempest. He vowed to be the most committed employee he could possibly be.

Steven stopped watching the clock and started thinking about getting projects done on or before deadline. He volunteered to help a team that was behind in getting a software update to a client. Steven joined a community technology group, where he met and networked with former colleagues. When a much younger peer asked him to lunch to ask advice about his fledgling career, Steven took that as a sign he might have turned the corner.

At his most recent performance review, Steven's supervisor expressed his appreciation for the change in attitude: *"Steven, everyone knows that you're one of the smartest guys in the business. But nobody wanted to work with you. I have to admit, when I first noticed your change in attitude I was skeptical. None of us were sure you could keep it up. But you've proved to all of us—and probably to yourself—that you can be an outstanding contributor when you put your mind to it. I'll be recommending you for the next available promotion."*

Steven smiled. The storm was beginning to pass, and he was proud he had charted his own course to safe harbor.

▶ TO ENGAGE OR NOT TO ENGAGE—WHO MAKES THAT DECISION?

As Steven's struggle reminds us, it's the employee who makes the decision to engage—or not. Even the best, most engaging leaders, managers, and employers may not be able to inspire those who are not ready and willing to be engaged. It may take a crisis in life or work for the decision point to arrive, but ultimately each employee must choose the path to engagement.

By devoting this book mainly to the six drivers that leaders and managers can wield, we are in no way disregarding the employee's responsibility for doing his or her part to stay engaged. Employees should never take away the message from any employee engagement initiative that they are absolved of the responsibility for keeping themselves engaged with the excuse that it's the manager who is being held accountable for it.

While the responsibility is shared, managers have to be highly motivated to engage each employee, because their own success and the success of their teams depend on it. So the question becomes, "How can managers make employees' self-engagement easier?" Our answer is to present techniques and tools that managers can use to challenge employees to take the self-engaging actions that no one else can take for them.

As we go through the guidelines in this chapter, reflect on your own level of engagement. As we have said before, if the manager is not engaged, it is less likely the manager's direct reports will be engaged. In fact, a recent Accenture study,[1] based on a survey of job satisfaction with middle managers, revealed that they are frustrated about several issues, including shouldering an increased workload (36 percent), not receiving enough credit for their work (32 percent), having no clear career path (31 percent), and receiving less support to work effectively (31 percent). These findings are disturbing and raise the crucial question, "How can we expect managers to positively influence others when they have negative feelings about important aspects of their jobs?"

So whether you are a manager or not, consider this an opportunity to assess your own level of engagement, and consider what you can do—independent of your own manager's actions—to enhance your commitment, enthusiasm, and performance at work for your own benefit and for those who report to you.

▶ DRIVING YOUR OWN ENGAGEMENT

As we have indicated, for the purposes of this chapter, you are the driver of your own employee engagement "bus." That doesn't mean you can't benefit from a road map, however. We understand that many readers may have difficulty knowing what they need to do to be more engaged at work. For most of us, it is easier if we have questions or checklists to which we can respond. You will find these below.

Assessing Your Own Level of Engagement

Begin by going to www.re-engagebook.com, and invest a few minutes completing the Self-Engagement Assessment. This will allow you to complete the following exercises with the benefit of knowing your own self-engagement "score."

▶ HOW CAN YOU GET MORE ENGAGED?

For readers with low self-engagement scores, we suggest you begin by responding to this straightforward question, "What can I do on my own to be more engaged—to be more passionate, enthusiastic, and fulfilled—at work?" List your ideas below:

▶ _____

_____

▶ _____

_____

Now ask yourself, "What can my manager or other leaders do that would inspire me to be more engaged?" List your ideas below:

▶ _____

_____

▶ _____

_____

▶ _____

_____

▶ _____

_____

List any actions you could take to influence your manager or other leaders to do the things you listed above:

▶ _____

_____

▶ _____

_____

Viewing Self-Engagement through the Six Engagement Drivers

We have organized many of the steps employees can take to boost their own engagement, grouped according to the "lenses" of the six engagement drivers. Before we present the action steps, first consider which of the six drivers is most important to you in determining the degree you are willing to give your best effort and enthusiasm at work. Rank them 1 to 6, with 1 being the most important to you in your current work situation.

___ Trust and confidence in senior leaders
___ Manager effectiveness
___ Team effectiveness
___ Job enrichment and professional growth
___ Feeling valued and recognized
___ Personal well-being

A CHECKLIST OF SELF-ENGAGEMENT ACTIONS

What follows is a variety of suggestions for increasing your own engagement, organized by the six engagement drivers. Pay special attention to the drivers you ranked as most important to your engagement, and then place a check next to any suggestions that you believe you could benefit from doing.

Trust and Confidence in Senior Leaders

Ways to build more trust and confidence in the organization's leaders

You may feel that trust in senior leaders is built mainly from the top down, but there may be more ways than you think to deal with the situation constructively. If you believe that your distrust or lack of confidence in senior leaders is causing you to be less engaged than you could be, consider the following checklist of actions you could take (independent of what the senior leaders may do):

___ Check out your perceptions of senior leaders with trusted peers, as you may be lacking important information or misperceiving their behavior.

___ Speak up in meetings with your manager and other leaders, and assertively, but wisely, express your convictions and desires.

___ When you present your ideas, be prepared with a specific plan for improvement, and volunteer to be a part of implementing the plan.

___ Don't be too quick to dismiss the efforts of new leaders. Give them time to communicate and begin to execute their vision before judging it.

___ Focus as much as possible on building trust and confidence with your immediate manager.

___ When a leader asks for your input, ideas, or support, be prepared to respond positively and take the initiative.

___ Demonstrate an "ownership mentality." Learn how the company makes money, seek to uncover unmet needs you can help address, and find out what you can do to make it more profitable.

___ Look for ways to take the initiative to meet the customer's needs, or ways to improve your own skills, so that leaders will trust you to handle new challenges.

___ If you have observed unethical behavior, report it to a trusted higher-up.

___ Give honest responses and constructive comments on employee surveys, especially about leadership-related issues.

___ If you aspire to a leadership role, work to maintain the highest standards of trust-building and confidence in all your relationships.

___ Other: _____

_____

Manager Effectiveness

Ways to improve the quality of performance coaching and feedback you are receiving from your manager

If you feel that some of your manager's practices are causing you to be less engaged than you could be, consider the following checklist of actions you could take (independent of what your manager may do):

___ If you feel your manager is not giving you the feedback and coaching you need, ask for it.

___ Seek feedback from anyone with whom you interact, including customers, not just those who supervise you.

___ When seeking feedback, ask for specific examples of things you do well and need to improve. When problematic behavior is mentioned, ask for specific examples and suggestions for ways to make changes for the better.

___ Get to know your manager's top performance priorities and professional goals so you can better support them.

___ Take a more active role in your own performance planning and appraisal process by suggesting specific objectives and evaluating your own performance.

___ If you feel that your supervisor has given you performance objectives or appraisal results that are not clear, ask for clarification.

___ When changes need to be made in your performance objectives, request a meeting with your supervisor to update the objectives.

___ If you feel your strengths are underutilized, discuss with your supervisor ways to use more of your strengths on the job and spend relatively less time trying to improve weaknesses.

___ Ask for the opportunity to receive 360-degree developmental feedback from peers, superiors, and your own direct reports (if you have any).

___ Other: _____

_____

Team Effectiveness

Ways to be a better team member and promote better teamwork

___ Consider the team's mission and objectives first, then your own.

___ Volunteer to assist other team members in challenging and stressful times.

___ Get to know the other members of the team better.

___ Know what your teammates are working on and how they contribute to team goals.

___ Be willing to share information with other teams rather than guarding it out of a desire for power.

___ Be willing to give and receive honest, constructive feedback.

___ Openly admit your weaknesses and mistakes.

___ If you feel other team members are not pulling their weight, be prepared to have a difficult conversation, letting them know how you feel and assertively asking for specific changes in their behavior.

___ Be open to different perspectives and diverse team members.

___ Be candid and passionate in your discussion of issues.

___ Willingly make sacrifices for the common good of the team.

___ Quickly and genuinely apologize when you say or do something inappropriate or possibly damaging to the team.

___ Commit to the decisions that are agreed on, even if you initially disagreed with them.

___ Be willing to put the most important issues on the table regardless of how difficult they may be to resolve.

___ Be slow to seek credit for your own contributions, but quick to point out those of others.

___ Be willing and able to use Web 2.0 technology to collaborate with other team members.

___ Don't sacrifice face-to-face communication by overrelying on electronic communication.

___ Be willing to meet members of other generations (and others with different perspectives) halfway.

___ Expand your network, get in the loop, and build relationships in other functional areas.

___ Other: _____

_____

Job Enrichment and Professional Growth

Ways to create your own career growth or advancement opportunities

___ Keep your focus on mastering your current job before you focus on advancement opportunities.

___ If you feel your current job or assignment is not a good fit for your strengths and interests, take the initiative to meet with your supervisor to discuss your ideas for changing jobs, changing the way the job is done, or swapping jobs or assignments with a coworker.

___ Persevere until you find a job you love to do.

___ Set goals for things you want to learn and follow through by pursuing certifications and/or degrees; taking classes; attending webinars, seminars, and conferences; exploring information on the Internet; reading; and finding mentors.

___ Discuss with your supervisor the competencies and knowledge required for the job or role to which you aspire.

___ Before taking on a new job assignment, ask questions to make sure the job is one that will make good use of your talents.

___ If your career path seems blocked, or you can see no advancement opportunities, seek lateral or cross-functional assignments. Imagine ways you could actually create a new job or new assignment for yourself that meets the needs of the firm while making better use of your talents.

___ Learn how money flows through the organization, and what you can do to increase sales/profits or reduce costs.

___ Put yourself in the supervisor's shoes, and be prepared to explain how it would benefit your work unit or organization as a whole to change your job assignments, increase the variety of job tasks you perform, expand your responsibilities, or allow you greater autonomy.

___ Seek whatever training you need to earn the trust of your supervisor to delegate more to you.

___ Instead of getting too comfortable when you have mastered a job, keep yourself engaged by seeking new challenges.

___ Ask for feedback about performance issues that may be holding you back.

___ Informally interview people in positions to which you aspire, ask their advice, get a realistic understanding of their jobs, and seek a mentoring relationship with them where appropriate.

___ Explore the possibility of temporarily or permanently swapping jobs with a coworker.

___ Seek and propose mini-assignments that will help prepare you for a job that may not be currently available so you don't have to wait to try out pieces of the job.

___ Let your supervisor know your career aspirations, talents, and plans so he or she can understand how to help you.

___ Become an "intrapreneur" by identifying a new service or business idea that can make money for the company.

___ Think twice before quitting your job. First, meet with your supervisor (or a trusted coworker) to articulate your concerns, and ask for constructive ideas for resolving the situation.

___ Other: _____

_____

Feeling Valued and Recognized

Ways you can become more valued, better recognized, and rewarded

___ First and foremost, find out what your organization values and what specific results your supervisor expects from you.

___ Be honest with yourself as you consider whether you are willing to put forth the effort required to achieve those results.

___ Get your supervisor's input on what skills and knowledge you could acquire that will make you more valuable to the organization.

___ Give value to get value: look for ways to share information and be a resource to coworkers.

___ If you feel you are not receiving the information you need, ask your supervisor for the information directly and look for ways to stay plugged in through informal relationships throughout the organization.

___ Speak up when you have an idea that you believe could bring value to the organization and be well-received by your manager.

___ Let your supervisor know what form of recognition (e.g., public versus private, written versus spoken) you most appreciate.

___ To get a better feel for the impact and value of your job, ask to sit in on a meeting with a customer or client.

___ Ask your supervisor what criteria he or she uses to determine raises and variable compensation.

___ When asking for a raise, think first about the value you have added and will add ("what's in it for them" instead of "what's in it for me").

___ If you see a need for additional tools or equipment to do your job better, first do a cost-benefit analysis before you approach your manager with your request.

___ When you have reached a goal, reward yourself with a special treat: take a day off, get a massage, or buy something you've been wanting.

___ Other: _____

_____

Personal Well-Being

Ways to increase your own sense of well-being

___ When you are justifiably annoyed, angry, or frustrated, speak up and assertively ask for what you want instead of suppressing your feelings.

___ Realize your limits when dealing with stress and understand that you can choose how you respond to stress. A stress management class or seminar may help you learn to make those choices in a more conscious and controlled way.

___ Take a time management class or seminar, or read a good book on the topic.

___ When you can, delegate more of your work to reduce your workload to a manageable level.

___ If you are in the habit of bringing work home with you every night, it could be a sign you need to delegate more, get help from coworkers, learn to manage your time better, or find more efficient ways of getting work done.

___ Rein in the need for absolute perfection—know when good enough is good enough.

___ If the demands of your job have become overwhelming, pursue possible solutions with your supervisor, including making potential changes in organizational work processes, eliminating unnecessary paperwork, taking a more efficient and organized approach to the job, managing time better, reassigning some job activities to others, or being reassigned to a less demanding position.

___ When you need to have uninterrupted time to finish a large project or to complete several smaller tasks, block out the hours or days on your calendar ahead of time.

___ Give yourself more uninterrupted time to get work done by resolving not to constantly check your e-mails and/or voice mail messages. Don't always answer the phone when it rings; let voice mail pick it up when you are extra busy.

___ Plan your vacation and reserve your vacation days as far in advance as possible. Then take your vacation! You earned it and you need it.

___ If you are a chronic multitasker, you may be burning yourself out and actually becoming less competent. Try doing one thing at a time and giving it your full attention.

___ Pursue outside interests or activities that relax and reenergize you.

___ Get out of the office for lunch or walks to break the routine and clear your mind.

___ Lead a more healthy lifestyle: monitor more carefully what you eat and drink, exercise more, get more sleep, get plenty of sunlight, and lose weight if necessary.

___ Other: _____

_____

Prioritizing to Take Action

Go back and review all the actions you checked, select three actions you are ready to take now, and list them below:

1. _____

_____

2. _____

_____

3. _____

_____

Questions to Stimulate Career Self-Management

For managers who want to challenge employees to become more engaged by taking charge of their own career management in the organization, and, as well, for individual employees who need to challenge themselves, here are some questions that may be helpful:

1. What talents or abilities would you most like to use at work?
2. What abilities or skills would you like to develop?
3. What have you done lately to develop or improve your skills and abilities?
4. What kind of new challenge would you like to take on?
5. What would you most like to learn?
6. What obstacles do you face in learning what you want to learn?
7. Based on the objectives you set in your last performance review, what actions have you taken to reach those objectives?
8. Do you know what others think of your performance and attitude? If not, how can you find out?
9. Do you know whether you are satisfying customers (either internal or external)? If not, how can you find out?
10. How does your work increase customer satisfaction? How do you know for sure?
11. What more could you do to increase customer satisfaction?
12. What ideas do you have for better serving customers?
13. Have you asked others for their feedback or taken part in a 360-degree feedback process?
14. Would you like to be mentored? If so, in what competency or topic?
15. Have you built good relationships with coworkers?
16. Have you thought about a new way to address a challenge or problem we have?
17. Are you doing everything you can to master new technical challenges, processes, or tools?
18. Have you attended a professional seminar in the last six months? If so, what did you learn?
19. Do you read or listen to audiobooks or podcasts? What have you learned lately?
20. Have you considered joining professional associations as a way to learn and grow?

21. Is there anything you are good at in your leisure time that you could do more of at work?

22. What was the best job you ever had and why?

23. Would you say you have responded positively to changes in the work environment in the last year?

24. Who do you think has greater control over your career progress, you or someone else?

Overcoming Habits of Mind and Behavior That Limit Your Engagement

Sometimes the obstacles to increased self-engagement are more deeply embedded. The fact is, many people engage in self-sabotaging behavior that their managers are ill-equipped to help them resolve.

COMMON SELF-LIMITING BELIEFS OR MINDSETS

As we have emphasized in our discussion of senior leaders' mindsets, the thought is the father of the action. This holds true for all of us as we face our daily challenges at work. Below we have listed just some of the beliefs that can limit our effectiveness, grouped within the six engagement drivers. There may, in fact, be certain circumstances where employees may be justified in holding some of these beliefs. But as you will see, all of the beliefs can be dysfunctional when they indicate an overly cynical or naïve outlook, as the case may be. In either case, the employee holding these beliefs may be seriously distorting reality.

Self-limiting beliefs about senior leaders

▶ All senior leaders are dishonest.
▶ I cannot trust anyone in authority.
▶ Senior leaders are only motivated by greed and self-interest.
▶ Leaders are always right.
▶ Leaders are always honest.
▶ Leaders don't care about employees. They only care about the bottom line.

Self-limiting beliefs about managers

▶ My manager's job is to keep me motivated.
▶ If I need feedback, my manager will provide it.
▶ Management will initiate career discussions and plans charting my career progress.
▶ My manager is too busy to meet with me.
▶ My manager isn't interested in my ideas.

Self-limiting beliefs about teamwork and coworkers

▶ I can't trust any of my team members. They are all only looking out for themselves.
▶ Everyone on my team is incompetent.
▶ The only way to get something done is to do it myself.
▶ If I share information with coworkers, they will use it against me.
▶ People who work from home or in remote locations are not really part of the team.

Self-limiting beliefs about job and career growth

▶ I own my job.
▶ That's not my job.
▶ If I perform well, I should get a promotion.
▶ After a certain amount of time in a job, I should get a promotion.
▶ When I complete my degree, I should get a promotion.
▶ All opportunities for promotion or horizontal movement in the organization will be posted.
▶ I should be paid or promoted based on job tenure.
▶ I can depend on my employer to provide opportunities for continual learning.
▶ Career paths and ladders should be defined and clear.
▶ If there are no job vacancies in the organization, it's unlikely a job can be created.

▶ My success depends more on improving my weaknesses than leveraging my strengths.

Self-limiting beliefs about being valued and recognition

▶ I don't deserve praise . . . I'm just doing my job.
▶ Praise is counterproductive—it just goes to people's heads.
▶ If I don't hear from my manager, it means I'm doing a good job.
▶ I'm not paid what I'm worth.
▶ No one cares about my ideas.
▶ People in lower-level jobs or support roles are a lot less valuable.
▶ New hires have to earn respect.

Self-limiting beliefs about personal well-being

▶ I must work as many hours as possible, even if it means sacrificing my health and time with my family.
▶ I cannot delegate for fear that the work won't be done right.
▶ "All work and no play" makes me more valuable to my employer.
▶ I can't afford to take vacation time.
▶ To keep up, I have to take work home every night.
▶ If I don't work when I'm sick, my work won't get done.

Other self-limiting beliefs

▶ Life should be fair.
▶ Change scares me and I must resist it.
▶ My employer will take care of me.
▶ I can expect long-term employment with my current employer.

You may have other self-limiting beliefs to add based on your own work experience. Our point in showing these is to bring to the surface some underlying assumptions that put a ceiling on our own capacity to self-engage and to provide a list of issues for managers to openly explore with employees.

COMMON SELF-DEFEATING HABITS

In survey comments, we found ample evidence that employees and their managers are acting in ways that sabotage and complicate their relationships and thus undermine their own efforts to stay engaged and cause others to disengage. We have observed these same negative habits of thought and action in our years of professional coaching. We present them here as a checklist to help you evaluate whether any of them may be inhibiting your own efforts to self-engage, or the efforts of those around you. We also show actual selected survey comments, some referring to the respondent himself or herself, and others to a manager or coworker, that serve to illustrate each of the habits:

___ **Avoiding conflict**
Fearing escalation of emotion or possible rejection to the point of avoiding confrontations necessary for moving forward

Illustrative survey comment

"Those of us who are not comfortable speaking up publicly or have questions need to trust our managers; knowing they will in turn deliver our message/ suggestions correctly without divulging our identity or adapting/editing the message for the benefit of the receiving party."

___ **Win-lose**
Needing to win so badly that someone else must lose; making every interaction an adversarial one

Illustrative survey comment

"My manager does not pull her weight. She always wants others to help her do her job—she's a bully, bossy, disrespectful, insulting, always trying to put fellow employees down by insulting them."

___ Perfectionism

Feeling a need to be perfect to the extent that it may create fear of failure, extreme self-criticism, or criticism of others

Illustrative survey comment

"My manager perpetuates and reinforces a negative work environment, admonishing all who did not meet the perfection he expects."

___ Entitlement mentality

Feeling too much reward too quickly with too little effort

Illustrative survey comment

"There is also a noticeable sense of entitlement or a false sense of importance amongst some of my coworkers in my immediate area leading to minimal, passive work and short attention spans on their duties."

___ Victimized

Blaming outside circumstances or other people for not taking action

Illustrative survey comments

"I've been struggling with standing up to coworkers who take credit for work I have done, and then the supervisors encourage their behavior. It would be wonderful if we knew who to talk to in times where work conflict arises."

"I feel like I am being taken advantage of every day.

___ Stuck in the comfort zone

Having a need for security that is so strong that it inhibits the need to take risks, change, and grow

Illustrative survey comment

"Managers need to empower associates to be risk takers. They can preach it, but sometimes they don't practice it all that well."

___ Rational to a fault

Lacking empathy and having difficulty accepting human foibles and failures

Illustrative survey comment

"The leaders of the organization inspire employees through executing effectively on a day-to-day basis, but do not inspire through strong conventional management techniques like empathy, career pathing, and any kind of personal connection."

___ Emotional volatility

Losing control of emotions and abusing coworkers, taking unreasonable risks, or making impulsive decisions

Illustrative survey comment

"My supervisor needs to be better with people. He is very disrespectful and seems to verbally abuse people who are not so aggressive. He rarely shows respect to low-level employees when his supervisors are not around."

___ Knowing it all

Having an excessive need to be right and impress others with knowledge

Illustrative survey comment

"My manager is a technical expert on how to do my job. Unfortunately, that means he only allows me to do things his way, which he believes is the only right way. That makes the job less interesting and me less motivated."

___ Withholding information

Hoarding information to gain power instead of sharing it to gain trust and teamwork

Illustrative survey comment

"Information flows up, but honest information does not flow down. Favoritism and the 'Good 'Ol Boy' network is very prevalent."

___ **Withholding praise**
Being reluctant to recognize others or express appreciation

Illustrative survey comment

"I love working here, but I wish I could be recognized every once in awhile by the doctors on a job well done."

___ **Faultfinding**
Having a negative and overly critical attitude in general and toward others' ideas and initiatives

Illustrative survey comment

"I speak for all of the cooks when I say that we do not feel appreciated when we do a good job, and we get negative criticism when we make a mistake instead of positive. There is too much negative vibe in the kitchen, especially coming from the executive chef."

___ **Sucking up**
Being so concerned about how they look to higher-ups that they focus on looking good at the expense of actually achieving something

Illustrative survey comment

"I feel managers are overwhelmed with those who play favoritism to them, and do not see the little guy who works hard and gives it their 100 percent and more."

___ **Talking too much**
Violating confidences or simply turning people off by talking when they should be listening

Illustrative survey comment

"My immediate supervisor does not exercise confidentiality. She talks about other workers with other coworkers."

___ **Passing the buck**
Failing to take responsibility for oneself or blaming others for our mistakes

Illustrative survey comment

"The goals set by managers are at times unrealistic, and then we as a department feel the blame will be put on our laps rather than the person who set the goal in the first place."

___ **Claiming unearned credit**
Taking credit for others' ideas or accomplishments

Illustrative survey comment

"It is hard when you do your best and someone else is always taking credit for the job you did."

Did you see a few habits that come close to describing some of your own past behavior? If so, you are not alone. Most of us must "own up" to behavioral tendencies that we would like to change, but struggle to do so. We suggest that you select one or two to work on and ask a trusted coworker to help monitor your behavior and give you feedback and support when you slip into old, self-defeating habits.

Common Self-Engagement Challenges: The Four Generations

Each employee's challenges are individual ones, not generational, as we have emphasized before. Nevertheless, there may be value in presenting a few of the more common challenges that arise among various age groups. Our intent in the lists below is to alert you to needs that frequently occur and should be addressed, not to reinforce assumptions and stereotypes that may not necessarily apply to any given employee within these generations.

Traditionalists (born 1945 and before)

▸ They may feel that younger leaders do not value their knowledge and experience enough to tap it before they retire.
▸ Rigid organizational policies may inhibit flexibility regarding options to full retirement that would allow them to continue to contribute.

Boomers (born 1946–1964)

▸ Because some often judge Millennials and Xers as lacking their work ethic and initiative, they may be reluctant to engage with and mentor them, or be mentored by them in new technologies.
▸ They may be cynical about how seriously the organization is about capturing their knowledge and providing ways for them to leave a legacy.
▸ Some are frustrated by organizational practices that limit their options for phased retirement and continuing part-time or consulting options.

Gen Xers (born 1965–1980)

▸ Independence may cause some not to identify with and be loyal to the organization.
▸ Need for autonomy may cause some to be reluctant team players.

▶ They may be easily discouraged by fewer career path options and feel blocked as older Boomers postpone retirement.

Millennials (born 1981–1994)

▶ Some may initially struggle without sufficient performance coaching, feedback, and mentoring.

▶ Without clearly stated goals, some may flounder and not take the initiative.

▶ Because many are more oriented to immediate gratification and short-term timelines, they may have difficulty focusing on long-term goals and rewards.

Self-Engagement Challenges in Turbulent Times

We have touched on most of the issues below in previous chapters, where we presented actions that leaders and managers can take to address them. Now we suggest that you consider these challenges from your perspective as an individual employee. As you review the list, ask yourself, "What could I do, independent of any action higher management might take, to claim some sense of mastery over the situation?"

▶ You may be less likely to take the risks necessary for creating the innovative ideas needed to survive tough challenges.

▶ Your fear of job loss may result in being increasingly distracted and spending more time worrying, swapping rumors, and speculating in hallway conversations about what might happen.

▶ Strong emotions may result in increased conflict with co-workers.

▶ Budget cutbacks may increase turf battles and in-fighting over limited resources.

▶ Staff reductions will increase individual workloads, which may lower morale and lead to burnout.

▶ Increased workloads may lead to less time spent exercising, unhealthy eating and drinking habits, sleep loss, less time spent with family and friends, and overall reduction in personal well-being.

▶ A natural tendency to withdraw in times of crisis may inhibit you from expressing your concerns and ideas.

▶ You may assume that stalled company growth will mean little or no career growth.

▶ You may switch your focus to seeking new job opportunities elsewhere.

▶ Fewer opportunities to celebrate individual and team success may reduce the level of "psychic reward" that motivates continued achievement.

▶ The organization's failure to confront poor performers may become even more demotivating to you and other better performers.

▶ THE CHALLENGE OF CLAIMING FULL PERSONAL POWER

Despite our best intentions and efforts to be more engaged and fulfilled in our work, all of us are capable of undermining ourselves. There are common mindsets and patterns of behavior that are particularly self-sabotaging, which we will present in this section. First, to pave the way for assessing those behaviors, we address the funda-

	Can Control	Cannot Control
Take Action	Mastery	Ceaseless Striving
No Action	Giving Up	Letting Go

Figure 10.1   The Personal Power Grid

mental questions of "What can I control?" and "What actions can I take?"

The Personal Power Grid (Figure 10.1) is basically a tool for diagnosing how constructively and effectively we are dealing with the challenges we face. Whatever the issue may be, we either have some control in addressing it or we have no control. Another choice we have is to either try to take action to deal with the challenge or take no action. Depending on our choices, we find ourselves in one of the four situations indicated by the quadrants. There are two healthy choices: Mastery (taking action on the things we can control) and Letting Go (not trying to control what we cannot control). The other two choices are problematic: trying to take action on what we cannot control (Ceaseless Striving) is a recipe for frustration, and not taking action on what we can control (Giving Up) is abdication. These last two quadrants represent choices that allow the individual to stay in the realm of "victimhood," where it is easier to blame one's circumstances, one's employer, one's manager, or one's coworkers rather than try to master the situation or let it go.

What follows is an example of a dilemma faced by an employee who feels frustrated about her career goals and must make a decision about whether and how to constructively engage. As you can see, four options have been identified:

Challenging Situation *Employee wants a promotion from an hourly to a salaried position, but feels she has been unfairly discounted as unqualified.*		
	Can Control	**Cannot Conrol**
Take Action	*Employee researches skill gaps and discusses with her manager how to improve.*	*Employee complains about the situation and randomly applies to unrelated job postings.*
No Action	*Employee just waits for manager to recognize her potential.*	*Employee resolves to make incremental job moves instead of one big move to the desired position.*

As you think about a dilemma that is standing in the way of your own engagement or the engagement of a direct report, consider using the blank grid below to flesh out the decision to be made and confront the responsibility we all have for taking constructive action if we can.

The Challenging Situation		
	Can Control	**Cannot Control**
Take Action		
No Action		

We hope this worksheet helps in identifying specific actionable goals and results in employees taking more responsibility for their own self-engagement.

▶ THE LIMITS OF SELF-ENGAGEMENT

Despite our best efforts, some employees will not rise to the level of full engagement. They may simply be in the wrong jobs, too distracted by personal life challenges, or too resistant by reason of their beliefs or work ethic. As managers, the trick is not to give up on disengaged employees too soon—not without having explored ways to effectively address these issues.

We need to also acknowledge that the wisest and most adaptive decision for some employees may be to pursue employment in other organizations where the fit may be better and they can start fresh with a new manager.

Where does self-engagement end and engagement attributable to manager or leader actions begin? We will never know the answer, but we must always pursue it. As Ferdinand Fournies has pointed out, there are 16 reasons why employees don't do what they are supposed to do, and only one of them lies outside the power of the manager to influence.[2]

▶ FINAL THOUGHTS

Psychologists describe patients who exhibit self-defeating behaviors to which they rigidly adhere as having character disorders. To the great frustration of those around them, they don't see their behavior as dysfunctional or unacceptable, often being perplexed and defensive when others question their actions. They tend to resist well-intentioned attempts to help them examine and address their behavior, often leaving them socially outcast.

In our many years in consulting we've seen our share of employees with what might be called "engagement disorders." These employees are typically quite unhappy with their lot (at work and often in life) and go out of their way to express their displeasure to any and all around them, including customers who (surprise, surprise) are not crazy about hearing their stories of woe. They seem to live by that old aphorism: "Chaos, panic and disorder—my work here is done." Even the best of managers can be frustrated by their immovable attitudes, leaving these miscreants in an inevitable slide that ends with a pink slip and two weeks' severance pay.

Don't succumb to engagement disorder!

Like many of your colleagues, you may have had a tough break or two in your career—horrible manager, corporate downsizing, or incompetent leadership at the top of the house. And we know that getting a paycheck from an employer who is passionately working to develop the six universal drivers we've discussed would make your work life a lot more productive and enjoyable. Many workers are in the same crowded boat these days. This doesn't mean that you or your coworkers have to suffer from an engagement disorder. The truth is:

▶ In spite of these bad breaks you still have a choice about how you comport yourself.
▶ You can still go to work with the attitude that you will do the best you possibly can.
▶ You can continue to learn and develop your skills.
▶ You can find others at your place of work who share your interest in creating a better workplace and would be willing to champion and work toward this important goal.

And if these efforts don't help you succeed at your current place of work, you can rest assured there are places where a self-engaged employee is valued. We hope that whatever situation you find yourself in right now, you will see that much of what you do, and how you respond to the environment around you, is in your hands.

The choice, ultimately, is yours.

► **CHAPTER ELEVEN**

Becoming a More Engaged Workplace

All elegant strategies eventually deteriorate into work.
—PETER DRUCKER

If you want what you never had, you must do what you have never done.
—SEEN ON T-SHIRT AT 24-HOUR FITNESS

▶ WHAT DO WE DO NOW?

Some of you may have seen the movie *The Candidate*, in which Robert Redford plays a young, upstart politician vying for the United States Senate. The final scene, where Redford's character has just learned that his fledgling candidacy has been victorious, is particularly compelling. He has invested significant time and effort into the campaign, and just before he delivers his acceptance speech, he turns to one of his staff members and says, "What do we do now?" From the look on his face, it's clear he truly doesn't know what his next move is—a look we occasionally see from leaders who have just received their employee engagement survey results, a look that says, *"What do we do now?"*

This chapter provides insights into what your organization can do to initiate steps to become a better workplace, not just to win an award, but to put in place the particular talent management practices that will support your particular business strategy. We also will introduce our *Employee Engagement Planning Matrix*, a tool that will help you identify the long- and short-term actions that will increase the engagement of the people you depend on to achieve your business objectives.

It bears repeating that the ultimate purpose of becoming a better place to work is not just to make your corner of the world a better place, but to serve the business goals and strategies of your organization.

▶ LINKING SIGNATURE DRIVERS AND PRACTICES TO YOUR BUSINESS STRATEGY

There is a reason we don't push the idea of reflexively implementing employee engagement best practices of other *Best-Places* employers—as we have said, they may not serve your business objectives or leverage your talent in a way that fits your culture. As you can see from the following table, the *Best-Places* winners that scored highest on the six engagement drivers are implementing practices that embody those drivers and support the business strategies to which they are committed.

Best-Places Employer	Business Strategy	Signature Driver	Signature Practice
Quality Living, Inc.	Build reputation for providing highest standards of caring service	Trust and confidence in senior leadership	Application of leadership principles and mindsets (practices)
Winchester Hospital	Increase patient satisfaction and loyalty by building strong management culture that inspires employees to give great patient care	Competent and caring managers who keep employees aligned and engaged	Intensive training and coaching of managers to build their people management skills

Nalley Automotive	Build customer loyalty and repeat business through great service and word of mouth	Building team effectiveness and commitment	Structuring of service tech teams
Rackspace Hosting	Grow through referrals from satisfied customers served by employees we support and invest in	Job enrichment and professional growth	Encouraging role-changing and horizontal moves
Joie de Vivre Hospitality	Build reputation for providing world-class service and a unique customer experience	Valuing employee contributions	Commitment to annual awards and ongoing recognition of employees for exceptional service
Vertex Pharmaceuticals	Innovate and commercialize breakthrough drugs	Employee well-being	Four weeks' paid vacation per year and overall focus on employee wellness

These exemplary employers are also putting their own spin on their practices in ways that fit and express their unique cultures. This is why we chose to describe their key drivers and practices with the word "signature." By implementing specific people practices in their own way, these companies are putting their distinctive signatures on drivers that are universally effective in all organizations, but are particularly applicable to their own strategic business objectives.

We should also note that all six employers scored high on all six of the Universal Engagement Drivers, further reinforcing our point, first stated in Chapter 3, that the six drivers are not independent of each other, but, on the contrary, are interconnected, overlapping, interwoven in the fabric of the organization's culture, and exert strong mutual influence on one another. It would be hard to imagine a winning company scoring high on one and low on another, as in high on senior leadership and low on employee well-being, or high on job enrichment and growth, but low on valuing and recognizing employees. Indeed, we have not been able to find any such high-low pairings among any of the winning employers in our database since 2004! What we did find (among second-tier non-winning employers that scored in the sixtieth to eightieth percentiles) were high scores on some drivers paired with average scores on others.

Best Places to Work, where employees genuinely believe they are lucky to be employed, can be likened to fine diamonds, which grade high on all six qualities on which they are rated—shape, clarity, cut, carat weight, color, and certification. Or for more musically inclined readers, the six drivers can also be compared to the six strings on a well-tuned guitar that resonate and harmonize to create the desired sound. A missing or out-of-tune string destroys the effect. Still, depending on the tune being played, some strings are more important than others, and, just so, some drivers are more important depending on the employer's business and talent strategies.

▶ WHERE TO BEGIN

We know of no employer that has a perfect score on any of the six engagement drivers. So there is always room for improvement. Here are some questions that senior leaders and HR executives need to be asking:

- ▶ Is our business strategy clear enough that we can easily identify which functional units or locations and which positions are most critical to the achievement of that strategy, both short term and long term?
- ▶ Are our business objectives clear enough—in all units and locations and at all levels of the organization—that we are

able to identify what knowledge, skills, and abilities will be most critical in achieving them?

▶ Are we willing to focus our attention, time, and budget on attracting, engaging, and disproportionately rewarding people in key positions?

▶ What key and supporting staff will we need to hire from the outside versus train, develop, and promote from within?

▶ What specific knowledge, skills, and abilities are required in the key and supporting roles?

▶ Recognizing that different employees are more motivated by some engagement drivers than others, which of the six drivers are *generally* most important to the current employees, succession candidates, and future hires who will fill these roles?

▶ Which one (or two) of the six engagement drivers is most critical in supporting our key business objectives and the kind of culture that will support those business objectives? The answer may vary from one unit, location, or position classification to another.

▶ Where would we rank our company as an employer (or specific divisions, functional units, or locations) on the six engagement drivers, from strongest to weakest? If you are not sure how your employees would respond to this question, ask them—via a companywide engagement survey, focus groups, open forums, small-group or one-on-one conversations, or all the above.

▶ How well are our current people practices and initiatives and our overall culture supporting the employee engagement drivers that are most critical in achieving our business objectives?

▶ What new engagement practices should we consider based on our response to the above question?

To assist you in answering this last question, we provide the following employee engagement planning matrix:

Employee engagement planning matrix

	Short-Term Actions (Climate)	Longer-Term Actions (Culture)
Enterprise-Directed Actions	What short-term actions (within one year) can senior leadership (including senior HR leaders) take to increase employee engagement?	What longer-term actions (one year or more) can senior leadership, in partnership with HR, take to increase employee engagement?
Manager-Driven Actions	What short-term actions can individual managers, in partnership with HR, take to increase employee engagement?	What longer-term actions can individual managers, in partnership with HR, take to increase employee engagement?

Let's define and discuss each of the variables in the matrix:

▶ Enterprise-directed actions. As discussed in Chapter 4, some employee engagement practices are primarily the domain of senior leadership. A decision to change the copay for a health insurance plan, investments in improvements to a facility, or changes in internal job-posting guidelines, for example, are generally the domain of the senior leadership of an organization.

▶ Manager-driven actions. As discussed in Chapter 5, several employee engagement practices are primarily driven by direct managers and supervisors. For example, it is within the realm of managers to provide meaningful and appropriate recognition to their employees, resolve conflict among team members, and coach employees about their performance and career interests.

▶ Short-term actions (climate). Some decisions and their associated actions can be made and implemented within a year or less. These can have an impact on the climate of the organization, which, like the weather, is more subject to change. For example, the changes in internal job-posting guidelines previously mentioned can be implemented within a short period. Some training programs, such as those designed to help managers build conflict management skills, might also be conducted within that same time period.

▶ **Longer-term actions (culture).** Some issues and their associated actions require a much longer time period to fully implement. The rule of thumb here is that these decisions will take at least a year, or several years, of effort. These decisions are designed to change the culture of the organization and usually take more time to realize their full impact. They are typically not as subject to changing conditions as climate issues are. Although we presented training on conflict management as a short-term action, it requires a longer-term commitment, such as codifying new learning and manager practices into the annual performance appraisal process and following through to hold managers accountable for a few years to assure that they truly embrace and use the new skills.

Initiatives designed to improve employee engagement usually require effort in each of the four quadrants. What follows is an example of how the engagement matrix can be used to establish a comprehensive plan:

Example A: Completed employee engagement planning matrix

ISSUE: *Feedback from our employee engagement survey indicates we are at risk of losing talented employees because they do not see career opportunities.*

	Short-Term Actions (Climate)	Longer-Term Actions (Culture)
Enterprise-Directed Actions	*Change job posting guidelines. Authorize funds for training of managers and employees.*	*Change performance appraisals for managers to increase emphasis on employee development.*

Manager-Driven Actions	Managers provide information at staff meetings about changes. Introduce new training program for career development.	Managers fully implement initiative requiring that each employee has an Individual Development Plan that is reviewed and updated annually.

In the preceding example, the use of the matrix created the focus to consider a wide range of initiatives that may address this common but important issue.

Here is another example:

Example B: Completed employee engagement planning matrix

ISSUE: *Feedback from our employee engagement survey indicates the overall quality of frontline supervision is negatively impacting employee productivity and retention.*

	Short-Term Actions (Climate)	Longer-Term Actions (Culture)
Enterprise-Directed Actions	Identify managers who are not effective, and lay out a six-month performance plan; reassign, coach/train, or terminate as appropriate. Announce supervisor development initiative. Identify criteria for successful supervisors.	Establish a dual career path for employees who don't want to manage or aren't capable of managing. Change compensation system to support dual career paths.
Manager-Driven Actions	Solicit feedback from employees about managers' effectiveness. Start conducting more productive staff meetings.	Implement and sustain manager mentoring program. Follow up with 360-degree feedback and developmental coaching.

This matrix may not help you identify or solve all the issues raised in employee survey data, but it can certainly help when the matters are complex and several variables must be considered. You may also choose to complete a different planning matrix for each division or functional unit in addition to the one you complete for the overall organization.

The following is a blank version for you and your colleagues to fill out.

Your organization's employee engagement planning matrix

ISSUE:

_____

_____

_____

_____

	Short-Term Actions (Climate)	Longer-Term Actions (Culture)
Enterprise-Directed Actions		

	Short-Term Actions (Climate)	Longer-Term Actions (Culture)
Manager-Driven Actions		

▶ TANGIBLES VERSUS INTANGIBLES

As you consider what actions to take, keep this in mind: actions that produce decidedly tangible outcomes, such as increasing pay or benefits or hiring more staff, are more tempting to select. Why? Because of their very "tangibleness". We can point to them as evidence to the workforce that we have done something immediate, real, and concrete. If you have evaluated that these tangible actions are indeed the right ones—the most likely to engage targeted talent, the most supportive of business objectives, and cost effective—then you can feel some confidence in implementing them.

But it is highly likely that you will need to also implement some less tangible practices—for example, communicating company goals more clearly, recognizing managers who allow valued employees to move elsewhere in the organization in order to remain challenged, or training managers to conduct "stay" interviews with their direct reports. If dissatisfaction with pay is your issue, the engagement actions may be both tangible and intangible; increasing pay would be the tangible action, and communicating more clearly about how pay decisions are made would be the intangible action.

In reviewing your engagement planning matrix, check to see if your actions reflect a balance between tangible and intangible actions as well as between short-term and longer-term actions and between those that are enterprise driven and those that are manager driven.

▶ ENTERPRISEWIDE VERSUS FUNCTIONAL UNITS

With all our emphasis in previous chapters on the engagement scores of entire organizations, we cannot emphasize enough in this final chapter that engagement can differ widely from department to department, division to division, and location to location within the same organization. We strongly recommend to our clients that when conducting employee engagement surveys, they collect and analyze data by functional unit. Only then can managers be held fully accountable for creating and executing initiatives and practices that will move the employee engagement needle upward.

Human resources and training staff also have important roles to play as partners to managers who need and want to engage more of their direct reports. And certainly senior leaders need to question whether they are creating the right conditions to engage the managers whose unit engagement scores are not what they should be.

▶ TARGETED ENGAGEMENT VERSUS EQUAL FOCUS ON ALL EMPLOYEES

One of the more controversial topics in discussions about human capital today is how much to differentiate among employees as we allocate our limited energies and budgets to attracting, engaging, training, developing, and retaining them. Many companies still follow the

"20-70-10" tiered-performer model that is based on evidence that top performers produce disproportionate value and should be rewarded disproportionately. Some disparage this system as "rank and yank," forcing managers to cut muscle instead of fat after the initial rounds of eliminating bottom-tier performers, thus risking demoralizing the workforce and inviting lawsuits. Others argue that too much differentiation can destroy teamwork by reinforcing "we-they" distinctions and can lead to overlooking individuals in frontline, customer-facing positions who may be the real heroes in the organization. Our own view is that better employers achieve differentiation while still valuing all employees.

Recall our observations in Chapter 2 that *Best-Places-to-Work* winners were able to maintain significantly higher engagement scores at all position levels "from the mailroom to the boardroom" than were the nonwinners. Based on our discussions with representatives of many of these winning companies and our analysis of survey comments, the truly elite employers have managed to be successful at targeting and investing in key high-value talent while also creating a culture that consistently values every employee.

Another word of caution to senior leaders: in discussions centered on determining which employees are most critical to the company's strategy, not all members of the senior team may agree about which employees actually bring the most value and are most critical. As we know, engineering executives may believe engineers that do great technical work are the key to business success, while those with business development responsibilities may see things very differently.

▶ ENGAGEMENT PLANNING AND YOUR EMPLOYER BRAND

As the job market and recruiting challenges become more competitive, employers naturally become more concerned about how they are perceived by the outside world in general and by potential recruits in particular. In past years some employers have tried to address this concern by simply creating recruitment advertising or Web pages presenting a desired image as an employer. One retail chain advertised itself as "the place to fast-track your career," but new recruits realized within a few months that the company could not deliver on that promise and that their career advancement would be much slower than anticipated. The result: disillusionment, disengagement, and much higher-than-average first-year turnover.

Before You Brand: A Reality Check

The retail chain noted above could have avoided this result by not skipping the reality-check phase of employer branding, which consists of:

Step 1. Assessing the reality about how both the outside world, including targeted recruits, and your current workforce see your organization as a place to work.

Step 2. Getting clear about the kinds of talent you will need to achieve your business objectives.

Step 3. Understanding the engagement drivers that most attract and retain the people you need.

Step 4. Working to shape your culture and put in place the kinds of management practices that will enable you to offer an "employment value proposition" that is authentic and will truly meet the needs of your employees and prospective hires.

And finally . . .

Step 5. Advertising and publicizing the genuine brand you have built from the inside out.

The key here is that step 5 must come only after you have successfully completed steps 1 through 4 (you may have already gone through steps 1 through 4 in a less formal, more intuitive way, as many employers we know have done). If you begin your branding process by declaring an "aspirational brand" without aligning it with the reality of employees' daily work experience, you are in danger of writing a check your culture can't cash.

For example, let's say a bank has determined that having customer service representatives (CSRs) cross-sell and up-sell bank services in addition to providing services at teller windows is a key piece of its business strategy. That means that in addition to training current CSRs to be more sales oriented, the bank must also attract and hire CSRs who are able and willing to both sell and serve customers—a rarer commodity. Because the CSR job will now be more demanding than before and the right candidates harder to find, the bank may decide to raise pay, or provide sales training, or create new flex hours.

Whatever new enticement it decides to offer and advertise, the bank needs to make sure it delivers what it promises. If it doesn't, new employees will quickly become disengaged and leave. This is the cardinal rule of employment branding (along with its corollary: be careful what you promise), but it is dismaying to consider how often we have seen it broken.

▶ THINGS CHANGE: BAD NEWS AND GOOD

You don't even need to have read Nassim Taleb's thought-provoking and sobering bestseller, *The Black Swan: The Impact of the Highly Improbable*, to understand that things can change quickly in today's business world. We have seen companies turned upside down and destroyed since the economy began its meltdown in September 2008. Companies that used to show up on *Fortune*'s "100 Great Places to Work" list year after year have since dropped off.

Voices of Disappointment

We saw much evidence of wrenching change in the comments of employees on the *Best-Places-to-Work* surveys. The following comments show that some change originates with external factors, and some may be traced to internal problems:

▶ *"I do not feel the company is 100 percent stable like I did three years ago."*

▶ *"I feel that in the last few years we are slipping downward and management finally sees that there are problems. They now are in a panic to try and overcome these problems that have been here for years. There has been a lack of communication for years, and I had hoped it would improve."*

▶ *"This company has gone so far downhill, even since the last time we did another survey like this last year. This company has set its goals so high for the sales staff that it is making people dishonest and cheaters. They have blinded management into thinking that they are wonderful employees when in reality they do things half-fast and wrong. They sneak credit life and disability into loans, are cutthroat about getting their loan goals."*

▶ *"If I knew then what I know now, I would have not taken this position. Many things were misrepresented to entice me to take the position."*

▶ *"A few years ago I would have had nothing but positive things to say about the company. I loved the company and was proud to be part of it. I realize that change cannot always be helped, and I understand why the business has changed. But the company has stopped investing in employees. They no longer provide classes for building our strengths. And the raises keep getting smaller."*

▶ *"I was drawn to this company by the high value they placed on the family. I feel this has slipped over the years. Compensation and benefits affect my family in a big way."*

Voices of Pride

We also came across comments, though not as many, testifying to the fact that change may also be for the better, as some employers strive to become better places to work or to maintain that enviable status:

▶ *"This is my second time with the company, and I must say, the current environment (last five years) is so much different. It's like a different firm. The flexibility, work-life balance, and personal challenges are something that will keep me here for the rest of my career."*

▶ *"I left here to make more money (a lot) and ended up deeply regretting it. The benefits did not compare, and neither did the recognition."*

▶ *"I've gone from patient transporter to nursing assistant and now clinical researcher here, starting from when I was 15. I've seen the hospital at its worst in 2001, and now as it is becoming a major competitor to hospitals with whom we were never able to compete before."*

Our point in showing these comments is simply to illustrate that some employers are thrown off course by the winds of change more than others, and many by their own doing. The main issue we see is that when faced with frightening prospects, many employers hunker down just when they need to be demonstrating more commitment to their workforces. Leaders reduce their focus and investment in the engagement of employees—cutting training, limiting communication, eliminating benefits, and even losing their ethical bearings. The good news is that some employers do make dramatic changes for the better. Since 2004, we have seen several employers significantly increase their engagement scores and become *Best-Places-to-Work* winners over the course of a single year. Many have realized increased business success as a result.

▶ NEEDED: LEADER COMMITMENT

Becoming a better place to work is not easy. It usually means that managers need to have courageous conversations, that human resources professionals become more strategic business partners with executives and line managers, that employees accept the challenge to take more responsibility for their own engagement, and that senior leaders make workforce engagement a priority.

In a conversation with three *Best-Places* winners in Omaha a couple of years ago, there was agreement among the senior leaders from winning companies in all three size categories that as their businesses were growing, they each had experienced a gut-check moment. They each told their separate stories about reaching a pivotal point when they knew they could have gone on achieving financial success without continued attention and focus on some of the key leadership values that had elevated them to financial success.

One of the executives recalled that his company had started out with the foundational value of taking care of family and putting family needs in line with business needs. He recalled an incident when an employee asked for some time off in the middle of the company's busy season to attend a sporting event in which her child was playing. The executive thought about rebuking the employee. But he recalled how important it was to spend time with his own children when they were growing up and how he had taken time off work in the past for similar events. He knew this was one of those make-or-break moments. Was he willing to acknowledge the needs of an employee related to that key value—or not? He decided to let the employee take the time off. Not surprisingly, the employee got the work done on time anyway and was grateful that the company had "walked the talk."

All three leaders agreed they could probably sacrifice some people values and still be successful. But all agreed that deviating from their chosen path would have probably prevented them from achieving the same level of success. Further, all three agreed that if they gave up on those values, they not only would be selling out but also just wouldn't have as much fun.

So the question arises, are you succeeding because of your commitment to engaging your workforce or *in spite of* hedging on that commitment? Another way to pose the question—how much more successful could your company be if you launched new employee engagement initiatives that were fully aligned with your workforce plan and strategic business objectives?

We came across a comment from one survey respondent who was obviously in serious doubt about the commitment of his own company's executives:

> *The company has been making tremendous strides to become a "Great Place to Work"—the biggest hurdle that we are still working through is getting all senior leaders on board (i.e., walking the talk) of the human capital plan. It might stem from certain leaders' inability to coach/lead to achieve results after the training has been accomplished. When the ability is low, these individuals do not see the ROI and thus are reluctant to invest in their people. I have been told by one person in senior leadership that they are fearful of investing "too" much in us, because we might leave the company shortly thereafter. It's getting better, but the Human Capital Plan hasn't really made it to all individuals in the company in a way that is effectively providing ROI.*

Such comments testify to just a few of the obstacles that we face in launching new workforce engagement initiatives. Of course, most workforce initiatives have a built-in disadvantage: the costs are immediate and definite, but the benefits can only be realized with effective "soft-skills" execution and are not typically realized until some vague point in the future.

Assess Your Degree of Difficulty in Becoming a More Engaged Workplace

It's not just the three crosswind factors we have addressed throughout the book that can impede your journey to becoming a better workplace. A dangerous variety of mines may be floating in the ocean ahead. Answering any of the following questions in the negative may indicate the ones that could sink your plans:

___ Are senior leaders and the board of directors committed to making the company a better place to work?

___ Do senior leaders and the board understand the business benefits to be realized from employee engagement initiatives?

___ Does the company have the financial resources to invest in employees?

___ Are senior leaders willing to make long-term investments in workforce engagement?

___ Are workforce engagement initiatives linked to key talent and driven by well-planned workforce and business strategies and objectives?

___ Do your scores on the engagement driver assessments (Chapters 4 through 9) indicate that the company is within striking distance of achieving *Best-Places-to-Work* status?

___ Is there a culture of trust in the organization as a whole and in all divisions, functional units, and other locations?

___ Are senior leaders prepared to conduct an organization-wide employee engagement survey and take action based on survey findings?

___ Have you identified other indicators (a dashboard, so to speak) for measuring improvements in employee engagement that link to and support your business objectives?

___ Do you have the necessary support staff—human resources, training and consulting expertise—to launch new engagement initiatives?

___ Is the company undergoing other changes that must be dealt with before new engagement initiatives can be realistically undertaken?

▶ ENGAGING ONE EMPLOYEE AT A TIME . . . IN ALL TIMES

We have focused our attention in this chapter so far on the macro issue of creating a great workplace—the 50,000-foot perspective and the strategic responsibility that senior leaders and HR executives must take. But we cannot overemphasize the importance of engaging and re-engaging one employee at a time, a responsibility that falls not just to direct managers but to senior leaders, HR professionals, and employees themselves. Each employee is motivated more by one or two of the six drivers than others, so matching the right drivers to individuals, teams, units, divisions, and whole, sometimes global, organizations can be a complicated challenge. We hope that the many ideas and suggestions we have presented throughout the book will spur new and more effective actions and that you will implement the ones that fit your business objectives and the differing needs of individual employees. All employees are alike in one sense: they are interested in getting their needs met at work—needs that are encompassed by the six Universal Engagement Drivers, one or two of which, to each employee, are more important than the others.

It is up to managers and supervisors to find out each employee's primary and secondary intrinsic needs and figure out a way to simultaneously satisfy the person's needs and the organization's. This is no mean feat, and if an organization's senior leaders are serious about becoming a better place to work, they must understand that it will require them to free up managers to manage!

The great American novelist Thomas Wolfe once wrote: "If a man has a talent and cannot use it, he has failed. If a man has a talent and uses part of it, he has partly failed. But if a man has a talent and somehow manages to use the whole of it, he has won a triumph few men ever know." (It should go without saying that we believe the quotation, written in the 1930s, applies equally to women.) When we consider the unused and wasted talent in the world today, especially in light of the economic, social, and political challenges we face, it is truly scandalous that we cannot figure out how to harness more of the talents of the people who work in our organizations.

Has there ever been a time when having an engaged workforce was more important than it is right now? Having a largely disengaged workforce is clearly unacceptable, and yet in so many organizations, we have simply gotten used to it, developed a tolerance for it, and now accept it as the status quo.

Whether you believe employee engagement is a leading indicator of business success, as serious studies have shown, or you simply believe keeping employees engaged is your moral and professional responsibility as a manager, your motivation is secondary. The primary issue is the strength of your determination to do everything you can to bring out the best in those who report to you. If you and your colleagues can do that, you will achieve new heights of business success. But before you can do it, the leaders in your organization will probably need to begin doing things differently.

One of the most important things you can do is to have "check-in" discussions with individual employees, which we often refer to as "stay interviews" or "re-engagement conversations." As Figure 11.1 indicates, disengagement is a "slippery staircase." At any given moment,

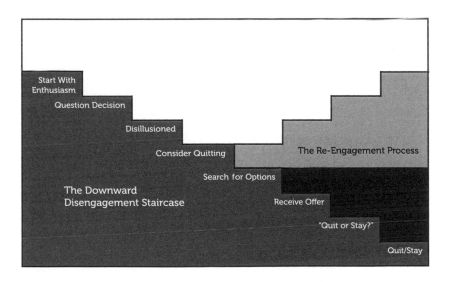

Figure 11.1

employees may be in various stages of disengagement, from mild to more serious, to actually leaving the organization. As one study indicates, 71 percent of employees who had made up their minds to leave the organization admitted that they gave less effort at work during the weeks and months before they finally departed.[1]

The good news is that many employees can be re-engaged with a sincere and concerted effort on the manager's part that begins with the simple words: "I've noticed that you don't seem as engaged or enthusiastic as you were a few weeks ago, and I'm concerned about that. You're a valuable part of the team, and I'd like to know if there's anything I can do." In some cases, this opening will lead to tough conversations; a manager may need to apologize for not having been available as a coach or mentor, or may have to uncomfortably confront an employee's poor performance. Chances are, a courageous conversation is all that stands in the way of re-engaging the disengaged.

Finally, we must keep in mind that employee loyalty is not what it used to be, and perhaps it never has been. Hiring is not like getting married—no vows are exchanged, and so they cannot be renewed. All employees are strictly volunteers. If there is such a thing as loyalty, it is something that happens day to day because we have made the commitment as employers to provide each employee with an engaging employment experience.

▶ NOTES

▶ CHAPTER ONE

1   For a complete review of the Quantum employee survey, a list of communities where annual events are conducted, and other information about the *Best-Places-to-Work* events, please go to www.re-engagebook.com, Appendix A.
2   Blake E. Asforth, Glen E. Kreiner, Mark A. Clark, and Mel Fugate, "Normalizing Dirty Work: Managerial Tactics for Countering Occupational Taint," *Academy of Management Journal*, 2007, Vol. 50, No. 1, pp. 147–174.
3   The Conference Board study of employee engagement, 2006.
4   Corporate Leadership Council report of employee engagement, "The Effort Dividend: Driving Employee Performance and Retention Through Engagement," 2004.
5   J. M. Crant, "Proactive Behavior in Organizations," *Journal of Management*, Vol. 26, pp. 435–462.
6   Press release from Quantum Workplace at *PR Newswire*, June 25, 2009.

▶ CHAPTER TWO

1   Malcolm Gladwell, *The Tipping Point: How Little Things Can Make a Big Difference* (Bay Back Books, 2000).
2   Ibid., p. 179.
3   Ibid., p. 181.
4   Ibid.
5   Ibid., pp. 184–185.
6   "Millennials Usher in New Kind of Work Life," *Omaha World-Herald*, June 16, 2008, p. D2.
7   Copyright 2009 Quantum Workplace, Goldenrod Consulting, Inc., and Keeping the People, Inc.
8   In estimating the variance for the model, a Taylor-series estimate was used.

9 On a six-point Likert scale, the average gap between the youngest and oldest generations is .27 when overall engagement is in the bottom quartile, and .13 when the overall engagement is in the top quartile. This difference is statistically significant.

10 "Jobless Claims in State on Rise," *Omaha World-Herald*, Nov. 27, 2008, p. B1.

11 "Pink Slips Report," compiled by Klaus Kneale, *Forbes.com*, Jan. 28, 2009.

12 Survey from William Mercer Company, as reported by Matthew Quinn, *Financial Week*, Feb. 3, 2009.

13 Clifford Kraus, "Auto Dealerships Teeter as Big Three Decline," *The New York Times*, Nov. 28, 2008.

14 "Caveat Vendor," *Forbes.com*, Nov. 30, 2008.

15 Ray Baumruk and Ted Marusarz, "Is There a Recession?" *Conference Board Review*, Vol. 45, No. 3, May/June 2008.

16 Dina Berta, "Leadership IQ's Murphy: De-Stress Layoff Survivors," *Nation's Restaurant News*, Feb. 2, 2009.

17 Personal interview.

18 Personal interview.

19 Personal interview.

▶ CHAPTER THREE

1 "Universal Engagement Drivers" is a trademark of Goldenrod Consulting, Inc., and Keeping the People, Inc.

▶ CHAPTER FOUR

1 "Second Annual Poll on Leadership," *U.S. News & World Report* and Harvard Center for Public Leadership, 2006.

2 Ibid.

3 "Senior Managers Play a Role in Employee Satisfaction Too," *PRNewswire–FirstCall*, Wednesday, Nov. 14, 2008.

4 Roger Maitland, "Support for Company Strategy Is Essential to Employee Engagement," *People Management*, 13586297, Vol. 13, No. 5, Mar. 8, 2007. ISR's 2006 database included both quantitative and qualitative information from 1,956,600 employees from 242 organizations in 108 countries. There were 33 high-performance companies (with 581,180 staff) and 21 transitional firms (with 297,500 employees).

5 Rita Zeidner, "Employers Increase Communication about Finances," citing study, "Communicating to Employees during the Current Financial Crisis," *HR News*, Dec. 30, 2008.

6 Joe Rei and Leigh Branham, "Changing of the Guard: How to Avoid a Leadership Shortfall," citing a research study by the Advanced Management Institute, *FMI Quarterly*, Summer 2008.

7 Beth Kowitt, "How Are Other Companies Using Web 2.0?" *Fortune*, Sept. 15, 2008.

8 Stephen Baker and Heather Green, "Beyond Blogs," *BusinessWeek*, June 2, 2008.

9   "Most Companies Step Up Communication to Ease Workers' Recession-Related Stress, Watson Wyatt Survey Finds," *PR Newswire* news releases, Dec. 19, 2008.

10 John Chambers, "How I Work: 'Lights! Cameras! Cue the CEO!'" *BusinessWeek*, Aug. 21, 2006, p. 27.

11 Patricia O'Connell, "Don't Let Top Talent Get Away," *BusinessWeek.com*, February 2009, p. 38.

▶ CHAPTER FIVE

1   Jim Clifton, "Engage Your People," *Leadership Excellence*, 2007.

2   *Gallup Management Journal*, Sept. 13, 2007.

3   Charlotte Rayner, "What Does Bullying Cost Your Business?" *People Management*, 13586297, Vol. 12, No. 24, Dec. 7, 2006.

4   "Uncertain Economy Weighs Heavily on US Workers, Accenture Study Finds: Middle Managers Cite Workers' Low Morale and Concerns about Job Security," Accenture Newsroom, Nov. 13, 2008.

5   Maureen Moriarity, "Workplace Coach: Leaders Can Help Layoff Survivors," *Seattle Post-Intelligencer*, March 2009.

6   Douglas McGregor, *The Professional Manager* (McGraw-Hill, 1967).

▶ CHAPTER SIX

1   Lynda Gratton and Tamara J. Erickson, "Eight Ways to Build Collaborative Teams," *Harvard Business Review*, November 2007, pp. 100–109.

2   Ibid.

3   David Pauleen and Brian Harmer, "Away from the Desk . . . Always: A New Breed of Workers—Independent, Autonomous, Out of the Office—Requires a New Breed of Manager," *The Wall Street Journal*, Dec. 15, 2008, p. R8.

4   "Embrace the 'Dwight Schrutes' in Your Workplace," *Newswise*, Mar. 27, 2009.

5   Ellen McGirt, "Cisco Gets Radical," *Fast Company*, January 2009, p. 88.

▶ CHAPTER SEVEN

1   From the Rackspace corporate Web site at www.rackspace.com.

2   A registered mark of Rackspace.

3   For more information about this concept, see *The Ultimate Question: Driving Good Profits and True Growth* by Fred Reichheld Harvard Business Press, 2006.

4   *The Business Journal* (Phoenix), Vol. 25, No. 11, Dec. 10, 2004, p. 48.

5   "Best Places to Work in the Bay Area," *San Francisco Business Times*, Apr. 27, 2007, p. 19.

6   *Business Courier* (Cincinnati), Vol. 21, No. 30, Nov. 12, 2004, p. B8.

7   "Best Places to Work," *Business First*, Nov. 11, 2005, p. 29.

8   "Best Places to Work," *Kansas City Business Journal*, Oct. 28, 2005, p. 16.
9   Ibid., p. 22.
10 "Best Places to Work in the Bay Area," *San Francisco Business Times*, Apr. 27, 2007, p. 19.

▶ CHAPTER EIGHT

1   Ferdinand Fournies, *Coaching for Improved Work Performance* (McGraw-Hill, 1999), p. 37.

▶ CHAPTER NINE

1   "Hewitt's Best Employers in Canada Study Finds Link between High Engagement and Employee Health and Well-Being," Hewitt Newsroom, Feb. 18, 2009.
2   Will Dunham, "Health Spending Takes Rising Share of U.S. Economy," Reuters, Tuesday, Feb. 24, 2009, www.reuters.com/article/healthNews/idUST RE51N0W120090224?feedType=RSS&feedName=healthNews&rpc=69.
3   Reed Abelson, "Health Care Costs Increase Strain, Studies Find," *The New York Times*, Sept. 25, 2008.
4   Karen Sloan, "Omaha's Health Care Costs May Soar in '09," *Omaha World-Herald*, Sept. 9, 2008.
5   Pedro Nicolaci da Costa, "Americans Increasingly Insecure about Retirement," Reuters, Wednesday, Feb. 25, 2009, www.reuters.com/article/topNews/idUST RE51O3Z320090225?feedType=nl&feedName=ustopnewsearly.
6   Linda A. Johnson, "Study Puts a Total on Diabetes Cost: $218 Billion," Associated Press, Nov. 18, 2008.
7   David Tuller, "Kidney Disease Takes a Growing Toll," *The New York Times*, Nov. 18, 2008.
8   Kevin Sack, "Health Care Benefits Inspire Rush to Marry," *The New York Times*, Aug. 13, 2008.
9   "More Employers Ponder Dropping Health Care Benefits," *Employee Benefits News*, March 2009, ebn.benefitnews.com/asset/article/2672391/ebn-industry-inbrief-030509.html.
10 "Applying the Obama Test to Healthcare: SimplyWell Cited as Top 10 Best Practices by Center for Healthcare Transformation,"*Bio-Medicine*, Jan. 30, 2009, www.bio-medicine.org/medicine-news-1/Applying-the-Obama-Test-to-Healthcare-3A-SimplyWell-Cited-as-Top-10-Best-Practices-by-Center-for-Healthcare-Transformation-35309-1.
11 Kathleen Koster, "Study Links Healthier Workers with Improved Productivity," *Employee Benefit News*, Mar. 31, 2009, ebn.benefitnews.com/news/study-links-healthier-workers-with-improved-productivity-2671963-1.html.
12 Ibid.
13 Milt Freudenheim, "Building Better Bodies," *The New York Times*, Sept. 30, 2008.
14 Kathy Gurchiek, "Organizations Dig in for Grim Days Ahead," *SHRM Online*, Dec. 18, 2008, www.shrm.org/Pages/login.aspx?ReturnUrl=%2fPublications% 2fHRNews%2fPages%2fOrganizationsDigIn.aspx.

▶ CHAPTER TEN

1   Cited in "The Art of Re-Engagement: 9 Personal Engagement Tips," *The Engagement Factor Blog*, Mar. 4, 2009.
2   Ferdinand Fournies, *Coaching for Improved Work Performance* (McGraw-Hill, 2000).

▶ CHAPTER ELEVEN

1   "Decision to Leave" Web survey results, 2004–2008, Keeping the People, Inc., 2008.

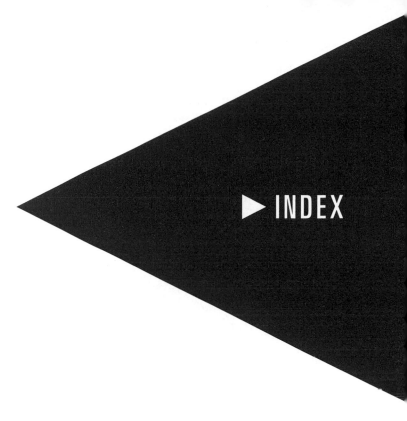

▶ INDEX

ABOUT THE AUTHORS

Leigh Branham is principal and founder of Keeping the People, Inc., in Overland Park, Kansas. His firm helps clients analyze root causes of employee disengagement and turnover and implement strategies to grow revenues and profits by becoming better places to work.

His book, *The 7 Hidden Reasons Employees Leave: How to Recognize the Subtle Signs and Act Before It's Too Late*, was selected as one of the top 30 business books of 2005. He is also the author of *Keeping the People Who Keep You in Business* (AMACOM, 2000).

Leigh has consulted with multinational companies and has spoken at human resources and leadership conferences in China, Poland, Argentina, Paraguay, Canada, and Malaysia. He has been interviewed on National Public Radio and has been widely quoted as an expert on employee retention in *BusinessWeek*, *The Harvard Management Update*, and by the Associated Press. He publishes a quarterly free subscription e-newsletter, the *Keeping the People Report*, available at www.keepingthepeople.com.

Mark Hirschfeld is principal, SilverStone Group Inc. of Omaha, Nebraska. He has been actively involved in organizational development consulting for over 20 years. In his tenure with SilverStone Group, as well as serving as a vice president for the management consulting division of the Gallup Organization, Mark has assisted in the design and execution of human capital solutions for many growing companies.

Mark has written many articles on career management, leadership effectiveness, employee survey design and administration, and best practices of winning *Best-Places-to-Work* employers. He has conducted extensive research on winning companies that participate in the *Best-Places-to-Work* program in the United States, and his consulting activities include work in Australia and Canada, as well as a one-year assignment in the United Kingdom.